M000235288

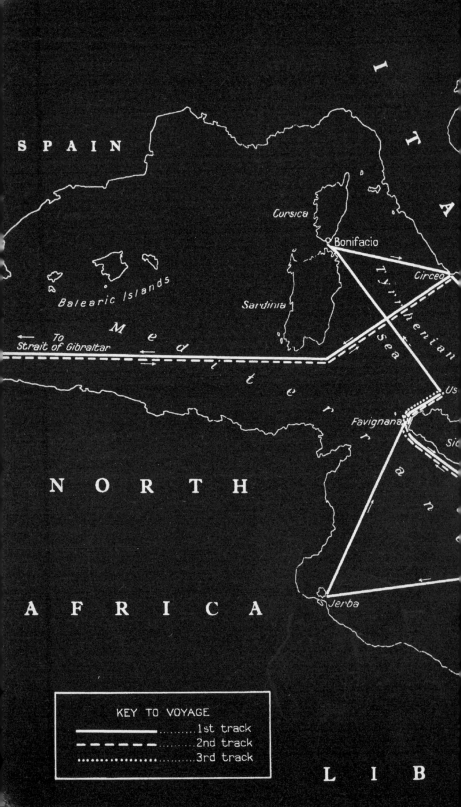

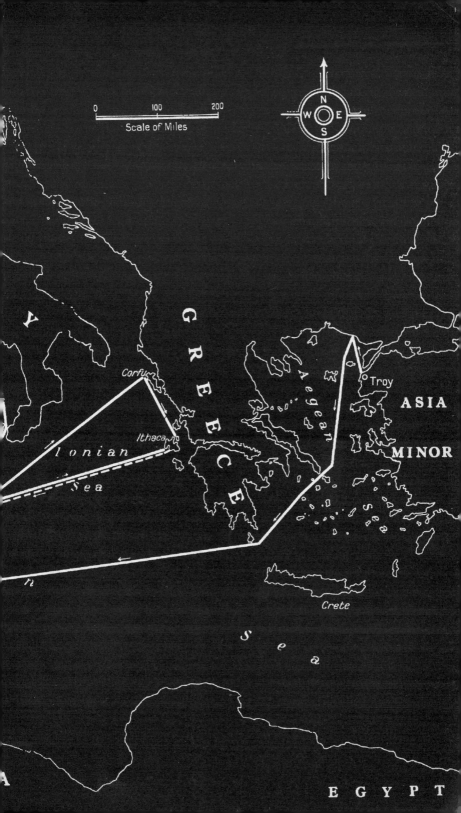

ULYSSES
FOUND

ULYSSES FOUND

ERNLE BRADFORD

SUTTON PUBLISHING

This book was first published in 1963 by
Hodder and Stoughton Ltd.

This edition first published in 2004 by
Sutton Publishing Limited · Phoenix Mill
Thrupp · Stroud · Gloucestershire · GL5 2BU

Copyright © Ernle Bradford, 2004

All rights reserved. No part of this book may be reproduced, stored
in a retrieval system, or transmitted, in any form, or by any means,
electronic, mechanical, photocopying, recording or otherwise,
without the prior permission of the publisher and copyright holder.

British Library Cataloguing in Publication Data
A catalogue record for this book is available from the British Library

ISBN 0 7509 3725 4

Printed and bound in Great Britain by
J.H. Haynes & Co. Ltd, Sparkford.

They are not dead, they are not dead!
Now that the sun, like a lion, licks his paws and goes slowly
   down the hill:
now that the moon, who remembers and only cares
that we should be lovely in the flesh, with bright, crescent feet,
pauses near the crest of the hill, climbing slowly, like a queen
looking down on the lion as he retreats.

Now the sea is the Argonauts' sea, and in the dawn
Odysseus calls the commands, as he steers past those foamy
   islands
wait, wait, don't bring the coffee yet, nor the *pain grillé*.
The dawn is not off the sea, and Odysseus' ships
have not yet passed the islands, I must watch them still.

The Argonauts   D. H. Lawrence

Acknowledgements

I SHOULD like to express my particular thanks to A. R. Burn, Esq., and to Captain John Tothill, D.S.C., R.N. (Retd.), both of whom were kind enough to read the book in manuscript, the one eliminating my grossest classical mistakes, and the other checking my geography and navigational details. The emendations and improvements are theirs, the errors remain mine.

I am indebted to the Society for the Promotion of Hellenic Studies for permission to make use of their library and their unrivalled collection of classical photographs, as also to the Trustees and Authorities of the British Museum. My thanks are due to E. V. Rieu and the Penguin Classics for permission to quote extensively from E. V. Rieu's translation of *The Odyssey*. As is shown in the notes at the end of this book, I have used this translation in all places where a major geographical description is given by Homer—this, so that I might not be suspected of translating or adapting the poet to suit my own convenience or theories. In other places, the translation is my own. My acknowledgements are due to Laurence Pollinger Ltd., and the Estate of the late Mrs. Frieda Lawrence for permission to quote D. H. Lawrence's *The Argonauts* from *The Complete Poems of D. H. Lawrence* (William Heinemann Ltd.) at the front of this book. Other writers and classical authorities, whose works have been quoted, are acknowledged in the notes to each appropriate chapter.

E. B.

Introduction

EVERYTHING in this book may well seem both to lovers of poetry and to classical scholars an unnecessary gloss upon the *Odyssey*. In one sense it is, for it is clearly unnecessary to attempt to trace the voyage of Ulysses when millions of people, for thousands of years, have been quite happy to read the *Odyssey* as if it was only a fable. At the same time every single accretion—however small—upon a monument so enduring may serve some purpose. It is fair to argue that: "Poetry, in a word, should be centripetal, not centrifugal, and its serious business is not with caverns in Cashmere, or Upas trees in Java, or alligator-holes in Florida, but with what is common to our kind." The same writer, however, goes on to say: "That is sound doctrine, to which I heartily subscribe. But it is doctrine which is sometimes pushed so far as to exclude its essential complement. What seas washed the insubstantial shores that harboured Circe and Calypso, and on what chart is Prospero's island found?"

I do not think that anything is lost by attempting to find a skeleton—however magnificent the cupboard that hides it. I have seen coral formations disguising the old bones of ships, but I did not feel less amazed by the beauty of the coral just because I had found the timbers and iron frames which the polyps had disguised and decorated.

My quest for Ulysses began a long time ago. It started in Alexandria. I was just nineteen and an ordinary seaman, proud possessor of a uniform, an identity number, and a place on a gun's crew, when I first entered the Averoff bar off Mehemet Ali Square, and met Andreas. I sometimes wonder what has happened to Andreas since 1941; in those days he must have been in his middle thirties. He was about six feet tall, but with a belly that disguised his height, and a dark, twirled-up moustache in the Edwardian manner which proclaimed him a happy and healthy 'masher' of the old-fashioned vintage. He was resting his belly on the marble slab of the counter when I first saw him. He was sipping a long glass of Zibib, so well diluted with water that it was only a faintly clouded colour.

I was near enough the schoolboy in those days to be still under the influence of all that I had been taught. Alexandria to me was the city of the great Greek conqueror. It hardly existed as a 19th-century French and Anglo-Egyptian collaboration. It was myth and mystery, Antony and Cleopatra, the Bull of Serapis, Pompey's Pillar, bearded anchorites, the Pharos, and a vague suggestion of infinite sexual sophistication. I was eager to transform my recent acquisition of classical Greek in the Upper Sixth, into a language that could be of some practical use in this city to which the exigencies of fate and fortune had driven me. It was no more than this fact, this desire on my part to expand my so recently acquired knowledge, that caused me to say; "Kalee Spéra" to Andreas.

I spent a pleasant evening before going down to the harbour in a gharry. I caught my ship's liberty boat back aboard, and watched the wake curl out through the scummy, sewage-ridden water. Smoking was forbidden in the boat, but once aboard—preparatory to turning into my hammock—I lit a Papastratos that Andreas had given me. Its light straw-coloured smoke scented the air in the passage way where I slept. I carried few books with me in those days, for one travelled light as a sailor. In the rack which supported the electric light cables over my head was stowed my entire library. Andreas had spoken of Ulysses. It was for that reason only that I reached for the first volume of the Loeb *Odyssey*, and held it out above my head in the swaying hammock. (A little swell still set into the harbour after the long day's wind from the north.)

In those days I needed to refer less to the English translation than ever since, and I liked to feel that my comprehension of the language of the Greeks still kept me in touch with a sanity that had long since deserted all the things I read daily in my own tongue. Andreas had never read Homer, but he knew the story of Ulysses almost by heart. This was not surprising, for in the Greek schools boys learned about the Homeric hero in much the same way that in England they learned about Alfred the Great, or in America about Lincoln.

Andreas had spoken of Ulysses as 'the wily man'—a kind of Greek Pantagruel. This was an idea which at that time was not immediately clear to me. He was in Andreas's reckoning the Artful Dodger, not the Romantic Hero. He was the kind of Greek who could still make a living in Alexandria after all the others had gone to the wall. Ulysses was the shopkeeper with his thumb on the scales, and an eye to the girls, handy with a knife in a dark alley, and at the same time in some strange fashion or other, capable of honesty—or was it of great consistency?—over most of the major issues.

Ulysses, from that moment on, became to me a comrade in adversity. So I lived with him in my kitbag, in the same sea and under circumstances somewhat similar to those which he had known. Even when I became a petty king myself—the navigator of a destroyer, and able to keep my ears unplugged while the men at the oars were not allowed to hear the siren voices—those two pale green Loeb volumes followed me around. Transferred now from sailor's kitbag to officer's battered suitcase, they went with me to Sicily and Crete, to the Dodecanese, and to Lemnos in the far north of the Aegean Sea. They went to Malta and Sardinia, the Aeolian Isles, and many times through the straits where Scylla and Charybdis yielded so easily to the 40,000 horsepower of a destroyer.

But it was Andreas who first put me in touch as it were, with the man beneath the myth. It was Andreas, standing at his small bar on that hot afternoon—his shirt open, the sweat trickling over his matted black chest—who first said: "My mother came from Ithaca, you know."

When you have sailed the Mediterranean at the age of nineteen with the *Odyssey* in your kitbag, and when you have come back, of your own volition, to the same sea in your twenties and thirties—and still kept the same book at the foothead of your bunk—it is not surprising if you come to wonder whether some of it may not be true. This is particularly the case if you find, out of your own experience, that great sections of the poem seem to read like accurate reportage.

I spent most of the years between 1950 and 1960 sailing the Mediterranean, the largest vessel I owned being an old 20-ton cutter and the smallest a 7-ton sloop. For one period of two-and-a-half years while sailing in the central and eastern Mediterranean I only slept ashore on five nights. I grew to know this sea, and in doing so I also grew to know the *Odyssey*, almost as thoroughly as the charts that led me through the Messina strait, or across the Ionian to the islands and to Ithaca. In the course of my wanderings I came to a number of conclusions about Homeric geography and the navigations of Ulysses.

It is proof, perhaps, of the vitality of the hero that such apparently recondite matters can still concern anybody in the 20th century, at a time when space travel has become an accepted fact. A future Ulysses has probably been born. One can only hope that he will be seeking to return to his Ithaca, and not fleeing from the ruins of 'a Troy' that encompasses the whole world. He will, in any case, be more than fortunate if the story of his voyage is framed in such a way, and in such a language, that men will read about it 3,000 years after he is dead.

But it was Andreas, 'whose mother came from Ithaca,' who first lifted the hero for me out of the world of poetic fantasy and set him fairly and squarely in the Mediterranean that still exists. For this reason alone I owe him a deep acknowledgement before anybody else.

E. B. 1963.

CONTENTS

MAPS

Foreword

It is always flattering to be asked to read a manuscript or write a Foreword; and indeed, to be so honoured, rather than avoided like the plague, when one has annotated the author's Sixth Form essays twenty-five years ago, is almost a ground for feeling that one has not lived in vain. It is a pleasure to wish good luck and a friendly reception to Ernle Bradford's essay in the geography of the Odyssey, *Ulysses Found*.

A French scholar once asked a friend, who had announced his intention of writing on another hero of antiquity, whether the book was to be *plutôt scientifique*, or *plutôt lyrique*? Mr. Bradford's book is clearly *lyrique* in conception and quality; but he would wish us to judge it *du point de vue scientifique*. Here the judicious reader must make up his own mind; and the present writer must confess that he approached the MS. in a mood of the deepest scepticism. After all, Homer himself does not say, *propria persona*, that his hero had these adventures, but only that this is what Ulysses told the Phaeacians, when dining out on the strength of them. Some of the stories, too, and even details which give geographical hints, such as the short summer nights, or the mention of the Kimmerioi (*if* that is what Homer wrote, and not *Cheimerioi* or *Kerberioi*) have clearly been borrowed (as Mr. Bradford is aware) out of another saga—that, in fact, of the famous *Argo*, which is mentioned in the *Odyssey* at xii, 70. However, Ulysses' wanderings clearly are placed 'out west'; for he steers homeward from Calypso's isle by keeping the Great Bear on his left. Scholars now generally date Homer after rather than before 750; and Chios, his traditional home, is not far, for a travelled man, from Aeolic Cyme, whose sailors founded the other Cyme, Cumae on the Bay of Naples, about 750, and "first brought tin from the Tin Islands," and were the predecessors, in western exploration, of their neighbours, the Phocaeans. The poet could have heard about the west from practical seamen; he could even, in his young days, have sailed with them. Mr. Graeme Ritchie pointed out in his fascinating Zaharoff Lecture, *Chrétien de Troyes and Scotland,* that even the original Waste Land where Chrétien's knights ride is not just nowhere. It is, in fact, in that newly discovered region of northern Britain, with which some Normans had become acquainted when the knightly David, King of Scots, held court at Carlisle. If the Holy Grail has its links with mundane geography, then in all conscience, why not the much more mundane, anthropologically interesting, pre-agricultural people of the Cyclopes?

Anyone can enjoy the *Odyssey,* even seated by the fireside of his northern home; but there will always be some who, like Samuel Butler, (an explorer of fabulous lands in his own right) will desire to 'find Ulysses'; some, too, who on Mediterranean high seas have met him, or nearly, like J. E. Flecker or L. S. Amery. If one is to embark on a methodical search, it is clear that Ernle Bradford has gone the right way about it, not in public transport but as his own master, in small boats, in those seas and little harbours where the hero's spiritual and professional descendants are still to be found. That world has four dimensions; very likely more, but that is a question for yogis; four, certainly. In Greece in the special conditions of 1940–41, one was continually prompted to say to oneself "This is exactly like something out of Greek history," and to receive the disconcerting answer "This *is* Greek history; and you *may* be there for the next chapter; or not." And with that, it only remains to wish fair winds to a new book on its travels, and to all who sail in our author's company.

A. R. BURN
Senior Lecturer in Ancient History,
Glasgow University.

Go, little boat, and sail the dangerous west.
Whether in faery or on solid ground
Among rank sea-smells, those who rightly quest
Shall see, at some day's end, ULYSSES FOUND.

A. R. Burn

1
Ancestry

WHEN the Greeks came down to their long, dark ships, leaving the ruins of Troy still smouldering behind them, Ulysses was a man in early middle age. We do not know exactly how old he was, for Homer is indifferent to such details. What we do know is that Ulysses had left a wife and a young son behind him in his island kingdom, and that he had been engaged in the long siege of Troy for ten years. He was to be detained a further nine whole years wandering the Mediterranean before he was restored to his own island. Yet, as we find out from his actions on landing in Ithaca, and from the vigour of his revenge upon the men who had been ruining his kingdom, the Ulysses who returned to Ithaca was in the prime of life. We also know that Ulysses' father, Laertes, was still alive when the wanderer returned home, and—although he is described as an old man—it is unlikely that an 'old man' in those days was much more than sixty.

It seems likely that the Ulysses who came back to Ithaca was in his forties. At the time when Troy finally fell to the Greeks, he was probably somewhere in the middle or early thirties. He was the ruler of a small kingdom which he had not seen for ten years, and as eager as all the other Greeks to put war behind him and return to the administration of his island.

When men return from a war it is their record as fighting men which usually determines their immediate position in society.

I

Inevitably within a short time the standards of judgement change, so that often the war hero turns out to be a peace-time failure. But at first the only test by which returned soldiers can be gauged is by how they have conducted themselves in the recent battles. Ulysses, who was to become known for all time as the sailor and the wanderer, had many other claims upon the attention of his contemporaries. He had had, by any standards, a most remarkable 'war record'. His reputation was very different from that of warriors like Ajax and Achilles. The goddess Athene, when she is being her most flattering to Ulysses, refers to him not as 'lion-hearted' or 'first in combat', but as 'a many-coloured mind ever framing some new craftiness'.

Sometimes a man's ancestry may give a clue to his life and actions. At other times men of genius and ability seem to have sprung, self-formed, from obscure origins. But then, "Happy is the man that knows his own father," and if we knew for certain the true parentage of our heroes and men of genius many apparently inexplicable talents would be revealed as having a comprehensible genetic background. Ulysses had a comparatively straight-forward family tree, one attested by many early sources and classical commentators. If ever a man's breeding was a clear indication of the type of character that he would bear through life, we have such a case in Ulysses.

His father was Laertes, the king of Ithaca, and his mother was a lady called Anticlea. A man's ancestry can only be traced with any certainty through the maternal line, and Anticlea did not have an entirely blameless reputation among early genealogists. In fact, some of them suggested that "she had lived on intimate terms with Sisyphus" before she married Laertes. It is for this reason that we find Ulysses sometimes referred to as 'the son of Sisyphus'. Now Sisyphus was the king of Corinth who was famous for having promoted navigation and commerce, but who was also renowned for having been avaricious, fraudulent, and deceitful. It was for these latter faults that he was condemned in Hades to be forever rolling up a hill a marble block which, as soon as it neared the top, always escaped him and rolled down again. He sounds in many ways a likely parent for the wily Ulysses. All the same, I think Anticlea's reputation can be cleared, for Laertes himself came from exactly the right kind of stock to father the hero. But it is his mother's ancestry that is of the greatest importance.

A great deal of the secret of Ulysses' nature is made clear when one realizes that his maternal ancestry was far from ordinary. His mother was the daughter of the master-thief of antiquity, an almost legendary figure, many of whose exploits were transferred in later centuries to his famous grandson, Ulysses. This maternal grandparent was Autolycus. He lived on Parnassus, and his name meant 'The Very Wolf'. The name Autolycus is of the greatest importance in this search for Ulysses, for it is from his mother's father that Ulysses' own name derives.

His Homeric name, Odysseus, meaning the 'Son of Wrath', is appropriate enough for a man destined to become an avenger. In the west—and especially in popular speech—he was generally known as Olysseus, which Latin writers were to render as Ulysses. Now the name Olysseus derives, as does that of his maternal grandfather, from the Greek, O Lukos, 'The Wolf'. So we find that, whereas Autolycus means 'The Very Wolf', Olysseus means simply 'The Wolf'. This wolf strain is apparent in many of the tales about the hero. But Ulysses was also a smooth talker, a man nimble with words. This is clear enough in Homer and is repeated many centuries later by Ovid: "Ulysses was not beautiful, but he was eloquent."

Before leaving this side of his ancestry it is important to note that Autolycus, The Very Wolf, was reputedly the child of the god Hermes by the nymph Chione. This in itself is evidence of the extraordinary logicality of the Greeks when it came to establishing genealogies—even when the genealogies ran back

3

into myth and mystery. For if the crafty hero is the grandson of a notorious robber and cheat, his great grandfather is Hermes himself, the God of Lying and Thieving who was known in early mythology as 'The Cunning Hermes'. This Hermes was a far remove from the later classical god, the youthful herald and grave conductor of souls. Under this early aspect of his nature he was regarded as the patron saint of thieves. The nymph Chione, who bore Hermes Autolycus, was famous for her beauty. With the arrogance that beauty brings, she was later rash enough to compare herself with the goddess Artemis, who immediately killed her. Further back in Ulysses' ancestry than Hermes one need not go, except to note that Hermes was the son of Zeus, king of the Gods, by the nymph Maia, whom Zeus raped in a grotto of Mount Cyllene in Arcadia.

If Ulysses' maternal ancestry reveals quite clearly from which side of the family he inherited his quick wits, smooth tongue and loose morals, it is his father's side which shows how the salt sea got into the hero's blood. Laertes, his father, came from the royal line of the kings of Argos. On this side, then, Ulysses was related to the house and blood of the most important kingdom in the Greek Peloponnese. He may have been no more than the ruler of a small island, but his connections help to explain how it came about that he was the leader of the chieftains who went to Troy from the Ionian islands.

Laertes has another and far more important claim on our attention than his descent from the kings of Argos. He was one of the last remaining Argonauts, and had sailed with Jason on the great voyage in quest of the Golden Fleece. Now the *Argo* was reputedly the first war-galley ever built, and the men who sailed in her were all to become legendary heroes and demigods to the later Greeks. Laertes had taken part in the greatest voyage of adventure and discovery then known, and could claim to be one of the pioneer sailors of the ancient world. It seems right that he should have had Ulysses for a son. It is for this reason that I ignore the

4

slander of ancient commentators who have found Laertes' wife Anticlea guilty of having palmed off on Laertes, as his own, her bastard son by Sisyphus. Ulysses traditionally had seafaring and royal blood on his father's side, and a violent and somewhat crooked strain (even if reputedly of divine origin) on his mother's.

2

Youth

ULYSSES was short-legged and red-haired. He was probably red-faced too, and almost certainly he limped a little. He had a fierce, tip-tilted beard of the type which the Greeks called 'pogon'—a word they also applied for obvious reasons to certain peninsulas. Strong in the arms and shoulders, he was what we might call 'barrel-chested', and it is likely that with his short legs, and after his long years at sea, he walked with the sailor's traditional roll.

Anyone less like the fair-haired, noble-browed, cleanshaven Greek of imagined antiquity it would be hard to find. More amorous than Nelson, he had little of the latter's gentleness. He was no abstract navigational theorist like the Portuguese, Prince Henry the Navigator, nor was he an ascetic. In appearance he was probably more like Sir Francis Drake than any other famous sailor of history. In temperament Ulysses may have resembled John Paul Jones a little, but it is certain that, given the latter's opportunities, he would have been a great deal more successful with Catherine the Great than was the American hero.

Little is known about Ulysses' early life until we first hear of his being wounded by a wild boar on the slopes of Mount Parnassus. The accident occurred when Ulysses came over to the mainland of Greece to stay with his grandfather, Autolycus. In the course of a day's hunting on the mountain, Ulysses was attacked by a boar and gashed in the thigh. He bore the scar to the end of his life.

Although it is quite likely that he was wounded in a boar

hunt, there is something more, perhaps, to the wound of Ulysses than a simple hunting accident. This wounding in the thigh seems to equate him with a number of eastern gods, Tammuz, Adonis, and Cretan Zeus, all of whom were wounded and killed by a boar. These stories all stem from a Phoenician source and seem to derive from the legend of the 'year god' whose death occurred after harvest time. The cult arose in prehistoric times, when the sacred king was put to death as a sacrifice to the earth mother. In this connection, Ulysses' visit to Hell (which is one of the few incidents that almost certainly has no place in his true historical wanderings) has crept into the poem from an earlier source. His wound in the thigh suggested his identification with the God of the Year. It is for this reason that some scholars have maintained that Ulysses was no more than a Solar God, and that the story of his wanderings is only the myth of the Sun God's travel throughout the twelve months of the year. Although I agree that some of this mythology has crystallized around the figure of Ulysses, I am equally convinced that the hero was a real man. His travels have a completely straightforward geographical interpretation.

Autolycus looked after his grandson until his wound had healed, and then sent him back to Ithaca laden with gifts. It was from Autolycus that Ulysses received his other name—Odysseus—meaning The Angry One—"For", said his grandfather, "I am at present angry with many men"—naming him, as was quite customary then, for something that was applicable at the moment. Ulysses, in fact, does not seem to have suffered noticeably from illtemper, or if he did he was usually intelligent enough to disguise his feelings. It may be that his red hair led to the story of his having a violent temper, to this day redheads being accredited with a quickness to anger. When I was living in Sicily where—rare in a Latin country—there are a number of redheads, I remember hearing that they were generally reputed to be 'men of violence'.

When the time came for Ulysses to marry, his father sent him to Sparta where he knew that the Spartan King, Oebalus, had a granddaughter of marriageable age. It was natural for Laertes, with his Argive background, to wish for an alliance in the Peloponnese, natural too that he should want to secure a link between his small island kingdom and the powerful state of Sparta.

Oebalus' granddaughter was called Penelope. To judge from other tales, like that of Atalanta, it seems to have been the custom to hold a kind of athletics contest to determine who should be the husband of an eligible young woman. In the case of Penelope it took the form of a race down one of the streets of Sparta, and was won by Ulysses. Some uncharitable commentators later asserted that the race was 'fixed' by Penelope's uncle who had taken a fancy to Ulysses.

Penelope was accordingly married to Ulysses in Sparta and the couple prepared to leave for their home in Ithaca. But Penelope's father, Icarius, was unwilling to let his daughter go and begged Ulysses to stay in Sparta. Ulysses, for his part, was already tired of the plains of the Eurotas and the heat of the Peloponnese. He longed, no doubt, to see his rocky island again, to feel the wind blow cool from the north, and hear the waves slap against the sides of the lean ships. A typical family row developed at the moment of departure, for just as Ulysses had harnessed the horses in the chariot, Icarius made a last appeal to his daughter. Unwilling to delay any longer, and aware no doubt that a woman likes to know who is master in the house, Ulysses turned to Penelope and said: "Make up your mind now! Either come to Ithaca with me, or stay behind in Sparta with your father!"

For answer Penelope covered her face with her veil to hide her blushes, thus intimating to her father that she intended to go with her husband. Icarius at last accepted the loss of his daughter, and even raised a statue to her which showed a young woman veiling her face. Known as the statue of Modesty, this became a well-known landmark in Sparta and was remarked upon by the Greek traveller and geographer, Pausanias, when he visited the

8

city in the 2nd century A.D. The young couple returned to Ithaca where, as next in line to the kingdom, they set up house in the palace of Ulysses' parents, Laertes and Anticlea. After a time Penelope was delivered of a son. He was called Telemachus, or Fighter Afar—a prophetic name for one who was to help his father as an archer in the battle against Penelope's suitors.

About 1200 B.C. the city of Troy was sacked and burned after a ten-year siege by a combined army from the Peloponnese and the islands like Ithaca which owed allegiance to the rulers of mainland Greece. "At the beginning of the 12th century," writes H. L. Lorimer, "contemporaneously with the collapse of the Hittite empire and the advance of the Sea-and-Land-raiders against Egypt, (City) Vlla was destroyed by fire. . . . There is nothing in the archaeological record to suggest that the destruction of Troy by Greeks was a subsequent fiction; on the contrary it is established as an historical event which occurred while Greeks and Trojans had relations with each other. . . . That it rests on ancient tradition is unquestioned; that which it embodies ascribes the destruction of Troy to a confederation of Greeks of the mainland and a few of the islands, and this was implicitly believed by Greeks of all periods. There is no counter-tradition."

Some time, then, in the years before 1200 B.C. Ulysses, son of Laertes, king of Ithaca, was married to Penelope and lived with her in his island. During this period there was, no doubt, considerable discussion among the Greeks as to the advisability of attacking Troy. Ulysses may quite likely have heard the subject debated while he was staying in Sparta. For, whether the rape of Helen was an historic fact or not, the attack and destruction of Troy certainly was, and the principal reasons for it are not hard to find.

The kingdom and city of Troy, situated just south of the Dardanelles on the mainland of Asia Minor, controlled the trade route between the Aegean, the Sea of Marmora, and the Black Sea. This route was important to the Greeks, and so long as Troy was friendly to them, all was well. But the moment that the Trojan state became hostile or indicated its intention to close the Dardanelles, war became inevitable. The Trojans may well have threatened to levy a toll on shipping passing through the straits; or to increase an existing toll; or it may have been no more than forethought which prompted the Greeks to eliminate this threat to their trade route before it developed. At any rate, in the decades before 1200 B.C., the subject of an attack on Troy was undoubtedly being mooted among the kings of Argos, Mycenae, and their dependants and feudal tributaries. Finally the die was cast, and Agamemnon, king of Mycenae and the most powerful prince in Greece, decided on war. He called on all the princes and rulers who owed him overlordship to furnish their quota of men and ships for the attack on Troy.

Among those whom Agamemnon visited was Ulysses, who had already acquired a reputation for bravery and skill which made him a natural asset to any army. Now Ulysses had been warned by an oracle that if he went with the invasion force to Troy he would not return for twenty years, and that when he did reach home again he would be alone and destitute. Such a fate naturally seemed unpleasant to a young man, happily married, and enjoying the regency of his island kingdom. As soon as he heard that king Agamemnon, together with his brother Menelaus, and Palamedes, son of the king of Euboea, had landed on a recruiting mission, Ulysses knew that he wanted no part in their war.

He was strong and active, so he could not escape on grounds of physical unfitness. He decided that he would pretend to be mad. When Agamemnon and his followers left the palace, having been told that they would find Ulysses busy at work, they came upon a strange sight. There was the man they had come to find —the future ruler of Ithaca, and lord of the other near-by islands —ploughing the sand on a beach, and dressed like a peasant. He was wearing an old conical felt hat and trudging behind a plough with a sower's sack at his waist. That was extraordinary enough in itself, but then they saw that the team which Ulysses had yoked together consisted of an ass and an ox. They hailed him, but he seemed not to recognize them. Now they noticed that he was sowing the beach, not with seed, but with handfuls of coarse salt. His behaviour and his appearance clearly suggested that he was mad.

It was at this point that Palamedes—who had perhaps grown wise to the fact that a number of the Greeks were reluctant to leave their homes and go to war—hit upon a stratagem which inevitably reminds one of the judgement of Solomon. Seizing the infant Telemachus from the arms of Penelope who was standing near by, he laid him on the ground directly in front of the advancing team. To avoid killing his only son, Ulysses immediately reined in his team and picked up the child. Unmasked by the sanity of this action, he was compelled to join the expedition. No doubt Palamedes smiled to think how he had scored off this cunning young man. He little knew what a terrible revenge Ulysses would take.

Three islands, Doulichion, Same, and Zakynthos, the modern Zante, came within the domain of Ulysses. From them and from Ithaca he furnished twelve ships, together with their crews and fighting men, for the expedition against Troy. Leaving the Ionian sea behind him, the reluctant hero sailed south with his squadron and rounded the promontory of Malea at the south of the Peloponnese. He made his way up to Aulis, the harbour in the Euboea channel where the Greek fleet had arranged to muster before setting sail across the Aegean to Troy.

It was during these months of preparation that Ulysses was despatched by Agamemnon on a recruiting mission. Agamemnon no doubt appreciated the irony of sending Ulysses on such a task, and realized that no one makes a better recruiting officer than a man who has himself been unwilling to go to war. Ulysses would be determined that no one should manage to 'dodge the draft' when he himself had failed.

Surprisingly enough, Achilles, greatest of the Greek heroes, was another one who was trying to avoid taking part in the war.

His mother Thetis had a foreknowledge that Achilles was destined either to gain eternal glory but die young, or to live long but ingloriously. With a woman's innate realism, she decided that a long life, however unimportant, was better than a short one. Accordingly she had arranged for Achilles to be disguised as a girl, and to be hidden among the women in the palace of the king of Skyros.

The island of Skyros lies about twenty miles east of Euboea, and rumour soon reached Ulysses and his companions that Achilles was hidden there in the king's palace. The task of unmasking Achilles was not an easy one, for the women's quarters were forbidden to men, and it would have been impossible to detect the lithe form of Achilles among the other veiled and long-robed figures. While Nestor and Ajax, who had also been sent to Skyros, hesitated as to what course to follow, Ulysses showed that it is guile and quick wits which triumph. Lycomedes, king of Skyros, allowed them to search his palace, protesting all the time that he had no knowledge of the man whom they were seeking. When the search had proved as fruitless as he had expected it, Ulysses apologized to the king—saying, at the same time, that he would like to leave some presents for the ladies of the court.

Embroidered dresses, jewellery, perfumes, and other suitable gifts, were accordingly brought into the hall of the palace and the ladies were asked to take their choice. Rather incongruously included among these gifts was a spear and a shield. Now Ulysses stood back and watched while the women came forward. Then, at a prearranged signal, a trumpet blast was sounded outside the hall. Ulysses' men-at-arms who were stationed outside began to clash their swords and shields together, and to make all the sounds as if an armed band was attacking the palace. While the women ran back screaming to their quarters, one of them was seen to tear off her veil. She stripped herself to the waist, and seized from the pile of gifts the spear and shield that Ulysses had so thoughtfully provided. Achilles was unmasked. There was nothing left for him but to accept the will of the Gods—a short life but a glorious one.

Throughout the course of the war it was by the use of his wits, where others relied solely upon their physical courage, that Ulysses won his great reputation. He was certainly brave in battle and Homer recounts numerous stories of his exploits—so much so, that at times it is difficult to tell whether Achilles is really the hero of the *Iliad*, or Ulysses. It was Ulysses, in company with Diomedes, who stole the Palladium, that ancient image of the goddess Athene upon whom the safety of the city depended. It was Ulysses who devised the stratagem of the Trojan horse. It was he who, when Helen tried to trick the hidden warriors into revealing their presence, prevented them from making any sound.

The man revealed in the story of the *Iliad* is one of the most unusual heroes in history. The poet has depicted him warts and all, and it is for this reason that Ulysses seems a far more credible human being than many others who are much nearer to us in time. One of the most unpleasant 'warts' was Ulysses' revenge on Palamedes. He bribed the latter's servant to conceal a letter from Priam, king of Troy, beneath his bed. Palamedes was accused by the Greeks of being a traitor, and was stoned to death. As he was to show in the long story of his wanderings, Ulysses was not a man to be trifled with, nor one who would forgive an injury.

3

The Black Ship

THE island of Tenedos lies a bare two miles off the coastline of
Asia Minor. Between the island and the shore the fast-running
current still sluices down from the Dardanelles, just as it did when
the Greeks set sail from Troy. Now known as Bozcaada, it is
one of the only two Turkish islands in the Aegean and is of little
importance today. Indeed, its whole history has been a happy
one—happy in that it has hardly featured in the bloody chronicles
of the Aegean, except on the one famous occasion when the
Greeks pretended to abandon the siege of Troy. When, on the
instructions of Ulysses, the Greeks had burned their camp and
retreated to their boats as if in defeat, it was towards Tenedos
that they set sail. It was nightfall when they left, and on the
following morning the Trojans coming out from their city
found the Greek camp burned and deserted, and only the mysterious wooden horse left behind on the shore in front of Troy. The
Trojans looked seaward, but there was no sign of the enemy
fleet, so they assumed that the Greek ships were already hull-
down, bound for their homeland. Little did they know, as they
dragged the horse across the sun-dried land and into the walls of
Troy, that the Greek fleet was lying concealed behind the low
bulk of Tenedos.

It is not a mountainous island, and its most prominent feature
Mount Sana is less than 400 feet high. In those days, though,
like the rest of the Aegean islands it was doubtless green and
spiky with trees. Little more than three miles long, it could

14

still afford anchorage to quite a large fleet on its south-western coast. On this side of the island there are innumerable small bays and coves where the ships would be safe from northerly winds, and from the southward-flowing current of the Dardanelles. If the stratagem of the wooden horse was largely the product of Ulysses' fertile mind, it was undoubtedly he who pointed out to Agamemnon where the ships could lie in safety out of sight of the Trojans. Not for nothing had Ulysses spent his youth in the Ionian islands—the home of pirates right up to the 19th century. There can have been few Greeks who knew more than Ulysses about winds and weather, suitable places for ambush, and anchorages where sea-raiders could bide their time.

On the night when Ulysses and the other Greeks emerged from the belly of the wooden horse to open the gates of Troy, Agamemnon and the fleet rowed silently back from their shelter behind Tenedos. They beached their ships, and made their final victorious assault on the sleeping city of their enemies. It is likely that the Greeks anchored their fleet in the small bay just south of Yukyeri Point. It is still a good anchorage for small vessels, with a bottom of sand and weed, and a beach protected from the north by a small headland on which now stands the ruins of an old fort. Even though the coastline may have changed a little during the past three thousand years, it was probably here that the Greek fleet was drawn up during the siege of Troy. The low peninsula still provides shelter from the prevailing winds and the current runs more slowly at this point. Out in the centre, between Tenedos and the mainland, it can run as fast as two-and-a-half knots, a considerable hazard for ships which under sail or oar are unlikely to have made more than four or five.

It was from this beach that Ulysses embarked with his comrades after the sack of Priam's capital. Behind them the city on the plain still smoked, and the ruined walls collapsed with a sighing fall. A south-easterly wind was blowing, hot off the mainland, as they hauled in the sleeping-stones which served them for anchors and cast off the stern hawsers that they had made fast to rocks on the beach.

For ten years Ulysses was now condemned to wander the scrolled waters of the Mediterranean, knowing dawn and sunset always to the same background of sea-smell, and pitch-pine, and wet wood. Even the places where he was detained during his travels were no more than small anchorages, humped shoulders of rock, scrub and trees, from which the sea was always visible. His ship, which in those years he grew to know better than other men know their houses, was similar in some respects to the Viking craft which in later centuries were to cross the North Sea and the Atlantic—and even make their way into those warm stretches of the Mediterranean around Sicily, where Ulysses was now destined to sail.

Unlike the ship which had carried his father Laertes in search of the Golden Fleece, the ship of Ulysses has no recorded name. Some authorities, and especially the supporters of Samuel Butler, have seen in this evidence that the writer of the *Odyssey* had little knowledge of, or interest in, the sea and seafarers. Nothing could be further from the truth, for the anthropomorphic habit of giving ships names is comparatively modern, although it is true we have record of ships' names in classical times. I have sailed out of Trapani and the Aegadian islands west of Sicily in recent years, in boats similar to those which the Homeric heroes used, and found on them only the official registration numbers which they were compelled to carry by the Italian Government. It is probable that some of these Sicilian boats are more like the Homeric vessels than are the caiques of the modern Aegean. Although they set a lateen sail—an inheritance from the Arabs— they are often engineless, and rely in calms upon the muscle-power of the men who crew them. Like the Homeric vessels they are open boats, shallow-drafted and keel-less, designed for being run up on beaches. Yet these 20th-century fishermen still go a hundred miles or more to fish the rich banks off the North African coast. They have a central rudder—something that

Ulysses did not have — and sometimes, but not always, a compass.

The number of men to each boat in Ulysses' squadron probably varied, but it seems unlikely that many of them were powered by more than twenty oars, ten to each side. This would necessitate a minimum crew of twenty, but since for long periods in the Mediterranean a vessel must be constantly under oars, each one almost certainly carried at least a double complement. The rowers could thus take watches. But, quite apart from ensuring a change of men, such a system would have been necessary to make certain that there were always fresh men available to provide landing parties when it came to the piracy that was an integral part of the Homeric chieftain's life. Presuming that Ulysses left Troy with twelve ships, the same number which he had brought with him from the islands, it seems reasonable to assess the total number of his force as about five hundred men. There could have been more, for some of the ships might have been bigger than others, but on this matter Homer is silent.

Greece was well-forested in those days and particularly rich in pine. Pine has always been a good wood for the planking and masting of ships, although oak is preferable for keels and frames, and may well have been used. Common epithets which are applied to ships in the Homeric poems are 'swift', 'well-balanced', 'hollow', and 'black'. 'Swift' in these terms is clearly used to distinguish a war-galley from the more beamy trading vessel. "Well-balanced' is still a nautical term for any vessel that handles well, particularly when it is applied to a sailing vessel. 'Hollow' will surely mean an open boat, or one that is not decked-in. This was basically true of the Homeric ship, except that it would seem to have had a partially-enclosed section at the bows and stern. The forepart was no doubt used as a storage space, and the after-part was where the master, the helmsman, and other people of note had their quarters. There was no truly enclosed cabin, such as one finds even in a small modern yacht. The Homeric ship was designed for short passages. Whenever possible, it was beached at night while the crew went ashore, made their fire for a meal, and slept out in the open, in a near-by cave, or sometimes under the mainsail which could be spread over a tent-like arrangement of oars.

The adjective 'black', so often applied to the ships, must certainly mean that they were tarred as a protection against wind and weather. The warm waters of the Mediterranean, then as now, were a favourable home for worm – the sinister, wood-loving *teredo* among others. Now tar has been used as a preventive against worm since the earliest days of navigation, and Ulysses was fortunate that one of the islands which came under his sway had its own natural pitch lake. 'Well-wooded Zacynthos' as it was always called, the modern Zante, lies about twenty miles south of Ithaca. Its pitch lake was first recorded by Herodotus in the 5th century B.C., but it is reasonable to assume that it had been in use since man first discovered the efficacy of pitch as a wood preservative. "The pitch wells of Zante are in accord with the island's elegiac mood. The pitch rises to the surface through small pools of water, being skimmed off when the tarry concentration is thick enough. It is curious to reflect that the pitch still serves the same purpose that it did when Herodotus first came here: It is used for caulking and anti-fouling the local fishing boats and trading vessels."

The Greek ships had been many years away from their home ports by the time that the siege of Troy was over, and one can only conclude that they brought with them large quantities of dried pitch for recaulking and anti-fouling. Under the hot sun of the northern Aegean, and in the lukewarm waters of midsummer, not a ship would have survived if they had not been carefully maintained by carpenters, shipwrights, caulkers and riggers. No doubt they made fires on the beaches and, once a year, melted down great slabs of pitch for repainting and preserving their vessels. (I have found worm in my own pine-planked sailing boat after only twelve months in the Mediterranean.)

Ulysses' ship is also sometimes described as 'blue'. No doubt her topsides above water were painted indigo, one of the earliest natural colours used by Mediterranean peoples. It is more than likely that she also had the 'oculus' or 'eye' painted on either bow. This custom which survives in the Mediterranean to this day derives from the ancient Egyptian Eye of Ra, the Sun God, which was painted on their vessels many centuries before the Homeric period.

Such was Ulysses' home then, a swift, well-balanced, hollow, tarred boat, with probably ten oars a side. She carried one mast, almost certainly a fir spar, from which she set one square sail. The sail itself may have been of linen or papyrus, both of which materials the Egyptians had been exporting for centuries. There is a reference to a rope of papyrus in the house of Ulysses, but whether his sail was papyrus or linen, it is almost certain that his cordage will have been of papyrus and in some cases of leather. The sail was only set in moderate winds, and not expected to stand up to the strains which seamen would later demand from canvas.

The mast was movable, as is the case in many Mediterranean sailing boats to this date. It was housed in a sort of three-sided tabernacle and could be manhandled down so as to rest in a cradle in the stern. Supported by stays fore and aft, the mast will not have been very tall, since it needed only to support a square sail on a simple wooden yard. Quite large fishing and trading boats in the Gulf of Genoa and elsewhere use a similar type of mast and rigging to this day. When in harbour, the mast is invariably lowered to reduce top-weight and thus make the motion of the boat more comfortable for the men on board. I have no doubt that Ulysses and his men, when at anchor, often took their siestas—as I have done myself—under the shadow of the sail stretched across the lowered mast.

The oars, like the mast, will have been of fir and would seem to have been very broad in the blade—at least if the Homeric comparison of them to 'winnowing-shovels' may be taken at its face value. Quite apart from anything else, this would certainly account for the difficulty they often seem to have experienced in rowing against the wind. There were no rowlocks in the modern sense of the word. The oars were worked either over the gunwale, or through small ports in the ship's side against thongs of leather. Most Mediterranean boatmen, from the Aegean to the Tyrrhenian Sea, still prefer wooden thole-pins and a leather or rope grommet to metal rowlocks.

Professor H. Browne in his *Handbook of Homeric Study* commented with some surprise that "The ships had not even a fixed rudder, but used a hand-paddle for steering, and consequently they could only sail before the wind, so that 'making points', and much more 'tacking' was out of the question." The rudder, as we know it today, was a north European invention, and probably originated in the Baltic. This axled, hinged rudder was still considered something of a modern invention when used in the caravels of Henry the Navigator in the early 15th century. It was unknown in the classical world.

The 'peedalion', or hand-paddle, used by Ulysses was mounted on a heavy wooden peg right aft in the vessel, and pivoted against the peg in a leather thong. There were two pegs, one to port and one to starboard, so that the paddle could always be shipped on the lee side, and it is possible that two steering paddles were fixed, one on either side. A 5th-century vase, now in the British Museum, shows Ulysses passing the Sirens and the helmsman grasping the port-side steering oar. It is noticeable in this painting that there are only seven oar-ports visible on the vessel, thus arguing a minimum rowing crew of fourteen. It is quite possible to steer very well in a sailing boat with something like a hand-paddle shipped over one side or another, as I have proved myself once when having to rig a jury-rudder of this type in a 28-foot sailing boat. That the vessel of Ulysses could not do anything except run before the wind, because she was steered by a paddle, rather than a rudder, is demonstrably untrue. Being square-rigged, she would of course be unable to sail at all close to the wind, but she would have been quite efficient with the wind anywhere on the beam, or abaft the beam.

I have sailed in the Aegean, and out of Malta and Sicily, in fishing boats much smaller but similar in their general lines to the Homeric craft. When the wind was on the beam or ahead of it, the men on the lee side started rowing. This prevented the boat from making a lot of leeway, or 'crabbing' down wind. It is true, of course, that nowadays these boats set a lateen sail, a much more efficient rig than the old-fashioned square sail of Homeric times. But I see no reason to doubt that Ulysses' ship was quite efficient with the wind coming from anywhere abaft the beam.

The oared galley, which was the type of ship directly descended from those of the Homeric period, survived in the Mediterranean right into the 18th, and even the early 19th, century. The oared sailing vessel did not, in fact, disappear until very recent years when the advent of the mass-produced diesel engine gave the Mediterranean fishermen an alternative to oars during the long calms of mid-summer. For centuries after the English and the Scandinavian races had discarded oared vessels they were still in active use in the Mediterranean. The last naval action in which the oared galley predominated was the battle of Lepanto in 1571. Two centuries later, galleys were still used in the Mediterranean squadrons of Louis XV. J. Forfait, a French marine engineer of the 19th century, who made a special study of the Mediterranean galley, reached the conclusion that in a flat calm it could maintain four and a half knots for the first hour, two and a quarter to one and a half for subsequent hours. The galleys of Ulysses were a great deal smaller than those which Forfait was discussing. They would, therefore, with their shorter waterline-length and less manpower most probably have had a top speed under oars of about four knots. Under sail, and running free with the wind from abaft the beam, they may sometimes have made six knots or more. In view of Ulysses' later adventures with wind and weather, whirlpools and tidal streams, it is important to bear in mind how slow and small was the craft that he was sailing. Things which are simple, and of little or no moment to a modern ship would have been terrifying and dangerous hazards to a sailor of the Homeric period. Quite apart from the size and comparative inefficiency of his craft, the early mariner was without chart or compass. He was venturing in a world where all was strangeness and mystery. It can hardly come as a surprise if his voyage came to be emblazoned with myth and fantasy by bards and story-tellers.

If I have compared Ulysses' ship to a small galley, the men who pulled the oars were far from being galley-slaves. They were free-born Greeks from the islands, and there was no conception at that time of the oar bench being a fitting place only for a slave. Ulysses refers to them as his 'friends', his 'companions', and his 'comrades', and there is never any suggestion that they were even of a lower caste than the hero himself. Centuries later, the Greeks who manned the galleys and defeated the Persian fleet at Salamis were all free men. It would seem that the galley-slave was a much later conception. Even at that the Roman galleys which defeated the Carthaginians in the decisive sea-fight off western Sicily in 241 B.C. were manned by freeborn Roman citizens, although Rome's sailors were, in general, Greeks from southern Italy. But, as anyone who has ever pulled an oar under the hot Mediterranean sun knows well, the degree of physical fitness and endurance required for long periods at the oar is immense. Whether one is a slave or not, the hardness of the life remains much the same. Jean Marteille de Bergerac, who was a French galley-slave in the 17th century, left some vivid descriptions of the life. "Picture to yourself six men chained to a bench naked as they were born, one foot on the stretcher, the other lifted and placed against the bench in front of him, support-ing in their hands a vastly heavy oar and stretching their bodies backwards while their arms are extended to push the loom of the oar clear of the backs of those in front of them. . . . Sometimes the galley-slaves row ten, twelve, even twenty hours at a stretch, without the slightest rest or break." Now Ulysses' companions were not slaves, and the oars they handled were much smaller than those which de Bergerac was describing, yet there is no doubt that there were occasions when they had to row for many hours without a break.

The planks of the boats may have been fastened with copper or bronze nails, or with wooden dowels. The boat will almost certainly have been carvel-built, the traditional Mediterranean technique which is said to have originated in the East. The term 'carvel' implies that the plank edges are laid flush, one on top of the other, as opposed to clinker building, which is of Scandinavian origin, where the planks overlap. Most of the fittings, as is the case in the eastern Mediterranean to this day, will have been wooden and extremely simple. But the hoops on which the square sail was fastened to the yard were probably of bronze. The sail could be brailed up to the yard, and in bad weather the whole yard and sail could be lowered down into the boat and lashed along the centre of the thwarts. The sail was attached to the yard by hoops, and by ropes which ran over the yard from the stern of the vessel. By hauling on these ropes the sail could be brailed up tight to the yard, while by checking away on them it could be lowered down to its full working span. A somewhat similar arrangement was to be seen until quite recently among a few west-coast Italian fishing boats, which carried a standing yardarm for the mainsail. The whole system was simple but, as most small boat sailors can confirm, the simpler is often the better. The very fact that the vessel was without a keel, and drew at the most only a few feet, meant that it could take shelter in coves, bays, creeks, and estuaries, where little but a rowing boat or sailing dinghy could go today.

In a more or less open boat, with no charts or navigational instruments, and largely dependent upon the strength of the oarsmen, it was natural that the Homeric sailors should stick close to the shore whenever possible. At the first sign of approaching bad weather it was their custom to look for a suitable shelving beach, run the boat ashore, and wait until the danger was past and the sea had subsided.

When Ulysses and his ships left Troy it is more than likely that they made straight for Tenedos across the narrow strait. They would certainly not have ventured directly into the open sea south of the island, and it is probable that they made first for the anchorage at the north-eastern tip of Tenedos, where the fishing village of Bozcaada now stands. There was certainly a south-easterly blowing when they set sail, for in Book XI of the *Odyssey* Ulysses tells how, "the same wind that drove me from Troy brought me to Ismarus, the city of the Cicones." Now the Cicones lived on the southern shores of Thrace, on that part of the mainland which faces across the sea towards the island of Samothrace. Their land lies north-west of Troy, so a square-sailed ship would need a south-easterly wind to be 'driven' to their shore. Something one cannot know is whether Ulysses had always intended to sail north and raid the Cicones. Perhaps in his opportunist's way he decided that the wind should not be wasted and that, while he and his men were in the northern Aegean, they might just as well do a little more looting before sailing home.

I incline to the view that it was a deliberately planned raid, for there was nothing to prevent the ships waiting safely at anchor to the north of Tenedos until the wind changed. After all, having spent ten years in the area, Ulysees knew that the northerlies were the prevailing winds, and knew also that the south-going current from the Dardanelles was all in his favour for making his way homeward down the Aegean. But his decision to attack Ismarus was natural enough, for he knew how prosperous the city was and that the Cicones made the best wine in that part of the world.

The Cicones had been allies of the Trojans during the war, but their own country had escaped devastation. It is possible that it was not only the thought of their prosperity which lured Ulysses, but the fighting man's natural dislike of those who have grown fat and complacent from sitting on the sidelines. Unfortunately, what should have been no more than a profitable diversion on the way home turned to disaster. The seal of ill-luck was set upon Ulysses' voyage from the very beginning.

4

In the Aegean

THE good wine of Ismarus was famous throughout antiquity. It came from the vines grown on the slopes of Mount Ismaro, still a prominent feature of the Thracian coastline to any vessel approaching the modern city and port of Alexandroupolis. The coastline in this part of Thrace is mostly low and sandy, easy of access for the ships and raiding party of Ulysses. To men hardened by years of warfare it must have seemed that the sack of this opulent city would be the simplest of matters. So it would have been, if Ulysses had been able to call off his men after the operation was completed. But, like many another commander, he found that it was no easy matter to control his troops once they had been let off the leash, and allowed to indulge a taste for wine and plunder.

Having dropped the island Tenedos astern of them, the most likely course for Ulysses will have been to the east of Imbros and Samothrace, and then to make a landfall near Cape Makri. Curiously enough there is no mention of Samothrace, a strange island where the cult of the twin Cabeiri was celebrated. But Samothrace must certainly have been used by Ulysses as a landmark, for its central peak, over 5,000 feet high, is the loftiest mountain in the northern Aegean until one comes to Holy Athos on the western mainland. But the poet is strangely silent about the islands and the geographical features of the Aegean—an indication, some have said, that he was unfamiliar with this sea; and others, that he did not bother to describe a sea which was

26

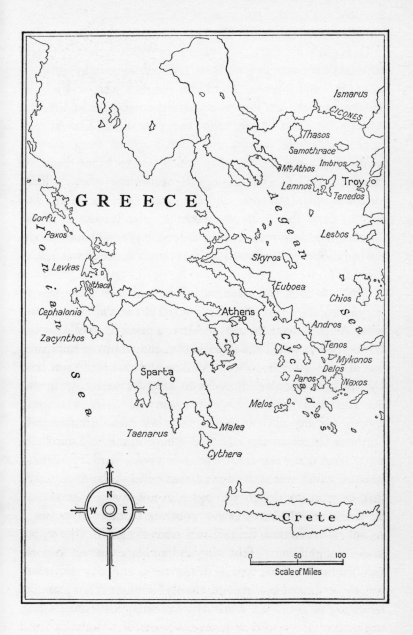

familiar to all his listeners. Samothrace, in any case, will have provided the Greeks with a useful landmark for their homeward run after their raid on the Ciconian coastline.

To begin with, the attack was a complete success. The Greeks beached their boats, swept ashore, and took the city by storm. "I sacked it," said Ulysses, "and killed the men who held it . . ." The women and the loot were divided among the raiders. But it was now, when Ulysses urged that they should leave at once before the whole country was roused against them, that his followers showed the stupidity which was to haunt them and bring them all to grief during the wandering years. Seduced by the women, the wine, and the pleasures of the shore, they delayed until they were overtaken by the vengeance of the Cicones who had roused their up-country neighbours. In the pitched battle that followed an average of six men was lost to every ship.

Ulysses himself had come out of the raid with a fine present of gold talents, a silver bowl, and seven jars of the best Ismarian wine. All these were the gifts of Maro, a priest of Apollo, whom Ulysses had surprised in a sacred grove, and whom he had spared out of respect for his office. "Mellow and unmixed" was how Ulysses later described the wine to king Alcinous, adding that one cupful of Ismarian wine to twenty of water was strong enough for any man. It is true that they make good wine in northern Greece to this day, and I have drunk in Samothrace a red wine that came from Alexandroupolis, hard by Homer's Ismarus, which was as good as any to be had in the Aegean. But that, as most winelovers will agree, is not saying a great deal, for the wines of Greece cannot compare to those of France. I do not refer to *retsina*, the resinated wine of modern Greece, but to the 'straight' wines of the mainland, or islands such as Santorin and Lesbos. But what type of drink was it, one may ask, which had to be diluted one part to twenty? Philippe Diolé, has the following to say: "We know approximately what these Greek wines were like, and their heirs, the wines of Campania. Small

28

quantities have been found in sealed glass flasks deposited in tombs. Such analyses as have been carried out show that the wine of the ancients . . . had little in common with what we call wine today. The peoples of antiquity were constantly devising methods of blending, sweetening and diluting, whereas what we most appreciate in wine is purity. To say that wine has not been 'adulterated' is, with us, to give high praise. They, on the other hand, were particularly free-handed in the matter of adding sweet-scented substances in order to obtain a beverage with the consistency of syrup which, as a rule, even hardened drinkers could not swallow unless it was well-watered. These 'wines'— not unlike certain Greek wines of today—contained a great diversity of elements, including honey, aloes, thyme, berries of the myrtle and sometimes even sea-water!" Ulysses calls the wine of Ismarus "red and honeyed," and adds that "its sweet fumes were irresistible." Whatever it may have tasted like, it was certainly highly alcoholic, as later events were to prove.

One misfortune which the Greeks did not suffer after their attack on Ismarus was to find themselves embayed by the southerly wind that had driven them there from Tenedos. A terrible gale from the north, "covering land and sea with dark cloud," proved something of a blessing. It sped them away from a coastline that was now thoroughly roused against these wandering pirates.

Driven rapidly southward down the Aegean, they were forced to lower the sails and yards into their boats to prevent further damage. Farrington, and others who uphold the theory that the *Odyssey* was written by someone without any real knowledge of the sea, have found evidence for their belief in the statement that, after the sails had been lowered, "we rowed the bare ships landward with all our strength." What seaman, it has been said, would act in such a way? Would he not, rather, stand out to sea for fear of losing his vessel on the rocky shores? The mistake that has been made here is to attempt to judge Homeric sailing techniques by those which have been evolved over centuries for completely different types of ships and boats. It is true that the last advice one would give a modern sailor, caught out in bad weather, would be to close the shore. But the vessels of Ulysses were not designed to ride out heavy weather at sea. Open, shallow-draught boats, they were totally unsuitable for weathering breaking seas—and the type of sea raised by a strong north-easter in the Aegean is highly dangerous even for a well-found modern sailing boat. Ulysses and his companions will have done exactly what Homer describes—rowed as hard as they could for the land. They will have found some point, cape, or island, that gave them shelter from the wind and weather, and then they will have hauled their boats ashore.

For two days and two nights the gale continued to blow, and they lay up in safety. There is no mention of what part of the coastline or in what island they took shelter, only that on the third morning, "there was a beautiful dawn." So they stepped the masts again, and took up their places in the boats, "leaving the wind and the helmsman between them to keep our vessels on course."

We do not know what time of the year it was when Ulysses set sail—storms from the north are quite common in the Aegean even in mid-summer—but we do know that now, as they ran southward, they were taking advantage of the prevailing wind over this sea. The Meltemi as the modern Greeks call them, or the Etesian winds to give them their technical name, blow over the Aegean throughout the summer, always from a northerly direction. As the hot air lifts over the Aegean and the Mediterranean south of Crete, so a cold air-stream flows in from Russia and the north to replace it. It was on the reliability of the Etesian winds—as reliable almost as the Trade Winds of the Oceans—that the Aegean civilization was based. In the early days of sailing and navigation they made possible almost regular communications between the coastal islands of Greece, the Peloponnese, Asia Minor, Crete, and even Egypt.

Ulysses knew the regularity of these winds. Later in the *Odyssey*, after he had returned to Ithaca and was pretending to be a Cretan sea-rover, he described a passage from his fictitious life when he had set out from Crete to raid the coast of Egypt. "We sailed off," he said, "with a fresh and favourable wind from the north. It was as easy as sailing down stream. And on the fifth day we reached the great River of Egypt . . ." Now from Messara Bay, the most sheltered harbour in southern Crete and probably the one Ulysses had in mind, the distance to the mouth of the Nile is a little over 300 miles. Since so many scholars and historians have poured scorn on the accuracy of the *Odyssey* in terms of navigational and sailing references, it is of the utmost importance to see what Homer makes Ulysses consider an ideal 'run' for his ship under favourable conditions. From Crete, he says that he reached the mouth of the Nile in five days or 'on the fifth day'. This gives him a daily distance made good of a little over sixty miles. His average speed from Crete, then, is roughly three knots, which is about what one would expect for this type of vessel running before a moderate wind under a simple square-sail. In my quest for the places Ulysses visited, and the route which he took, I shall show that there is little inconsistency anywhere in the Homeric account. An average speed of some three knots is just what Ulysses' ship does make under good conditions.

After the storm had blown itself out and the ship had got under way again, the poem gives no information about Ulysses' course down the Aegean, until he reaches Cape Malea at the southern end of the Peloponnese. It is still possible to hazard a guess as to his most likely route. After leaving Troy the main body of the Grecian fleet had sailed due south for Lesbos. Here they hesitated, debating whether to sail inside Chios—between the island and the mainland of Asia Minor—or outside the small island of Psara, and thus cut straight across to the safety of Euboea. Euboea is referred to more often in the *Iliad* and *Odyssey* than any other Aegean island, and the reason seems clear enough. The long Euboea channel, strong though its current is, provided the Greeks with a sheltered and easy passage. This was something they far preferred to hazarding their ships on the open stretches of the Aegean. So, if Ulysses had taken the Euboea channel on his way home after the gale, I think that we would have heard about it. What is far more likely, is that his ships were swept south past the island of Skyros, and through the Doro Channel at the foot of Euboea. Ulysses and his companions would now have been among the Cyclades islands.

There is only one reference in the *Odyssey* which provides a possible clue to Ulysses' course after leaving Ismarus and before sighting the island of Cythera off Cape Malea. Many years later when Ulysses is wrecked in the Land of the Phaeacians, and first sets eyes on Nausicaa, he compares her grace and beauty to that young palm tree which "I saw in Delos, springing up near the altar of Apollo." Now it is quite possible that Ulysses may have visited Delos before the Trojan war when he was sailing north-ward up the Aegean, on his way to the rendezvous at Aulis. It is equally likely, though, that he called in and anchored with his fleet off Delos on his way homeward. If so, he may not have come through the Doro Channel but due south to Mykonos, to drop anchor in the blue straits between Delos and Rheneia. Having spared the priest of Apollo when his men sacked Ismarus, and carrying in his ship the gifts that Maro had made him, it would have been natural to go ashore on the sacred island of Delos and make a suitable offering to the god Apollo.

When one sails through the Cyclades today it is their bare sculptured quality that makes them distinctive from all other Mediterranean islands. It was the blinding light of Delos that dazzled me when I anchored my small boat in the shadow of Mount Cynthus, protected by the ancient mole. Across the white-flecked strait, the sister island of Rheneia harboured a few sheep, and on Delos itself only a solitary goat-herd and his flock disturbed my silence. But these sun-devoured islands which the modern traveller knows are very different from the islands of the Homeric age. They were thickly forested in those days, and there were many more springs, green groves, and grassy places.

Seriphos, Siphnos, Milos, Santorin—I think of sailing past them, and of being blinded by the glare off their rocks after the cool, veined marble of the sea. But the islands which Ulysses knew were as rich and green as Corfu is today, or as the long valleys of Rhodes where the butterflies seem like specks of fire in the aquarium light beneath the leaves.

Putting the Cyclades behind him, Ulysses coasted down until Cape Malea and its outrider, the island of Cythera, opened up a needle's eye of channel before his bows. It was his intention to pass through the strait and then, hugging the western coast of the Peloponnese, make his way home to Ithaca.

5

Land of the Lotus-eaters

AHEAD lay Cythera, the sacred island where Aphrodite had emerged from the sea. On their starboard hand was the frowning headland of Cape Malea; then as now, one of the most lonely places in the Mediterranean. Beyond it the sea ran back blue and shining, into the Gulf of Lakonia. Out of sight, at the head of the gulf where the fishing village of Githeion now lies, there is a barren islet, called Marathonisi. Here, if Patrick Leigh Fermor's informant was correct, was the place where the 'momentous and incendiary honeymoon' of Paris and Helen began. Marathonisi was Homer's Kranae, where Paris dropped anchor on the first night of his elopement with Helen. I feel sure of only one thing, that if Ulysses knew the identity of that small islet, he spat to starboard and called down a curse on all faithless wives.

It was now that the swell, which runs down almost ceaselessly from the north, began to pluck the ships of the Greeks further and further from the land. Hard though they rowed, they found that they could not double the cape and get into sheltered water. The north wind piped up again, and the sound of the cliff-wash off the cape began to fade. The thyme- and fennel-scented headland drew away from them. The wind strengthened, and soon the ships were swaggering before a hard blow. Gregale or Grego, the Greek wind, is what the Mediterranean sailors call it. It was this same wind which, centuries after Ulysses, was to drive

St. Paul headlong from Crete to shipwreck on the bare flanks of Malta.

With wind and current both combining to drive them away from the land, Ulysses and his companions watched in despair as the shores of Greece faded. By nightfall they were south of Cythera, being carried away to the south-west through the empty wind-rinsed bowl of sea and sky. Above them to the north the constellation of the Bear mocked them—that one fixed point in all the turning heavens towards which they should have been steering if they were to reach their homes in the Ionian Islands.

". . . For nine days I was driven by those cursed winds across the fish-infested sea." The waters upon which Ulysses was now destined to spend so many years of his life were as strange to the Greeks of his day as was the Atlantic to the men who sailed with Columbus. It was the sea of myth and mystery, ending at the Pillars of the World, beyond which the unrelenting Stream of Ocean rolled eternally round the earth. If the Voyage of the Argonauts is the story of how the Greeks first discovered the trade routes to the Black Sea, the voyage of Ulysses, himself an Argonaut's son, is the story of how they first began to break into the western Mediterranean. Ulysses' voyage is comparable in many ways to that of Columbus. From the moment that he leaves Greece behind him, he becomes more than the hero of Troy— the cunning strategist who devised that city's downfall—he is now the archetype of all explorers.

During his voyage across the Mediterranean, Ulysses encountered no other ships. That in itself may not seem so remarkable. Even today, crossing in a sailing boat from Sicily to the Ionian Islands, I have seen no shipping for four days until I reached Corfu. But the extraordinary fact which confronts one on reading the *Odyssey* is that, from the moment of leaving the Aegean and being swept into the central and western Mediterranean, there is no mention of any ships other than those of Ulysses' squadron. Not a single sail lifts over the barren horizon. We meet men and monsters, priestesses and sacred groves, but we meet no other seamen. Ulysses and his followers are forced to fight with enemies on shore, but there is never a sea-battle. There are no other ships. The Greeks, it would seem, have a monopoly of knowledge about navigation and ship-building.

It is the strange silence and emptiness of the sea upon which Ulysses was now embarked that first puzzled me. In Book xxiii of the *Iliad*, Homer refers to Phoenicians being present in Greek waters as traders. Eumaeus, Ulysses' faithful swineherd, also tells how he was captured from the island of Syra by Phoenicians, and sold as a slave. The Phoenicians, then, were known to the Greeks of Homer's time. But when he comes to tell the story of Ulysses' wanderings outside the Aegean or the western coast of Greece, there is no mention of them. Ulysses, if we are to accept the evidence, was "the first who ever burst into that silent sea."

In the past, when comparatively little was known about the Phoenicians and their civilization, it was sometimes assumed that they had been navigating in the western Mediterranean many centuries before the Greeks. Since then the weight of evidence seems to suggest only that they were established in the central and western Mediterranean by the 8th century B.C. H. L. Lorimer writes: "Two Phoenician inscriptions found at Nora in Sardinia and dating to the first half of the eighth century constitute the earliest evidence for the presence of the Phoenicians in the West Mediterranean, but indicate a somewhat earlier date for preliminary exploration and settlement. This supports the statement of Thucydides, so far uncorroborated by archaeological evidence, that they had established depots all round the Sicilian coast before the Greeks planted their first colonies in the island. It also accords with the evidence of the *Odyssey*, in which the west coast of Greece is within the westward limit of Phoenician activity." On the other hand it would seem that the Phoenicians were visitors to Malta some centuries before this. The 12th century B.C. (which is the period that Homer is describing in the *Odyssey* and the *Iliad*) was a time when the Cretan, or Minoan, seapower had

collapsed before invaders from the north, and when the Phoenicians had not yet founded their colonies on the North African
coast.

Ulysses met with no other ships west of Greece—perhaps
because there were none. In his encounters with the inhabitants
of the lands and places which some scholars have called 'mythical'
it is noticeable that all these people are landbound. The story
of Ulysses is, it seems, the story of the first Greek sailor to explore
the unknown western Mediterranean. The reasons why so many
of the places and events described have been over-laid with
fantasy and myth is because even when Homer was writing,
some three or four centuries after the events described, this part
of the Mediterranean was still practically unexplored.

For nine days after being swept past Cythera, the Greeks were
at sea and out of sight of all land. On the tenth day they "reached
the land of the Lotus-Eaters." Before attempting to find this land
upon the chart, I must admit that both Ulysses and I are entering
upon a world of speculation—a world that was uncharted for
many centuries. It was one which neither Homer, let alone
Ulysses, could have defined with any accuracy. The 14th Edition
of the *Encyclopaedia Britannica* warns off all speculators and
navigators like myself with the words: "It should be plain enough
that the Lotus-Eaters and their country are situated in fairy-land;
but, besides allegorical interpretations, many ancient scholars
amused themselves by trying to identify them with some people
of Northern Africa, since that continent produces one or two
edible plants called λωτός by the Greeks. This foolishness has
been imitated by some moderns. . . ."

Despite this admonition, I shall persevere in trying to identify
the Land of the Lotus-Eaters. Both Herodotus and Scylax of
Caryanda identified this 'fairy-land' with a nation living in
western Libya, and the almost universal consent of antiquity places
them in, or in the region of, the modern island of Jerba.

Scylax of Caryanda in his Handbook or Pilot for mariners,
traced all the important places which were known about 350

B.C. around the Mediterranean coastline, and in particular Libya. His identification of the Jerba area with the Land of the Lotus-Eaters has at least a superior argument to that of modern sceptics, for he was living within a few centuries of the events described. The names given by sailors and peasants to certain areas tend to pass on, relatively unchanged, over many generations.

It is important to bear in mind that the ancient Greek tradition that Troy had really existed, and that its site was the mound of Hissarlik in Asia Minor, was disputed by Alexandrian geographers and historians in classical times. Centuries later, in Victorian scholastic circles, it could be argued that Troy had never existed at all and that the whole Homeric cycle was purely imaginary. It took the genius of Schliemann, acting largely on the Homeric poems, to find Troy in the very place where the earliest reports had said that it was. It also took the genius of Sir Arthur Evans, and others, to uncover the Kingdom of Minos—another fiction according to many once-reputable authorities.

If Jerba, or the near-by mainland of Libya, was the Land of the Lotus-Eaters, how would this match up with the ascertainable facts—the distance from Cape Malea and the speed of Homeric ships? Now, when Ulysses was driven past the island of Cythera, it was "the swell, the current, and the north wind combined" that sent him off course. He was driven before them for nine days across the Mediterranean. Only what we now call a north-easterly 'Levanter' is likely to have blown steadily—for so long —from the same direction, and a Levanter happens to be the predominant wind over this section of the Mediterranean. "They occur most often," says the Admiralty Pilot for this area, "with high pressure northward of Malta and low pressure southward." In general they do not last more than five days, but even after the main force of the gale has blown out, the wind often comes from the same quarter for several days more, while the whole surface-water keeps moving in a south-westerly direction for some time after the wind has dropped.

As we have seen from Ulysses' description of a voyage from

Crete to Egypt, the speed for his type of ship with the wind astern was about three knots. A speed of three knots for nine days and nights (216 hours) gives one a distance travelled of 648 miles. Now the island of Jerba lies approximately 650 miles from a point mid-way between Cape Malea and the island of Cythera. Ulysses, at an average speed of three knots, would accordingly have reached there on the tenth day — which is what the *Odyssey* says that he does. With a Levanter blowing, and in an open boat running before wind and sea, somewhere near the Gulf of Gabes (where Jerba lies), is exactly where one would expect to find Ulysses and his squadron. I see little reason why it should be considered 'foolishness' to agree with the ancient ascription that Jerba was the Land of the Lotus-Eaters.

One must now distinguish between the facts of the Lotus and the accretions of later legend. This was no Tennysonian land of 'amaranth and moly', although there is plenty of reason to think that after the storms of the Aegean and the long voyage across an unknown sea there were many sailors who would have agreed that:

> "We have had enough of action, and of motion we,
> Roll'd to starboard, roll'd to larboard, when the surge
> was seething free . . ."

If the Lotus was never a 'honeyed fruit' which drugged a man into a state of happy lethargy, it did indeed exist. It was a sweet object something like a grape which, when mixed with grain, could keep a man alive. Both the *cordia myxa* and the *rhamnus zizyphus* have claims to be the Homeric lotus: the first, a fruit that grows in clusters, was described by Pliny in his *Natural History*; the second is a kind of crab-apple from which cider can be made. It has sometimes been conjectured that it may have been the alcoholic cider that made the Greek sailors eager to stay ashore, forgetful of their homes. It is more likely, though, that it was the sloe-like fruit of the *cordia myxa* out of which the North African natives used to make a kind of mealy bread. In ancient times it was a staple article of food among the poor.

If it had been a drink which had seduced the sailors one can be sure that Homer would have mentioned it. The uses and abuses of wine figure largely in the *Odyssey*—sailors then as now, being fond of strong drink. But it is clear that the lotus was a food, not a drink. Ulysses' men were given some "honeyed fruit to taste . . . and all they wished for was to stay there, and eat the lotus, and forget that they had homes awaiting them." Even if the lotus was not as attractive as later romantics have imagined it, the sailors' reaction is not surprising. They were safe ashore; there was water in the land; and there was something to eat. The lethargic climate of North Africa is notorious. And if there were male Lotus-Eaters on the shore, there must surely have been women.

I was a sailor in a ship torpedoed off this stretch of coast during the last war, and spent nearly a week here waiting for transport back to Alexandria. If I had not been subject to the Naval Discipline Act, and if I had been provided with as many agreeable facilities as were Ulysses' men, I doubt very much if I would willingly have hazarded myself once more upon the sea. There are many worse things in life than resting in the shade when the sun is high; swimming in the cool of the evening; and contemplating the futility of "clanging fights, and flaming towns, and sinking ships, and praying hands." I do not think that it is only to the lotus that one must look for the sailors' reluctance to leave that tawny, sun-drenched shore.

The North Star

JERBA today is rich with olives and with date palms. It is a pleasant island, and one where the world could still be easily forgotten. Its inhabitants are Berbers, those light-skinned North Africans among whom one sometimes even finds a redhead. Their racial name seems to be pre-Homeric, at least if one equates them with the 'Barabara' mentioned in Egyptian inscriptions of 1700 and 1300 B.C. Some authorities have derived their name from the Greek 'Barbaros', a barbarian. It is just conceivable that Ulysses and his men first coined the word. I imagine him standing on the beach that faces across the narrow channel to the mainland, waiting for news from the scouting party he had sent out. Soon the word comes back that the land is inhabited and the people friendly, but that his men cannot understand their speech. It seems to them that it is nothing but—'bar-bar-bar'. Hence the word 'Barbaros', one who goes 'bar-bar', and is not civilized enough to speak Greek.

Three men were sent out on the scouting expedition and these were the only Greeks to eat the lotus. But the moment that he saw they were thinking of deserting and staying ashore, Ulysses took rapid action. He knew from his experience of war how quickly mutiny and desertion can spread. "I was compelled to use force to bring them back aboard. . . ." The men wept all the way as they were brought to the ships under escort. Ulysses was taking no chances, he was determined to show the squadron that he was firmly in command. "Once they were on board I had them dragged below the benches and put in chains." Presumably the Greeks had watered their ships by now, for Ulysses ordered everyone to embark at once and prepare for sea.

Ulysses knew that, after leaving Cape Malea, his ships had been carried far to the south. He must also have been aware that, as well as being a long way south of Greece, he was well to the west of it. How far to the west he will have had no way of telling. The Greeks of this period, as we know, were familiar with the land of Egypt, for it was one of their favourite raiding grounds. They will certainly have known that the land stretched as far to the west as anyone had ever been. When they sailed down to the delta-land of the Nile they could see the coastline shimmering away to the western horizon. No doubt some of the early navigators will have tried exploring it, only to give up in disgust before a featureless coast where there were no cattle to carry off, and no cities to loot. (It would be many centuries before Greek colonists would found cities like Cyrene and tame the rich tableland of Cyrenaica.) For a navigator of this early period, the only things upon which he could rely were his knowledge of winds and weather when in familiar waters, his lead-line or quant when in shallow waters, and the few signs of the sky with which he was familiar. He knew that the sun rose in the east and sank in the west. Other than this, he knew which part of the sky was north as soon as the stars came out. Ulysses could be sure of only one thing, that he had to get to the north.

The fact that the constellation of the Great Bear, or the Plough, "never bathes in Ocean's stream" but wheels round and round the Pole was known to these early Mediterranean sailors. An important part of Ulysses' later navigation depended upon this knowledge. Ulysses was the first man in recorded history to have made use of the stars for navigation. Often, sailing at night over the Mediterranean, I have acted as Ulysses and his helmsman must have done and kept a star steady on some fixed point of my mast and rigging.

Today Polaris is the 'fixed point' in the heavens, but this was not the case in the 12th century B.C. when Ulysses was sailing the Mediterranean. "The point in the heavens about which the whole starry pattern appears to wheel is not in actual fact a fixed point; it shifts through the centuries extremely slowly along an elliptical path which astronomers can trace out, so that we know how the stars appeared to observers in relation to the pole during different periods of history. The Great Bear, for example, is today no longer a non-setting circumpolar constellation for Mediterranean sailors, although it is for us in the north. And the bright star at which the Bear wheels—the star we call the Pole Star—was in Homer's day more than 12° away from the pole, and did not attract any particular notice."

The nearest star to the pole, and the one upon which Ulysses will have steered in order to make his way northward, was the star called Kochab, one of what are now called the 'Guards' of the Little Bear. But whereas Polaris in our own day is almost exactly due north, Kochab in the 12th century B.C. was about 7° east of the polar point. A 7° error would be considerable in modern navigation, but to the Homeric sailor in his small, slow boat such an error—even had he known about it—would have been of no great importance.

Since the star which Ulysses used as a guide was 7° east of the polar point, one would expect to find his next landfall somewhere east of north. Furthermore, since it is clear that he will have been trying to sail east as well as north—knowing that he had been carried many miles out of his way to the south-west—one will look to the north-east for his next landfall.

The common consent of antiquity, together with many later scholars and navigators, places the next sequence of the hero's adventures in Sicily. If, however, Ulysses had sailed *due* north from the island of Jerba or the coastline near by, he would have arrived after a comparatively short voyage in Tunisia, at the point where the coastline runs out to the peninsula of Ras Kapudia. A north-easterly course, on the other hand, will have given him a landfall on the southern shores of Sicily, most probably somewhere in the region of Marsala.

"So we came to the land of the Cyclopes, a fierce and uncivilized people . . ." Although the description would be bitterly resented, it is not so inappropriate to the southern Sicilian even today. Having spent a year and a half sailing all round these shores I find that the navigations of Ulysses from now on bear the distinct hallmark of truth. So many of the places, weather conditions, and even geographical descriptions seem to be accurate, that one is led to believe either that the author of the *Odyssey* had been a sailor in this part of the world, or that he had listened carefully to the story of one who had. I hold no brief for the first theory, any more than for similar theories that Shakespeare must have been a sailor, soldier, lawyer, or what you will, in order to write convincingly about naval, military, or legal matters. The artist of genius is as absorbent as a sponge of other men's lives and experiences. It was not necessary for Stephen Crane to go to war in order to write *The Red Badge of Courage*. What is perhaps the greatest sea poem in the English language was written by a man who had read widely, and listened attentively to tales about the sea, but who had no experience of it. ". . . It was six months after *The Ancient Mariner* was finished, that Coleridge for the first time went down to the sea in a ship, and then only to sail from Yarmouth to Cuxhaven. He is describing things which he could have known from books or tales of the sea alone. He had seen none of them." Whether Homer was a native of Ionia, whether he knew Ithaca personally, or whether he had ever sailed in the central Mediterranean are matters irrelevant to my quest. My concern is to discover the traditional sources of Ulysses' voyage, and the underlying truth beneath so much of the later myth-enshrouded story.

Ulysses, according to the *Odyssey*, did not immediately land in the country of the Cyclopes, but in an island lying just off their shores. Now the interesting thing is that there is only one place in all of southern Sicily which would suit the description, and this island lies exactly where one would expect it to do—hard by Marsala and Trapani. There is not another island along the whole of the southern coast until one comes to the minute Isola Correnti at the far eastern tip of Sicily. I have sheltered behind Correnti for forty-eight hours when a gale was blowing, and can confirm that it can in no way approximate to the Homeric description of the fertile 'Goat Island', with its stream and its trees, where the squadron of Ulysses made their first landfall after leaving North Africa.

The island of Favignana lies four miles off the western coast of Sicily. It is one of a small group now called the Aegadian Islands, but which were known in classical times as the *Aegates*, Favignana itself being called Aegusa, 'Goat Island'. ". . . a luxuriant island," is how Ulysses described it, "covered with woods, and the home of innumerable goats." It can hardly be coincidence that it was called Goat Island in classical days. Another factor in its identification is that from this island Ulysses and his men could easily see the smoke rising from the land of the Cyclopes (Sicily) lying just across the narrow strait.

The 280-mile voyage from the Land of the Lotus-Eaters to the Island of the Goats passed without incident, and there is no record of the time taken. Only one piece of information relating to the voyage is mentioned, the fact that the ships nearly ran aground on the island because the night was cloudy, there was no moon, and there was also dense sea-fog. Samuel Butler made great play with the fog that seemed to surround this coast to help account for his theory that the *Odyssey* was written at Trapani. But the fact is that fogs are not uncommon off this corner of Sicily, particularly if the wind is from the south.

". . . It was one of those heavy sea-fogs which you know will peel away when the sun gets up. I could hardly see the bows of the boat, and we seemed to be swimming not through water but through this strange thick air. The white clouds broke away before the wind of our passing and then closed in as dense as ever behind us." That is an extract from a log-book written when

I was sailing off this stretch of coast between Marsala and Sciacca. Now the strange thing is that sea-fogs are quite rare in the central Mediterranean, yet I have run into them three times when under sail round the western corner of Sicily. On another occasion when I was giving a hand at a *mattzana*—the tunny netting—off Favignana, the whole operation was delayed by a dense white fog which did not lift until the sun had been up several hours.

The fact that sea-fogs are not uncommon in this area is insufficient argument for Favignana having been Ulysses' Goat Island. But, taken in conjunction with the fact that it was known to classical geographers and writers as Goat Island, and that it fulfils all the geographical requirements of the story, the evidence seems to me conclusive.

There was clearly a south wind blowing when the squadron approached the shore, for "the long rollers were beating on the coast" where the Greeks ran their ships aground. A south wind, incidentally, would have suited them best for making the passage from the North African coast. They had been under sail, we know, for "it was not until the ships were beached that we lowered our sails." It is also worth stressing that it is when the south wind blows that one encounters sea-fog around this part of Sicily. Having hauled their boats up the beach, the Greeks lay down exhausted on the shore.

Goat Island

THE modern harbour of Favignana lies on the north coast of the island, but it cannot have been here that Ulysses landed. Coming up from the south in a thick sea-fog, his ships, as we know, ran aground before the Greeks were even aware that they were into soundings. Now there are three anchorages on the south coast of this seven-mile-long island; Cala Grande, Cala Rotonda, and a bay just to the east of Punta Longa. In all of them there are sand beaches and the bottom is sand and weed, but only one of them would really fit the description of "a safe harbour, in which there is no occasion to tie up at all." Even this would be something of an old sailor's yarn, for the harbour has yet to be invented where a man can leave his boat without any forethought or concern. I would incline to the view that Cala Grande may well have been the anchorage which is described. There is a small spit of land jutting out from the southern end, and just round inside it there is a shelving beach where "all your crew need to do is beach their boat and wait until the right wind blows."

There are four Aegadian islands, one of them, Isola Grande, lying so close offshore as almost to be part of Sicily, then Favignana about four miles west, Levanzo to the north of Favignana, and furthest out to the west, Marettimo. Only Favignana out of this small group has any harbours or anchorages worthy of the name. I spent several weeks off here one summer, exploring the islands and sailing between them. Favignana, the most prosperous, is still fertile and quite rich in trees; Levanzo is no more than a bony little island supporting a few vines and a number of rabbits; Marettimo is austere, presenting an iron-bound coast to the sailor, with only a landing stage on its north-eastern shore.

They are lonely islands still, and in Ulysses' days they were uninhabited, for he comments "The Cyclops [The inhabitants of western Sicily] have no boats . . . if they knew how to build ships they would have turned this island into a fine colony." Only of Favignana could it be said to this day that "there are meadows along the sea shore and land level enough to plough." Apart from Montagna Grossa, the main peak of the island, Favignana is low and cultivated. It is rich for this part of the world, and supports about 5,000 inhabitants between its fishing industry and its agriculture. I spent a happy day here, spearing fish along the southern coast and anchored at night in Cala Grande, tucked away behind the point where Ulysses and his men may well have landed. There is no spring now issuing from the mouth of a cave but there are springs on Favignana, something which distinguishes it from the other islands in the group—Levanzo, for instance, where all the water must be caught off the flat roofs of the houses during the winter rains.

Throughout my search for Ulysses I have always remained somewhat sceptical of minor geographical details like caves and springs. Such things can change considerably over the centuries, and the lapse of three thousand years can see landslides which close up caves, volcanic disturbances which destroy or alter old springs, and the sad process of deforestation which, as in Greece, can completely change a landscape. On the other hand, I take it that the main geographical descriptions in Homer's account of Ulysses' voyage are accurate. They read as if they were meant to be, and in fact they often bear an uncanny resemblance to our own *Admiralty Pilots*. The moment when myth and fantasy intrude into the story is immediately apparent, for there is about these passages a completely different atmosphere, a 'generalized' feeling. But whenever the poet sets himself out to describe a harbour, an anchorage, or some navigational hazard, there is a remarkable air of authenticity—something quite different from a poet's invention. Here is Homer's description of the island which I take to be Favignana.

". . . it is by no means a poor country, but capable of yielding any crop in due season. Along the shore of the grey sea there are soft water-meadows where the vine would never wither; and there is plenty of land level enough for the plough, where they could count on cutting a deep crop at every harvest-time, for the soil below the surface is exceedingly rich. Also it has a safe harbour, in which there is no occasion to tie up at all. You need neither cast anchor nor make fast with hawsers: all your crew have to do is to beach their boat and wait till the spirit moves them and the right wind blows. Finally, at the head of the harbour there is a stream of fresh water, running out of a cave in a grove of poplar trees." Here, for comparison, is Prospero's island in *The Tempest*:

"Thy turfy mountains, where live nibbling sheep;
And flat meads thatch'd with stover, them to keep;
Thy banks with pioned and twilled brims,
Which spongy April at thy hest betrims,
To make cold nymphs chaste crowns; and thy broom groves
Whose shadow the dismissed bachelor loves,
Being lass-lorn; thy pole-clipt vineyard;
And thy sea-marge, sterile and rocky-hard. . . ."

Shakespeare's island is in the imagination, it would indeed be a waste of time to try and find it on a chart. But Homer's description is pointed and detailed—it might almost be an estate agent's prospectus, or an inducement to colonists to set out and make something of this virgin territory. Whenever possible in the *Odyssey*, the nature of a harbour is described and its suitability in various winds and weather, while the mariner's second thought —water—is also mentioned.

"Throughout the twenty-five centuries of Mediterranean history which are known to us," wrote Bérard, "the sailors of each nation were continually borrowing from one another. . . . They stole or copied from one another the guides or sea 'road maps' which the French now call Nautical Instructions, the English, Pilots, and others *Portulans* or *Mirrors of the Sea*: in classical times the usual name for them was *Periploi*." The earliest *periplous* we possess dates from the 4th century B.C. but, in view of the extensive navigation that was taking place in the Mediterranean from the 8th century onwards, one may reasonably presume that much earlier ones did exist. It is not impossible that the writer of the *Odyssey* had such a mariner's *Mirror of the Sea* before him. But long before navigational instructions became committed to writing, they will have been passed on by word of mouth, or possibly in simple rhyming mnemonics such as those which still exist in English for the Rules of the Road:

> "When both lights you see ahead—
> Starboard wheel, and show your RED."

The *Odyssey* is the epic poem of a nation to whom navigation was all-important, so I do not find it strange that so much factual detail is incorporated into it. It is the very authenticity of the winds and weathers, ports and harbours, which acts as a solid backbone to the poem.

Can one imagine how Shelley, for instance, would have treated such a subject? Everything would have become blurred and diffuse, and it would indeed be 'foolishness' to try and identify a Shelleyan hero's voyage. If I take it that the basic geography of the *Odyssey* is authentic, I do not look for accuracy in small details such as caves and fountains.

The south wind still whirls the water up the buff-coloured sand of Favignana, and the slopes of Montagna Grossa still shelter their goats, relatively few today for the land is intensively cultivated. The shoulders of the island are enamelled with the pale green of vines and the flat plain to the east is ripe with fruit and wheat. The fishing boats which now shelter in the northern harbour have the *oculus* painted on their bows, and bright blue is

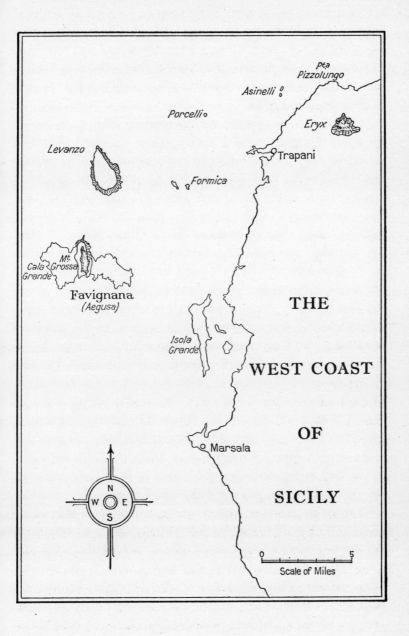

Pta
Pizzolungo

Asinelli ⸰

Porcelli ⸰

Eryx

Levanzo

Trapani

Formica

Mt.
Cala Grossa
Grande

Favignana
(Aegusa)

THE

Isola
Grande

WEST COAST

OF

Marsala

SICILY

N
W   E
S

0   5
Scale of Miles

still a favourite colour. From Montagna Grossa one can look right across the narrow strait to Sicily and the harbour of Trapani. Beyond them looms the high peak of Mount Eryx, where perhaps the Cyclopes lived. Ulysses remembered it all, and how "we gazed across at the neighbouring land of the Cyclopes and could see not only the smoke from their fires, but could hear the bleating of their sheep and goats."

When the Greeks awoke on the morning after their arrival their first thought naturally was to explore the island and then, as soon as they saw the mountain goats, to make sure of getting some fresh meat. Nine goats fell to each ship of the squadron, while Ulysses as the leader was given an extra one. They sat down afterwards to feast on this fresh meat and washed it down with the good wine of Ismarus. They still had plenty of wine left, for when they had sacked the city of the Cicones every man in the ships had "drawn off a good supply in jars." These jars, no doubt, were similar to the classical amphorae with which we have become increasingly familiar in recent years since skin-divers took to investigating classical wrecks. In the museum at Heraklion in Crete there are a number of Minoan jars from Knossos dating from an earlier period than those which Ulysses' companions had aboard their ships, yet such is the continuity of the Mediterranean world that I have seen modern jars being loaded aboard a Cretan caique which were identical in shape. Incised on their rough clay sides, these 20th-century jars bore the same vestigial rope patterns which decorated the Minoan ware.

The importance of finding fresh meat to these early mariners does not need stressing. They could take little enough provisions with them in their open boats—grain in jars or in hide bags, olives and olive oil, sun-dried fish, possibly sun-dried meat like the South African *biltong*, onions, cheese, and shellfish—the last three items are mentioned in the *Iliad*. Unlike most modern Mediterranean peoples, however, the Homeric heroes are notable for their large meat meals, an indication in itself perhaps of their northern ancestry. At the same time there are many references in the *Odyssey* to orchards and vegetable gardens, and it is the fruit and vegetables which now abound in Sicily and the other Mediterranean islands that Ulysses and his men will have missed. When they hunted the wild goats on Favignana they will have found no cultivated fruit and vegetables, not even the fruit of the prickly pear which now grows wild all over Sicily and the Aegadian islands. The prickly pear did not reach Europe until after the Spanish discovery of America. I have eaten *Opuntia Ficus-Indica*, 'Figs of India' as the Sicilian calls them, on the beach of Favignana. It was strange to reflect that this baroque, sinewy cactus—nowadays inextricably associated with the Mediterranean—was only a late-comer.

One thing which Ulysses and his sailors ate that will have changed little over the centuries was herb-flavoured meat stuffed, sausage-like, into gut. No doubt they will not have eaten all their wild goats' meat in one huge feast, but will have made up some with onions and herbs, washed out the goats' intestines in sea-water, and stuffed them with the forcemeat—just as they do in the Aegean to this day.

When picturing the voyage of Ulysses and his companions it is important to remember that these men were used to hardship and hunger, and that they could subsist on a most meagre diet for days on end. Greek sailors still can and do, as I know from travelling with them in their caiques. A handful of black olives, a piece of bread dipped in olive oil, maybe a slice or two of melon, and that is the day's food. (Two English acquaintances of mine who tried to run a caique commercially in the Aegean were defeated largely by the fact that, with their western ideas of how much food and drink a man requires, they could not compete with the Greeks who could live, in the phrase, 'on the smell of an oily rag.') In Ulysses' world men will have been used to hunger. But when fresh meat was available as on Favignana, they will have gorged themselves as wild animals do, to lay up a reserve against the inevitable lean days.

At dawn on the second morning Ulysses addressed his

companions. He told them that he intended to sail across to 'the mainland', and find out what kind of men they were whose fires could be seen across the strait. The other eleven ships were to stay behind while he and his crew carried out a reconnaissance. Ulysses did not know, of course, that Sicily was an island. He judged by its bulk, when compared with Favignana—a very typical 'island', about the same size as many of those in the Ionian and Aegean—that the shore across the strait was a mainland coast. His men now 'loosed the hawsers' and his ship put out to sea, leaving behind on the still water the snail-like track of her oar-thresh.

It is clear from the phrase 'loosed the hawsers' that the ship is pictured as lying at anchor off the beach. No doubt the Homeric sailors, whenever possible, adopted the same mooring techniques as their descendants do to this day. In the practically tideless Mediterranean, the best way for a boat to lie is with her stern made fast to the shore, and her bows held off by an anchor. Mooring—or sleeping—stones are still used by a number of small craft in this part of the world in preference to the conventional anchor. This is not only, as might be supposed, because of the cost of an iron anchor. The fact is that around many of the islands the sea-bed is foul or rocky, and a small boat's anchor is liable to get caught by its flukes under rock ledges, or in coral formations. A vessel of any size with a mechanical capstan can always break its anchor free, but not so a boat with an anchor that must be manhandled.

Sailing out of Levanzo on one occasion with a Sicilian crew, and wishing to anchor on the island's western coast, I noticed that they brought along with them their own anchor—a large sleeping-stone with a hole drilled through it, and a rope attached. When I asked why, they pointed out that I might well lose my conventional anchor in the rocky sea-bed. This Homeric anchor of theirs proved quite heavy enough to hold my 10-ton boat steady in the wind and swell that was running.

The high peak of Mount Eryx dominates all this western

coastline of Sicily, and at its foot lies the modern port of Trapani. Trapani derives its name from the Greek word, Drepanon, a sickle, after the sickle-shaped spit of land on which the port is built. There was nothing here when Ulysses landed. Many years were to pass before the Phoenicians established a trading centre on this coast. On Mount Eryx the Phoenicians would dedicate a temple to Astarte, the Goddess of Love, a temple which was later turned into the shrine of Venus Ericina. Today, the clouds which often veil the peak of Eryx drive their grey streamers round the Norman cathedral where the Sicilians bow their heads before the Madonna, the Star of the Sea. To the sailors on this coastline She remains the goddess of love and, as the votive offerings in the cathedral reveal, it is She who still preserves men from shipwreck on these narrow seas.

8

The Cave
of Polyphemus

TRAPANI has the feeling of a very old city. Century upon century of human beings have lived and died here, their dust is in one's nostrils, and the sea beyond the promenade is heavy with memory. Out there, beyond the paved sea-front where the local youth makes the *passegiata* in the evenings, the waters ran red with blood on March 10th, 241 B.C. when a Roman fleet of 200 ships defeated the Carthaginians, the hitherto invincible mariners of this sea. That battle brought to an end the first Punic war. The waters now are pleasant and idle, criss-crossed by a few errant merchant ships or decorated by the gulls' wings of fishing boats as they shrug their way offshore to the rich coastal banks.

This shore, this sea and this coast were already known to the first men whom we call the ancestors of our culture. In Levanzo, smallest of the Aegadian islands, there is a cave much older than the story of Ulysses. "The cave in Levanzo—like the famous caves of Lascaux and Altamira—is yet another of those strange temples of prehistoric art. But what makes the Levanzo cave unique is the fact that it is the furthest south that any trace of this early European culture has been found. Even more fascinating is the revelation of bulls and antelope and cattle on the walls of a cave in a tiny island that nowadays can only support rabbits. Levanzo, we now know, was once joined to Sicily, and the island was surrounded by a large fertile plain." Levanzo, in fact, was joined to more than Sicily. Between this western corner of the Sicilian coast and the Cape Bon peninsula in Tunisia there once lay rich and fertile valleys—

perhaps, who knows, long lost Atlantis? Levanzo, Marettimo, and the Goat Island of Favignana were three mountain peaks standing up out of this green plain where ran the bulls and antelope that the Levanzo cave-painters immortalized. Highest of all the peaks in this region, Mount Eryx must long have been a sacred place. Perhaps even when Ulysses landed on these shores there was some primitive shrine up there in the clouds where Astarte, Aphrodite, Venus, and the Madonna have had their subsequent temples.

The whole land looked quite blue when I stepped ashore here one spring morning. There had been a light rain overnight and the early sun was just beginning to wean the damp mist off the sown fields and thick carpeting of spring flowers. The flowers grew wild everywhere, bee-orchids, wild blue irises and cyclamen. Ulysses would have seen the cyclamen if he had been here in the springtime of the year. He was certainly the first Greek to set foot on this strange and beautiful coast. Curiously enough, if we can accept Virgil's authority for the story, the Trojan hero Aeneas was to land here later. The future founder of Rome, exiled from the city that Ulysses had helped to destroy, erected a funeral mound here to his father, Anchises, whom he had carried on his shoulders out of the blazing ruins of Troy.

In Trapani I have felt history as heavy as a plush curtain. This whole region is heavy with the past of man. One's own life is seen as no more than a minute drop of resin oozing from the trunk of some giant tree. Only if art, or accident take a hand, will it be preserved to form an amber bead, ten thousand years and more away. That happened to Aeneas and Ulysses, but only because the brief gales of their lives were immortalized by great poets. There is no record of the other men who jumped after Ulysses on to this fertile land and found themselves in the territory of the Cyclops.

We know how many men accompanied Ulysses ashore and went with him to the fateful cave of the Polyphemus. ". . . I picked out the twelve best men from my crew, telling the rest of my faithful followers to stand behind and guard the ship." They landed at the point on the coast nearest to the island. This was probably a little south of Trapani, but the whole of this coastline has changed considerably even since classical times, and to attempt an identification on such slim evidence would be a waste of time. Samuel Butler was more sanguine than I, and readily identified the Cave of Polyphemus with one to be seen to this day near Pizzolungo point, four miles north of modern Trapani.

If the day had been less hot when I was here last I would have prospected along the coast just south of the city out of curiosity. But it was high mid-summer, and the salt-pans to the south were like molten silver, the parched land shook with mirage, and even the sea was painful to the eyes. Sicily was delivered over to what her people called 'the lion-sun'. I value those deep drugged afternoons of the south, when even the beggar finds a shady porch in which to rest, and only the rich are still busy talking business with their counterparts in Naples, or trying to get the Chicago *mafia* on the transatlantic line. There are still bandits and robbers here, for Polyphemus has long been native to this corner of the island.

Butler's Cave of Polyphemus is still here. On the morning when I landed and went ashore to look at it the cave was un-occupied, although clearly it was still used as a sheep-fold, as are so many large caves in Sicily and elsewhere. Fenced off across the mouth by a stone wall, it is not difficult to imagine how—here or somewhere similar—a band of men could easily be trapped. There is no reason to take the giant size of Polyphemus too seriously, for this part of the tale has surely been embroidered by myth. Those who have escaped from great dangers are naturally prone to enlarge upon them in later years when they sit telling the tale to their children at home. Many who have served in recent wars must be ruefully aware of this mythopoeic function, and Ulysses, it is worth bearing in mind, was no Public School Briton trained in the habit of understatement and the 'stiff upper lip'.

When I went back to my boat to sail down the coast again to Trapani the sea was as simple-blue and as unstarred with sails as on the morning when the wily Greek came ashore. Around the foothills of Mount Eryx I could see the scattered dwellings of the Cyclopes and, like Ulysses, it was not only "the smoke from their fires" that told me the land was inhabited. I could also "hear their voices and the bleating of their goats and sheep." The morning mist had lifted off the peak of the mountain, and I could see the dark green of the trees that surround the town and its cathedral. It will have been more densely forested when Ulysses was here. It is interesting to note that his description of the giant Polyphemus brings in an appropriate image for this region of Sicily: "No one could have believed him to be a man who ate bread like ourselves. He reminded one of *some high wooded peak, lifting itself in solitary state out of the hills.*"

In deducing that this particular cave was the one in which the giant Sicilian was blinded by Ulysses, Butler made some play with the fact that the cave was still known locally as 'La Grotta di Polifemo'. I certainly found one or two of the Trapanesi who knew of the cave in these terms, but I cannot believe that an oral tradition could be preserved through all the vicissitudes of Sicilian history for three thousand years.

I fear that Butler himself may have helped to promote this attribution, for one of the people who referred to the cave as the 'Cave of Polyphemus' was the curator of the town museum, and he had read Butler's book. Throughout the Mediterranean most of these local ascriptions date from no later than the 19th century, when the first waves of foreign visitors with classical educations began to descend on these shores. Your Mediterranean-dweller, be he Italian, Sicilian, Maltese, Greek, or what you will, is only too happy to oblige inquiring visitors with tales appropriate to their demands. Very rarely can any of these stories be traced back earlier than the 19th century. Had I walked about Trapani asking for the Grotto of Polyphemus, I have no doubt I should have been shown a number of caves, and that my dark-eyed guides would soon have deduced from my questions what kind of a monster had lived there, and all the rest of the story. They would then have been ready for the next visitor who might have quoted them in evidence of the continuation of a traditional folk-lore.

This Mediterranean habit of producing the right answer is not, as some unkind Anglo-Saxons have suspected, entirely due to a natural duplicity. It is just as much due to a genuine love of the native birthplace, a desire that it shall shine in foreign eyes, and a kindly wish not to send the visitor away disappointed.

One sees an outstanding example of this in Capri, where the shadow of Tiberius—'Timberio'—has grown vaster, darker, and more omnipresent in the past thirty years. I daresay one hundred and fifty years ago he was practically unheard of in the island. Norman Douglas commented on the growth of these legends in his *Siren Land*—first published in 1911. If he could return from exploring 'the shadow and the dust', he would find plenty to amuse him in modern Capri. Some of Douglas's own exploits have been transferred to 'Timberio', while some of Tiberius's reputation has rubbed off on Douglas. A third shade has intervened—Dr. Axel Munthe. In the course of one day alone, an American friend of mine was informed that "Timberio was a doctor, fond of antiques and pretty ladies," "A white-haired old man fond of wine and pretty boys," and "an Emperor very fond of torturing lobsters."

Anything massive, of unfathomable age, and therefore attributed to gods or monsters was called 'Cyclopean' in classical times. 'The name Cyclopian," says the Classical Dictionary, "was given to the walls built of great masses of unhewn stone, of which specimens are still to be seen at Mycenae and other parts of Greece, and also in Italy." The ancient walls of Eryx are 'Cyclopean' for instance. A Greek tradition equated the Cyclopes with the assistants of the metal-working god Hephaestus. Since volcanoes were reckoned to be the workshops of the god, Sicily with its volcanic background and its mighty Aetna was long regarded as a 'Cyclopean land'.

I can find nothing in the *Odyssey* to suggest that the genesis of
the Polyphemus story was anything more than a real encounter
with a large and savage native of Sicily. I cannot even find that
he was necessarily one-eyed, and on this point I entirely agree
with Samuel Butler. "The name Cyclopes, for example, or
Round-faces—for there is nothing in the word to show that it
means anything else than this, and I see from Liddell & Scott that
Parmenides called the moon Cyclops—is merely an author's
nick-name. If μήλωψ means apple-faced', κύκλωψ should mean
'circle-faced'. As there is nothing in the word, so neither is there
in the *Odyssey*, to suggest that the Cyclopes were a people with
only one round eye in the middle of their foreheads. Such a
marked feature does not go without saying, and that it did not go
with the earliest Greek artists appears from the fact that they
always gave Polyphemus two eyes. It is not till later times that he
becomes monophthalmic, and the *Odyssey* gives him eyebrows in
the plural, which involves eyes in the plural also . . ." Robert
Graves in *The Greek Myths* refers to the ". . . pre-Hellenic
Cyclopes, famous metal-workers, whose culture had spread to
Sicily, and who perhaps had an eye tattooed in the centre of their
foreheads as a clan mark."

Clear evidence that the poet is embroidering on the encounter
with the Cyclops Polyphemus is provided by the fact that he
makes this wild savage understand and speak Greek. There can
have been no Greek-speakers in Sicily at the time that Ulysses
landed there—for Greek-speakers could only have reached the
island by boats, and this was one thing that none of the islanders
had. Yet Ulysses carries on a long dialogue with Polyphemus.
Furthermore, half the point of this story turns around the fact
that Ulysses gave his name as 'Oudeis', the Greek for 'Nobody',
and when the giant screamed out for help from his neighbours, he
shouted that it was 'Nobody' who was killing him. At this point,
they all went back disgruntled to their beds saying that if such
was the case there was nothing for him to do but get down and
pray.

61

The Polyphemus episode is one of the most perfect tales in all literature—and the genius of the poet is such that he can even make us feel sorry for this violent cannibalistic monster. When the last of the flock goes through the doorway in the morning—the huge ram with Ulysses clinging beneath its belly—the blinded giant wonders why on this day of all it should be the last to leave the cave. For almost the first time in literature, one feels the emotion of pity. And how arrogant is Ulysses! "The last of the flock to come up to the doorway was the big ram, weighed down by his own fleece and by me with my ever-active brain. . . ."

So, having blinded the Sicilian giant and escaped from the cave of death, Ulysses, and the six of his companions who were left alive made their way down to the shore and the waiting boat. Ulysses had succeeded in escaping, both by his agile wits and by making Polyphemus drunk on the wine of Ismarus. Ulysses is a man who, in the phrase, 'never misses a trick', and always manages to turn everything to good account. Even the rams, under which he and his men had escaped, were taken carefully back to the boat. These members of Polyphemus' flock would later serve to provide a feast for Ulysses and his companions on the Isle of Goats.

As soon as the seven survivors were aboard the boat they wasted no time, and all of them "ran to the benches, and plied the grey sea-water with their oars." But Ulysses could not bear to leave without taunting his blinded enemy. "Cyclops!" he called, "If anyone should ever ask you how you were blinded, tell him that you lost your sight to Ulysses—the Sacker of Cities, the Son of Laertes, the Man of Ithaca!"

9
The Island
of the Winds

THE enraged and blinded Cyclops picked up vast boulders and hurled them after the retreating Greeks. You can still see them there, if you are so minded, for the Asinelli, the Porcelli, and the Formica rocks, all suggest giant pieces torn from Mount Eryx and thrown by Polyphemus at Ulysses and his companions. But on the east coast of Sicily (where some maintain that the Cyclopes lived) they will equally well show you the Faraglioni rocks which, they maintain, were thrown by the one-eyed giant from his dwelling-place on the vine-green slopes of Aetna. I would not be so sure that they were wrong if I did not know that there is no island on the eastern side of Sicily that can even remotely approximate to 'Goat Island'.

The captains and crews of the other eleven vessels were waiting anxiously on Favignana. It was over two days since Ulysses had sailed across to the coast, and they could only presume that some disaster had befallen him. It is easy enough to imagine how they raised a cheer when they saw his vessel draw out towards them, and the oars beginning to dapple the sea. They had eaten well, they had had good wine to drink, and they knew the taste of spring water in the island. All that had been needed to restore their morale was the return of their leader.

Ulysses had a tragic tale to tell, of how six of their companions had perished at the hand of Polyphemus. I suspect that the three men who had tried to desert in the Land of the Lotus-Eaters only wished that they had been successful. The Land of the Lotus, of *dolce far niente* and friendly people, would have been preferable by far to the dangers of these new countries. I feel sure that Ulysses must now have stressed the perils of this new world that they were exploring, for the more he could impress on his followers the hazards that surrounded them, the more chance he had of making sure that there were no more attempts at desertion. I think the beginnings of the 'One-Eyed monster' legend can be traced back to the moment of Ulysses' return from Sicily to Favignana.

With the boom and sizzle of the surf in their ears, the sailors sat down on the small windy island and feasted off the fresh meat that Ulysses had brought back. They realized now that there was no hope of going ashore and settling down in the large fertile land which lay just across the straight. All that day, until the sun set, the Greeks made the most of the fresh meat. That night they slept out once more on the sea-shore.

I can picture them lying out under the sky in that sheltered cove, and I am sure that the time of the year was summer. It would be impossible to sleep happily on the shore of any of these islands in the winter months. Anchored in Favignana and Levanzo, I used to sleep night after night on the upper deck of my small boat, under one old army blanket. But that was in spring and summer. Returning this way late one autumn, I found that I needed the stove alight in my small cabin, and that a kapok-lined sleeping-bag was hardly sufficient to keep off the damp from the sea and the cold air from the land.

At dawn next morning Ulysses ordered his men to board their ships and get under way. It was only his determination that sent them back to the oar benches when they, for their part, would quite happily have stayed until the food or the wine ran out. Ulysses cannot be accused of being reluctant to get back to his wife and child, for what is the *Odyssey* but the story of one man's determination to return home at the end of a war?

One thing that strikes me particularly about the story of Ulysses is the sadness and the melancholy that seems inseparably associated with his seafaring. Although the Mediterranean is more often blue than any other colour, it is almost invariably described as 'grey'. Almost the only weather we hear about is bad. Storms, tempests, whirlpools, angry seas, these abound; but no easy, halcyon days. Even the later Roman poets, notoriously indifferent like all Latins to the beauties of the sea, can occasionally refer to it in kindly terms. Yet the Greek Homer—whoever he may have been—writing what has been called 'the greatest epic of the sea', never has anything to say about the sailor's life that could induce a single volunteer to ship before the mast. Contrast Homer's account of Ulysses' voyage with any one of the Norse or Anglo-Saxon sagas. Both abound with violence, with battle, murder, and sudden death, but the sagas exult where Homer complains. The distinction becomes very clear when one turns to descriptions of the sea itself. Here are Ulysses and his squadron leaving the Island of Goats:

"As soon as Dawn's rosy fingers showed in the East I woke my men and ordered them to go aboard and cast off the hawsers. They manned the ships at once, took up their accustomed places on the thwarts, and struck the grey sea-water with their oars. So we left that island and sailed on with heavy hearts. . . ."

Here on the other hand is *Beowulf*, written about A.D. 750, but describing a world very similar to the Homeric one: "A man cunning in knowledge of the sea led them to the shore. Time passed on; the ship was on the waves, the boat beneath the cliff. The warriors eagerly embarked. The currents turned the sea against the sand. Men bore bright ornaments, splendid war-trappings to the bosom of the ship. The men, the heroes on their willing venture, shoved out the well-timbered ship. The foamy-necked floater like a bird went then over the wave-filled sea, sped by the wind, till after due time on the next day the boat with twisted prow had gone so far that the voyagers saw land, the sea-cliffs shining, the steep headlands, the broad sea-capes. . . ."

It is not to disparage the *Odyssey* that I compare these two quotations. The *Odyssey* has had its fill of praise throughout the centuries—and *Beowulf*, perhaps, too little. The fact remains that, when it comes to dealing with the sea and seafaring, Homer adopts the tone of a tired and peremptory old man, warning his sons against the dangers of the mariner's trade. Is it, perhaps, as Butler and his followers have maintained, the voice of a poetess, of a woman who fears and hates the sea? I doubt their conclusion, for the very good reason that the voice of Homer can be heard in the Mediterranean to this day.

Greeks and Sicilians are still seafarers, but I never heard one who had anything remotely approaching the Anglo-Saxon outlook on the subject. Men who go to sea in the Mediterranean do so out of necessity, and for no other reason. Love of the sea would appear to be a Nordic trait. Often, when I and my wife were sailing around Sicily or in the Aegean, we were asked by local sailors what our reasons were for living aboard a boat. "The sea is brutal," remarked a coaster captain in Crotone. "It is no place for a woman. And only for men if they cannot make a living ashore." "I would never go to sea if I could avoid it," remarked a caique skipper in Naxos. "It is nice aboard your little *lordiko* in harbour. But be sure and don't put to sea when the Meltemis are blowing!"

It might be argued that few professional sailors, of whatever race, have much good to say about their trade, yet I have met dozens of fishermen, merchant naval, and naval sailors in northern Europe, who still retained an abiding love of the sea. I can hardly think of one, among innumerable Mediterranean sailors I have met over the years, who expressed any such regard. The Greeks, it is true, are far more 'sea-minded' than the Sicilians or the Italians. But, like Ulysses himself, it is only necessity that makes sailors of them, and the aim of every caique sailor is to earn enough to retire ashore. Similarly, the Maltese (whose language stems from the Phoenician, and who can thus claim to have some of the oldest seafaring blood in the Mediterranean in their veins), are more than reluctant sailors. Fishermen from Malta and Gozo will not put to sea in weather that would be considered no more than 'a good sailing breeze' in Cornwall or Devon.

I have come to the conclusion that Homer, when he is recounting the voyage of Ulysses, is a very typical 'Man of the Mediterranean'. It is quite unnecessary to attempt to prove that 'he' was a woman, or a citizen of the mainland who had a landsman's dislike of the sea. Homer is just as likely to have been an islander, familiar with the sea and all its ways from his birth.

Without any charts, sailing this unknown sea, Ulysses will still have had only one thought in mind—to make his way to the north-east. The one certainty he can have had, after being driven headlong across the Mediterranean from Cape Malea, is that he had been carried far to the south, and to the west. He knew also that he had made quite a lot of northing in his run up from Jerba, which had brought him to Goat Island and to the Land of the Cyclopes.

His next landfall was to be 'the floating island of Aeolus'. If we accept the fact that he will have been steering as far as possible to the north-east, there is only one island in this sea which can have given rise to the story of the home of the King of the Winds. About sixty miles due north-east from Favignana and the Aegadian group lies Ustica, a solitary and steep-to island. The fact that it is described as 'floating' in the sea has been taken by many to mean that we are now definitely in the realm of fairyland. But elsewhere in the *Odyssey* islands are described by an inverted adjective as swiftly-moving, meaning no more than that, in relation to the ship as it drew past them, they appeared to move.

Similarly the 'floating' Island of Aeolus only seemed to float upon the horizon—a good description of the way in which Ustica looms up alone on a fair day out of the blue haze of the Mediterranean. On this point Butler discerningly remarked: "[Ustica] shows no sign of having moved during the month that Ulysses stayed on it, and when he returns to it after an absence of three weeks, we have no hint given of its having changed its place."

There is no ancient authority for believing Ustica to have been the Island of Aeolus. The Aeolian Islands are, in fact, usually identified with the Lipari group which lies some eighty miles east of Ustica. Virgil refers to one island only, and this has been generally accepted as either the volcano Stromboli, or Lipara, the largest of these islands. The home of Aeolus, however, is clearly described as an island all alone in the sea, whereas the Lipari group consists of seven main islands, as well as a number of rocky islets, all quite close to one another. Furthermore, Ulysses would have had to sail right along the northern coast of Sicily in an easterly direction in order to reach them—something which he is unlikely to have done. Thirdly, the position of the Lipari islands is such that, when Aeolus made Ulysses a present of a fine west wind, it could only have blown him on to the Italian coast. But from Ustica, as we shall see, a westerly wind is quite acceptable for getting home to Ithaca. A further argument against the home of Aeolus having been in the Lipari group is, as will appear later, that these islands are quite clearly identified with the ones past which Ulysses had to steer on his way south to Scylla and Charybdis in the Straits of Messina.

Ustica, like the Lipari islands, is of volcanic formation. It is green and fertile, and terraced with vines, for here—as on all volcanic soil—the grape-vines thrive. There is a landing place today in the south of the island, where the village of Ustica lies. It is little more than a cove, but quite suitable for small modern coasters, schooners and yachts; vessels as large, or larger, than those of Ulysses. The peak of the island, Monte Guardi dei Turchi, is over 800 feet high and consequently very conspicuous to anyone sailing in these waters. I came up here one autumn in a high-powered diesel launch out of Palermo, and I was glad enough to tuck myself safely away in the small harbour. When the wind blows from the north, it has the full fetch of the sea all the way from Cape Circeo on the Italian mainland. Standing alone, thirty miles off the Sicilian coast, Ustica is exposed to every wind that blows. The Sirocco piles up the waves on its southern coast; the westerly brings a sea that has a clear run from the shores of Spain; and the easterly Levanter has a fetch of well over a hundred miles from the coastline of Calabria. "In many places," says the *Admiralty Pilot*, "the coasts are steep and inaccessible." Homer described it in the words, ". . . the cliffs rise sheer from the sea."

It is only when we come to Aeolus himself, to his children and the man-made surroundings of his home that myth and legend intrude. "Around this isle there runs an unbroken wall of bronze. . . ." It was beyond any technical capabilities of that time to construct such a wall. It is easy to dismiss this as no more than fantasy, but perhaps it is also an attempt to convey the inaccessibility of Ustica and its rugged coastline. British sailors use a strikingly similar phrase to convey a coast of this nature—'ironbound'. A literal-minded historian, deciphering our language a few thousand years hence, might find himself puzzled by this common maritime phrase.

The island, we learn, is inhabited by Aeolus and his wife, and by their twelve children. Six sons and six daughters—and "Aeolus has given his daughters to his sons in marriage." The incestuous relationship between the children of Aeolus is mentioned in order to show the listening Greek audience that the poet is describing some remote and completely 'unGreek' beings. Brother-and-Sister incest, as practised by the Egyptian Royal family, will almost certainly have been reported by Greeks who had visited Egypt or come into contact with Egyptians in the course of trading or piracy in the Levant. What more natural, then, that the poet should have transferred to his imaginary King of the Winds, and his family, the traditional 'royal incest' of Egypt?

Aeolus, king of the winds and weather, is introduced in order to provide a wind to carry Ulysses home to Ithaca. Now what Ulysses really required to reach Ithaca from Ustica was two or three days of northerly winds, followed by a long steady blow from the west to carry him right past Sicily, and home across the Ionian. On the other hand, a north-westerly would have taken him all the way there. Winds from the north-west, as it happens, are the commonest in this part of the Mediterranean, often blowing for several days or even a week on end. (Trying to reach the Balearic islands in the western Mediterranean from Trapani one summer I was held up in the Aegadian islands for five days while a strong north-westerly blew in my teeth.) Of this part of the world the *Admiralty Pilot* confirms: "North-westerly winds are in nearly all months the most frequent in this region, especially from June to August, when about one-third of all winds are from that direction; over the whole year nearly half the winds are from between west and north." It is more than likely, then, that Ulysses will have got his north-westerly from Ustica—especially when one bears in mind that it was almost certainly summer when he was here.

With a north-westerly he will have run down from Ustica, keeping the dangerous coast of the Cyclopes on his port hand. He will have altered course when he found himself once more to the south of Favignana, and then run due east across the Ionian for home.

The terms West and East have caused a great deal of argument among Homeric scholars and, when used to describe the geographical position of Ithaca relative to the other Ionian islands, have led to more controversy than anything else. This trouble largely stems from looking at modern charts which are marked with a compass rose showing the true and magnetic positions of the points of the compass. But the ancients had no conception of what the modern mariner or cartographer calls 'True North'. Indeed, all the cardinal points of the compass were somewhat hazy until the magnetic compass became a standard item in ships, and this did not happen until the 15th century A.D. North, as we have seen, was capable of being recognized by a sailor of the Homeric period by reference to Kochab, in the constellation of the Bear. For his definition of East and West, he had to rely upon the position of the sun at sunrise and at sunset. ". . . It is important to remember that this lack of precision was characteristic of the sailing world throughout the period before the magnetic needle.

A man might speak of 'between west and north', or 'a little north of east', but he was not thinking in terms of the bisection of angles, or of a precise arc of horizon, since he had no geometrical concepts."

When Homer, therefore, speaks of West or East, he is doing no more than indicating a general quarter of the sky. Greek sailors by classical times had, in fact, made a distinction between 'Summer' East and West, and 'Winter' East and West. There is no reason to believe that they did not do so in the Homeric period. In the Mediterranean world, lying as it does between latitudes 30° and 40° North of the Equator, there is a considerable difference between the bearing of the sun at sunrise and sunset at the two opposite periods of the year. The bearing of sunset in the Mediterranean in summer may be as much as thirty degrees North of West. A "west wind" in summer, therefore, is nearly North West.

All this is only to say that, when Homer describes Ulysses as being given the gift of a west wind, he only means 'a wind from a westerly direction'. It could well have been what we would call from the north-west, or even from the south-west. But since we know the prevailing system of winds over this stretch of the Mediterranean, I see no reason to doubt that it was with a north-westerly in his sail that Ulysses left the island of Ustica.

A north-westerly wind would have blown on his starboard beam as he ran down from Ustica to Favignana, would have come astern as he sailed along the southern shores of Sicily, and would have been on his port quarter as he crossed the Ionian Sea towards Ithaca. With this gift from the God of the Winds in their sails, the Greeks now began to retrace their steps across the Mediterranean.

10

To Greece and Back

THE distance from Ustica, round the western corner of Sicily, through the Malta Channel and across to Ithaca, is between 540 and 600 sea miles. The difference depends upon whether one goes east or west of the Aegadian islands. Assuming Ulysses' ships to have averaged three knots, it would take 200 hours to cover 600 sea miles. After nine days, or 216 hours, a ship maintaining a steady three knots should have completed the voyage. Referring back to the *Odyssey*, one finds that: "We sailed onwards [after leaving the Isle of Aeolus] for nine days, night and day. On the tenth we were already in sight of our homeland. . . ."

This does not prove that Ustica was necessarily the Isle of the Winds from which the Greeks took their departure. Nevertheless, taken in conjunction with all the other known facts, a nine-day sail from the north-western end of Sicily equates almost exactly with the Homeric story. If everything about the voyage of Ulysses is mythical, then it would soon become plain to all but the most obdurate of 'theory followers'. But the strangest thing about my search for Ulysses is that so many of the places described, and so much of the sailing itself, have fitted in perfectly with the known facts of modern geography.

If the poem had no basis in fact, Ulysses could have sailed forty-eight days—or what you will—to the land of the Lotus-Eaters, and with a wind from any direction whatever. But he took nine days with a north-easterly, which gives him a logical landfall somewhere in the Gulf of Gabes, near Jerba. Was it psychic intuition that made Homer place 'The Island of the Goats' within a few miles of Sicily? Was it chance alone that Ustica rises solitary in the sea at exactly the point where one would expect to find the Island of Aeolus? Was it again fortuitous that the length of time taken to get within sight of Greece should be almost exactly what one would expect of Ulysses' type of ship sailing from Ustica?

There is a saying: "Once is happenstance, twice is coincidence, three times is enemy action." I am not relying on the Bellman's technique: "What I tell you three times is true. . . ." For if there were no more in the *Odyssey* than three events, or series of events, which 'made sense' in terms of geography, and times and distance, then I would happily abandon any attempt to anchor the poem to recognizable places, people and islands.

"And on the tenth day we were in sight of our homeland. . . ." Ulysses is not made to say that they were in sight of Ithaca itself. This would have been unlikely, since the island lies tucked away behind what is nowadays called Cephallonia. 'The homeland' is obviously Greece, some section of the Ionian seaboard anyway, and it would be too much to believe that Ulysses' squadron could have made a perfect landfall at the entrance to the channel leading to Ithaca after weeks in unfamiliar waters.

The homeland to which he refers may have been any section of the western coast of Greece, or any of the off-lying Ionian islands. (Sailing from Syracuse to Corfu recently in a 20-ton yacht—with all modern equipment such as up-to-date charts, accurate compass, sextant and radio—I must admit to having been ten miles out in my landfall.) Nor had I, like Ulysses, "refused to let any of my men handle the steering of my ship but managed it myself all alone. . . ." But I take this to mean no more than that, like many a small boat captain, he had never taken a long uninterrupted sleep. He will have kept busying himself to check the ship's head against the sun and stars, to gauge wind and weather, and to chevy the crew about their duties of sail-trimming and steering.

With Greece in sight Ulysses now allowed himself a proper sleep and, so the story goes, the crew at once opened Aeolus' gift, the bag of winds, believing it contained treasure. All the winds immediately rushed forth, and a storm blew up and drove the ships away from the land. Now it is a known fact that the area around the Ionian islands is notorious for its sudden thunderstorms and violent squalls. These descend from the high hills and the rocky islands with practically no warning. "In all parts of the area where the coast is bordered by high hills or mountains, offshore coastal squalls are common, especially in windy weather. Many of these are white squalls, which occur in bright sunshine and often with scarcely a trace of cloud, and they are especially common on the western coasts of Greece and on the eastern side of the Adriatic, in the summer half of the year. When these squalls cross the sea they are indicated by the disturbed state of the sea surface, but in narrow channels, if the hinterland is bare and rocky, there may be no warning of their approach."

Sailing around these islands, between Ithaca, Levkas, Cephallonia, and Zante, I have several times run into this type of weather. There is no chance to reef, and the only thing to do is either drop one's sails at a rush, or bear off and run before the wind. Knowing how helpless even a modern sailing boat can be before the sudden blast of these island squalls, I can readily understand how an open boat, with only a square sail, would be completely at their mercy. There would be no question of tacking to windward, and the muscle power of twenty oarsmen or even more would be quite insufficient to drive a boat against the wind and weather.

It was off Ithaca in 1952 that I nearly came to grief in a 30-foot sailing boat: "When I came out on deck the northern hills of Ithaca were pale with sun-light. It was the last gleam before a thunderstorm came up against the wind and darkened the whole island. Just before the hills and foreshore were hidden under the driving cloud I took a bearing of the entrance to the Gulf of Molo. The island was not far away now, but we lost sight of it.

We steered a compass course through the low-flying spindrift, and the lightning was all about us. No sooner had the flash dazzled our eyes than the thunder spoke, hard on its heels. . . . There was a broken discoloured look about the water off our bows and the noise of the sea seemed to have changed. I had just got out the lead and line and was going forward to take a cast when a shift of wind disclosed the opening to the Gulf. The shore was less than a quarter of a mile away and the sea was slashing against the gap-toothed rocks. The cliff-wash had changed the pattern of the waves and that was the sound I had heard." Even with the assistance of my engine I found it difficult to make Port Vathy, the harbour of Ithaca. Any sailing boat, even a modern one—without an engine, could have done nothing but run back before the storm. Such was the fate of Ulysses' squadron.

I admit to feeling about this whole episode that it is no more than a poetic invention, designed to bring the hero within reach of his home, only to torture him like Tantalus by witholding the object of his desire at the moment it seemed within his grasp. Even so, nothing in this passage of the poem is impossible. Ulysses' ships would have taken about nine days under favourable conditions to reach the Ionian islands from north-western Sicily. A sudden storm, and the onset of a north-easter blowing off the mainland of Greece, would have prevented them making up to the land and would have driven them back before it.

It is noticeable in the *Odyssey* that it seems to be an accepted fact that a ship has no option but to run before any heavy weather, or strong winds. This accords with the known facts about these early vessels: that their squaresail could only be used with the wind from abaft the beam; and that their broad-bladed oars would have made rowing into a wind of any strength practically impossible.

Caught by the gale, and by a complete switch of wind, the Greek ships were blown away from their destination. Ulysses was driven right across the Ionian and south of Sicily. The memory of his homeland faded and was replaced by the images of the sea—the flare of sunlight on the water, the shine of fish-scales, the moon over barren hills, explosions of fish in still blue coves, and clouds swaggering over unknown shores. All the time the wind drove him relentlessly away from Greece, and back to the island of Aeolus.

11

In Search of
the Laestrygonians

"ONCE there, we disembarked and watered. . . ." While the crews took a meal on the beach alongside their ships, Ulysses begged the God of the Winds for a further gift. But a fair wind is something which is rarely repeated in the fickle sailing conditions of the summer Mediterranean, and it is little good praying for one. Few seas are more irritating to the sailor. For days on end a complete calm may fall, only to be succeeded by a thunderstorm, or a sudden gale that is too strong for canvas. This in its turn may take off after a few hours, leaving no working breeze behind it, but only an uneasy calm with an awkward sea and swell.

Ulysses and his men now found themselves faced with one of these long windless periods. There was nothing for it but to put the Isle of Aeolus behind them, settle down at the oar benches, and row. So, "for six days we forged onwards, never even lying up at night. . . ."

The remark in itself is interesting proof of the normal Greek practice of navigation at the time when Homer was writing. Night passages in a sea whose headlands and dangers were unmarked and unrecorded were always to be avoided. Whenever possible, they dropped anchor at nightfall. Exactly the same technique was adopted by the Portuguese mariners of Henry the Navigator in the early 15th century, when they were coasting down the unknown shores of West Africa. Even to this day in the Mediterranean, small coasters, fishing boats and caiques will often try to organize their passages so that they can anchor off-shore at night. On one occasion, when I was sailing from Crotone at the foot of Italy across to Corfu, I was advised by the captain of a 70-ton trading vessel to "Do as we do. Go right round the coast of the Gulf of Taranto, keeping near the shore. Then at night you can anchor and have a sleep." Upon my pointing out that if the wind went round into the south I should find myself on a lee shore, the captain merely shrugged. He considered it far more dangerous to set out direct across the open sea. Most sailors are conservative, and in the Mediterranean old habits die harder than almost anywhere else. The coastlines of this sea are littered with wrecks—dating from the Homeric period right up to the 1960's—many of which owe their origin to the Mediterranean sailor's habit of keeping close to the shore.

When Ulysses and his ships left Ustica for the second time there is no indication of the course they pursued, only that they were under oars: "My men's spirits were broken by the burdensome rowing." A natural course for them to have taken would have been back the way they had just come, round the corner of Sicily, and along the island's southern coast. They do not appear to have done this, and upon their next landfall hinges a major problem of Homeric geography. The location of Circe's island, the Siren rocks, and Scylla and Charybdis, have the consent of most ancient, and many modern scholars. The Land of the Laestrygonians, on the other hand, where Ulysses' squadron arrived after six days and nights under oars, has provoked much argument.

Of the various claimants to be the city and land of these terrifying cannibals the two blessed by antiquity were Leontini in eastern Sicily, and Formiae on the Gulf of Gaeta in western Italy. Leontini, on first investigation, would seem to be the more likely of the two. If Ulysses and his ships had retraced their tracks round the south of Sicily, they might well have continued to coast along up the eastern side. It is about 270 sea miles from Ustica to the nearest point on the coast to Leontini, and therefore within theoretical reach of ships making about two knots under oars for six days and nights.

Leontini, however, is some five miles from the sea. The town was founded about 730 B.C. by colonists from Naxos, and it was never a seaport. But the insuperable objection is geographical. There is nowhere on this coast which corresponds with the detailed description of the harbour into which the Greek ships sailed. ". . . an excellent harbour, closed in on all sides by an unbroken ring of precipitous cliffs, with two bold headlands facing each other at the mouth so as to leave only a narrow channel between. The captains of my squadron all steered their craft straight into the cove and tied up in the sheltered waters within. They remained close together, for it was obvious that the spot was never exposed to a heavy, or even a moderate sea, and the weather outside was bright and calm. But I did not follow them. Instead I brought my ship to rest outside the cove and made her fast with a cable to a rock at the end of the point. I then climbed the headland to get a view from the top, and took my bearings."

Apart from there being nowhere on the eastern coast of Sicily that corresponds with this detailed description, there is another objection to Leontini having been the city of the Laestrygonians. When Ulysses finally escaped from their land he sailed direct to the island of Circe, and the island of Circe was, as we know, north of the Messina Strait for the following good reason: At a later stage in his voyage, when Ulysses was about to brave the dangers of the Siren rocks and of Scylla and Charybdis, he was given detailed sailing directions by Circe which would take him past Scylla and Charybdis, and back into the Ionian Sea. Circe's Island, therefore must lie to the north of Scylla and Charybdis in the Messina Strait. It is inconceivable, if Leontini was the city of the Laestrygonians, that Ulysses would have made his way right back round Sicily again, going in the wrong direction to that in which he knew his home lay. On the other hand, he cannot have gone north from Leontini through the Strait of Messina to reach Circe's Island, or we would have heard of the terrors of Scylla and Charybdis at this stage in his voyage. Despite the fact, therefore, that some ancient authorities maintained Leontini was Telepylus, the city of the Laestrygonians, it must be dismissed.

The other ancient claimant to be Ulysses' next port of call is Formiae. Formiae has the backing of two such distinguished Romans as Cicero and Horace, the latter referring to Formian wine as "mellowing in a Laestrygonian" jar, while Cicero refers to tumult reigning at Formiae "no longer cannibal but political". Formiae lies north-north-east of Ustica, some 170 miles away across the open sea. The fact that it required an open sea voyage, something that Ulysses is likely to have tried to avoid, militates slightly against its claims. On the other hand, we know from the account that the ships never stopped to rest their oarsmen for six days and six nights. (If the ships had gone round Sicily in the direction of Leontini, it is inconceivable that they would not have made use of some of the sheltering coves and anchorages on the way.) Only an open sea voyage is likely to have accounted for his ships failing to drop anchor overnight. It is more than possible that, having now been twice right down the western and southern coasts of Sicily, the Greek navigators had come to the correct conclusion that it was an island. To set a north-easterly course, in their attempt to get back to Ithaca from Ustica, makes perfect sense. Only one thing stood in their way, the fact that Italy lay between. Like Columbus trying to discover a sea-route to China and the East Indies, only to come across America barring his passage, Ulysses in attempting to return to Ithaca may have discovered Italy for the Greeks.

Something else which disposed me to consider the claims of Formiae in preference to Leontini was the fact that it lay much nearer Ustica. To reach a point on the Sicilian coast near Leontini, after six days and nights of rowing, would entail an average speed of nearly two knots. Now Forfait in his study of the Mediterranean galley calculated that, after the first hour's rowing, the very most it could maintain was between two and a quarter to one and a half knots, and it is important to bear in mind that he was basing his calculations on the big mediaeval galley of some

180 feet long, with about 280 galley-slaves to drive it. A vessel of the type used by the Homeric Greeks would have been unlikely to maintain a comparable speed. Between one, and one and a half knots, would have been a good average over so long a period as six days and nights. One would expect, therefore, to find the Land of the Laestrygonians lying somewhere between 144 miles (one knot) and 288 miles (two knots) from Ustica. Formiae, 170 miles away, falls well within this range. It has the further qualification that it lies within easy reach of Circe's island—Cape Circeo—which is the principal headland at the northern end of the Gulf of Gaeta.

The modern town, now called Formia runs back inland noisy with industry, while the small port itself has become something of a summer resort for Romans. There are sandy beaches and high cliffs which trend out to the Scauri promontory on the east. To the west, the ancient city of Gaeta slumbers around the foot of its Angevin castle. This is one of the loveliest bays and coast-lines of western Italy, and when I sailed up here from Naples a few summers ago I felt confident that I was on the point of proving—or confirming an ancient tradition rather—that this was indeed the Land of the Laestrygonians. There was an old Volscian city here long before the Roman Formiae was founded, and it is clear that this indulgent coastline will always have been attractive to man. Behind the shores the mountains sweep up abruptly inland. Their slopes are charged today with the green of lemon and orange groves—something which the Homeric heroes will not have seen, for citrus fruits did not reach Europe until about the 13th century. The pomegranates which I ate in Gaeta almost reconciled me to this poetic-sounding but over-praised fruit, while the local wine is as good as anywhere in western Italy, superior to many of the better-known wines from the Naples area.

From Gaeta I sailed down to Formia itself. I left Porto Pescher-recchio—the Fishermen's Harbour—early one dawn when the coastal boats were coming back from their long night out on the bay. The barefoot sailors were treading about carefully between the fish and the seaweed in the bilges, and sniffing the damp, salt-sweet smell of newly-caught fish. They did not look much like their possible Laestrygonian ancestors, but neither do 20th-century Englishmen resemble the warriors of Boadicea.

Both the Cyclops Polyphemus and the Laestrygonians emerge from the Homeric account as 'anthropophagoi', or cannibals. Three thousand years ago there may well have been cannibals inhabiting parts of the Mediterranean Seaboard. In classical times Herodotus, Strabo, and others, record cannibalism among the Scythians who lived north of the Caspian sea. It is clear from the story that both Polyphemus and the Laestrygonians were 'food cannibals', and there is no suggestion of anything ritualistic in their practices. In both cases, however, they are described as inhabiting prosperous areas. One must therefore assume that they adopted the habit not out of want, but for the more sophisticated reason that they had acquired a taste for human flesh. "Food cannibalism for the satisfaction of hunger may occur sporadically as a result of real necessity or may be kept up for the simple gratification of a taste for human flesh. Cannibalism from necessity is found not only among the lower races, such as the Fuegians or Red Indian tribes, but also among civilized races, as the records of sieges and shipwrecks show. Simple food cannibalism is found in West Africa. Human flesh formerly was exposed for sale in the market, and some tribes sold the corpses of dead relatives for consumption as food. . . ."

There is no reason why there should not have been cannibals at one time on this coast. But one thing, which is attributed to the Laestrygonians that has clearly crept into the poem from some other source is the story that "In their land nightfall and morning follow so closely upon each other that a man who could do without sleep might earn double wages." This reference, which is quite explicit in the *Odyssey*, can only have come from some traveller's tale about the countries of the far north. Some commentators have attempted to explain it away by various ingenious means, but it is clearly a reference to the short nights of mid-summer in northern latitudes. It can have no application to any part of the Mediterranean.

If this coast around Formia was the Land of the Laestrygonians, then I knew quite well what I was looking for— a perfect natural harbour, "closed in on all sides by an unbroken ring of precipitous cliffs." The description of this particular harbour is one of the clearest and most definite in the whole poem. It reads exactly like a sailing direction, and I feel confident that this is exactly what it was based upon. However much the poet may have embroidered the tale with references to northern lands and to cannibals, the harbour is described so clearly that one should surely be able to find it to this day. So I thought, and so I still think. But I was to be disappointed in the Gulf of Gaeta. Although there are high cliffs here, and the promontory of Scauri seemed at first to promise me the cove I was looking for, I could in no way identify it. The harbour of modern Formia is an artificial one, as is the harbour of Gaeta. There is no perfect natural harbour anywhere on this section of coast, nor can there have ever been. I know well from other ancient ports and harbours which I have visited how the drying up of rivers and other coastal changes can often erase old harbours as if they had never been. (This is particularly the case at Selinunte in southern Sicily, where the classical harbour was tucked away behind a headland and in a river mouth.) But the harbour into which Ulysses' squadron sailed, to find themselves in the Land of the Laestrygonians, was clearly that rare thing in the Mediterranean—a natural cove, surrounded by sheltering cliffs, and with only a narrow entrance.

Try as I might, and I sailed back and forth along this pleasant stretch of coast, I could not equate the Homeric description with anything that I could find. I went inland and climbed the lonely promontory, which is starred with the sites of ancient Roman villas, to see whether I had missed some inlet or natural cove. I found nothing. This might possibly have been the Land of the Laestrygonians, but it was not here that the Greek ships were destroyed by rocks hurled down upon them from the heights above. It was not here that Ulysses made his ship fast at the entrance while the rest of his squadron sailed in and "made fast . . . in a spot that was never exposed to a heavy or even a moderate sea." Such places are rare in any part of the world, and the knowledge of them is handed on from one seaman to another.

Having failed to find the harbour anywhere near Formia I began to despair, and to wonder whether this was one place at least which existed only in the imagination. I went to Cefalù in Sicily which Samuel Butler believed to be the city of the Laestrygonians, but the beetling mountain conceals no harbour. There is only the short arm of a man-made breakwater, which can shelter no more than a few fishing boats when the weather is clement. Cefalù, in any case, could never have been the place to which Ulysses' men struggled after six days and nights of constant rowing. It is only sixty miles from Ustica.

All I knew was that, if the harbour existed, it ought to lie somewhere between 144 miles and 288 miles from Ustica. I had sailed all down the western coast of Italy and there was not a cove or headland that I did not know—even obscure little anchorages like the one at Cape Palinuro where a boat may lie at anchor provided always that the wind does not get round into the north. I had sailed right round Sicily twice, and had been up and down some parts of that tawny coastline more than a dozen times. The perfect harbour still eluded me. I crossed to Cagliari one summer and coasted up eastern Sardinia. Olbia had looked from the chart as if it might possibly be the place that I was seeking. But Olbia lies at the head of a marshy delta, loud with mosquitoes in summer, and formerly one of the most malaria-stricken places in this island of bandits and blood feuds. There is no natural cove surrounded by cliffs. There are enough shoals, rocks and islets to make the approach formidable, but it was not in Olbia that Ulysses lost eleven of his ships.

I found the Laestrygonian Land, as I suspect Ulysses did, entirely by accident.

The Excellent Harbour

On a summer day when a light easterly breeze was just stirring the sea, I sailed up the Straits of Bonifacio. Ulysses was far from my mind and I doubt whether I had glanced at the *Odyssey* for a year or more. I only found myself in that part of the Mediterranean by accident, having accepted a last minute offer to help crew a friend's sailing boat to Corsica and Sardinia.

The wind died towards noon and we sat idly about the deck until, with the first cooling of the land towards evening, an offshore breeze sprang up from Corsica and shrugged impatiently in the white folds of our mainsail. We decided to put into Bonifacio for the night. It was a harbour that none of us had visited before, so we busied ourselves over the *Admiralty Pilot* and a large-scale chart of the area.

I suppose my reading of the *Pilot* should have given me the first clue. "Port de Bonifacio consists of a cove, from three-quarters of a cable to one cable wide, formed by the peninsula on which the town is built: it affords excellent shelter to small craft. The harbour is entered between Pointe du Timon, the south-western extremity of the peninsula, and Pointe de la Madonetta, the southern extremity of a small peninsula. . . . The entrance is difficult to distinguish from a distance." As we closed the Corsican coast I could confirm the accuracy of the *Pilot*. Even with the aid of binoculars, it was a long time before I could make out the break in the cliffs that marks the entrance to Bonifacio.

The wind was gusty now, spilling off the high cliffs and causing us to tack constantly as we worked our way towards the land. It brought with it the scent of the *maquis*, that tangled undergrowth which carries the whole of the Mediterranean on its breath. I think it was not until we were right up to the entrance of the harbour that it dawned on me where I was. The cliffs stood high on either hand, and through the heart of them ran the knife-thrust of the sea. There were a few rocks offshore at the entrance to the harbour. We tacked, and came about again as we found ourselves at the mouth of the channel. Suddenly I recognized it—the place I had vainly sought in Sicily and Italy.

Bonifacio is unlike anywhere else in the Mediterranean. It would be an unique harbour in any country, but in this tideless sea where few rivers channel their way through the land, it is so rare a place that no sailor could avoid remarking on it. It is true there are other fine natural harbours—Grand Harbour in Malta for one, and Port Mahon in Minorca for another. But there is no other place like Bonifacio. I can think of only one other that remotely resembles it—the small harbour of Ciudadella in south-western Minorca, But Ciudadella, quite apart from its distance from Ustica, could never have been the home of the Laestrygonians. The creek which leads up to Ciudadella is no more than a channel winding through sandstone banks only a few feet high.

At Bonifacio, two bold headlands front one another and between them there is only this narrow channel. At the most, it is no more than 200 yards wide, and in places considerably narrower. So high are the cliffs on either hand that the channel appears even smaller than it really is. It is even more surprising to find how far back it winds into the land. The harbour itself, at the head of this channel, is indeed "closed in on all sides by an unbroken ring of precipitous cliffs". The channel bends round to the right, and once inside there is no sight or sound of the sea. This is truly a place where a vessel might lie and never be disturbed, whatever weather was blowing in the straits outside. This, I feel sure, was the harbour where the Greek squadron was ambushed by the Laestrygonians. This was the death-trap where Ulysses had lost all his other ships.

Later, when I read Victor Bérard's work on the *Odyssey*, I discovered that for quite a different reason he had come to the conclusion that the territory of the Laestrygonians lay in the straits of Bonifacio, but he placed it in a small cove on the Sardinian side. His reasons for this were philological not geographical—and geographically it does not fit the Homeric description. Bérard's theory was that Homer had based the wanderings of Ulysses on a Pilot, or *Periplous*, of Phoenician origin and whatever may be said for or against this argument, I find myself agreeing with one major point that he made: "To sum up, then, it would seem that Odysseus had ten important adventures in the seas of the West (The Phaeacians, the Lotus-Eaters, Cyclops, Aeolos, the Laestrygonians, Circe, the Land of the Dead, the Isle of the Sirens, the Island of the Sun, and Calypso) of these, seven take place in sea gates and all of them can be connected with these seven sea gates." I very much doubt whether Homer had any conception of where the Land of the Laestrygonians really lay. But what I do not doubt, is that his description of the harbour was based on the first-hand account of someone who had been into Bonifacio.

It is known for certain that Corsica was inhabited long before the period when Homer wrote, and before the period that he was describing. There are numerous megalithic monuments in the island, and near Bonifacio itself a number of megalithic burial-places have been found. Under their slabs of stone lie the skeletons of the savage men who were to be immortalized as the cannibal Laestrygonians.

It was here, then, that the Greeks came after leaving Ustica. Previously I had been following the false trails of Leontini and Formia because I had been trying to be logical as well as to follow classical tradition. I had looked towards the east and the north-east, because I knew that it was in that direction Ulysses should have steered. I had never really considered that he might have made a north-westerly course. I feel convinced, at any rate, that the harbour which is described in the *Odyssey* is Bonifacio in Corsica. So perfect a natural harbour, moreover, at one of the main 'sea gates' of the Mediterranean is certain to have been recorded by the first sailors who entered these waters. The Strait of Gibraltar, the 'main gate' into the Mediterranean, is described, and so too that other important 'gate' the Strait of Messina where Scylla and Charybdis lurk. At Bonifacio yet another of the most important Mediterranean 'gates' is accurately depicted.

Bonifacio, almost exactly 240 miles north-west from Ustica, is within the radius of a vessel making one and a half knots from Ustica and arriving on the seventh day after a steady passage. The fact that the harbour of the Laestrygonians lies to the north-west, and not where I expected to find it, does not worry me as much perhaps as it should.

That night, with our boat lying safe and still beside the old wall in the harbour, I knew that I had found the place where the Greeks met their doom. Bonifacio is formed by nature not only as a safe shelter in all winds and weathers, but as an ideal trap in which to ambush a ship or a squadron of ships.

Above my head, and all the way down the channel-mouth to the invisible sea, ran the towering cliffs from which a man could easily drop a rock on to the deck of a boat below. The Greeks, who entered this channel unsuspecting, perished to a man when the Laestrygonians, "standing on the top of the cliffs began pelting the ships with stones."

Only Ulysses escaped, for he had moored to one of the rocks off the entrance to Bonifacio. When the trap was sprung on his companions, he had only to cut the hawser securing his ship and stand out into the safety of the sea. "With the fear of death in their hearts my men settled down to row. It was with a sigh of relief that we sped out to sea, leaving those frowning cliffs behind us. . . ."

13

Circe's Island

"WESTWARDS I have journeyed to the parts of Etruria opposite Sardinia," wrote the Greek geographer Strabo. His *Geography* is the most important work on that science which has survived from antiquity. Consisting of seventeen books, it is interesting among other things for revealing how much credence Strabo placed in the *Odyssey*. He identifies many of the places mentioned in the poem and he has no doubt at all about the next landfall of Ulysses. "The Island of Circe," he remarks, "lies between the marshes and the sea, and it really is an island." The reason he emphasizes the point is because doubts had been expressed whether Mount Circeo, at the tip of the peninsula which bears its name, could really have been the home of the goddess. It had been claimed as such from time immemorial.

Cape Circeo lies 180 miles due east from Bonifacio. If the navigation which had taken Ulysses miles out of his way to the Corsican port was very faulty, his next landfall was, at any rate, in the right direction. Strabo notwithstanding, it is not an island —although the mistake of the geographer is easy enough to understand. Homer calls Circe's home Aeaea, and he describes how Ulysses in his surviving ship reached it 'in due course', after escaping from the Laestrygonians. A number of later scholars have disagreed with the identification pointing out that Mount Circeo is in fact joined to the mainland of Italy by a narrow neck of land. But if Homer is incorporating some sailor's first-hand account into his description, it is not surprising to find, on opening the *Admiralty Pilot* for the west coast of Italy: "Promontorio or Monte Circeo, of which Cape Circeo is the southwestern extremity, is an isolated and rocky mass, which rises steeply and is covered with sparse vegetation. The promontory is connected with the mainland by low flat land and when seen from north-north-westward, *it appears as a high conical and pointed island . . .*" (my italics). Similarly the *French Nautical Instructions* for this coast state: "Lying to the far south of the Pontine marshes, this mountain looks like an island when seen from a distance." I have twice approached it from sea myself, once coming from Fiumicino at the mouth of the Tiber, and once sailing across directly from Bonifacio. It looks exactly like an offshore island.

I remember on the second occasion how I made out the brownish-green hump of the cape long before any other shore marks were identifiable. Like "sweet Catullus all-but island, olive-silvery Sirmio," Mount Circeo is as near to being an island as is possible without actually having water on all four sides. I have also no doubt that, over centuries, the current which sweeps down this coast has brought much alluvial deposit from the Tiber to thicken the 'neck' joining the mountain to the land. It is not impossible that it was once completely separate. Bérard makes the comment that "In old times, sailors used to run their ships ashore on the west side of the island . . . a narrow channel leads in to an inner lagoon. In this lagoon, now called the Cala dei Pescatori (Fishermen's Port), the Romans established their port of Circeii. Surrounded on all sides by the forest and the dunes, it offers an admirable refuge to ships that find their way in." Unfortunately I sailed here in a cutter with a draft of nearly ten feet, so the nearest that I could get to Circe's home was some twenty yards offshore on the eastern side. It is a good anchorage if the Sirocco does not blow. And if it does, all one has to do is sail round the headland, and anchor close inshore to the north.

If I have found myself at variance with the writers of antiquity by placing the harbour of the Laestrygonians at Bonifacio, I

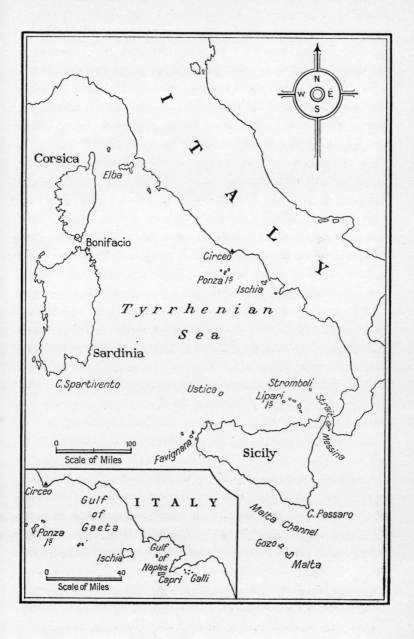

can find nothing to argue about their designation of this strange headland as the home of Circe. When I went ashore here on an early autumn day the smoke was rising from the little village of San Felice, blue against the brown of the land. A dog barked in the distance, and there were hawks hovering in the air currents which lifted around the mountain. Headlands of this type are nearly always graced by birds of prey, who find the updraughts and swirling eddies of air ideal for their purpose. Now Circe, or Kirke in Greek, means a small she-hawk or falcon.

Circe's mountain must always have been an important landmark for sailors along this coast. Ulysses, escaping with his companions from the destruction of the Greek squadron, would have made straight for the point once he saw it lift above the horizon. Approaching from the west he will certainly have believed it to be an island. Even if it was joined to the mainland in those days he will not have immediately discovered his mistake.

For two days and nights the survivors lay on the beach near their boat, "suffering not only from exhaustion, but also from the horrors through which we had passed." On the third day, which was heralded by a beautiful dawn, Ulysses took his spear and sword and went inland to reconnoitre. "I climbed a rocky height which promised a wide view, and on reaching the top I was able to see the smoke rising from the distant spot where Circe's house lay screened by the dense oak scrub and forest trees. . . ."

Although today Mount Circeo is almost devoid of trees, there are the remains of an old forest down in the low-lying land at the neck of the peninsula. There are still oaks among the other trees. That this forest was extensive as late as the mid-19th century is revealed by the French writer and traveller, Mercey: "This fine forest is merely an extension of Fossa Nuova forest, where oaks grow—evergreens or cork trees and magnificent elms. . . . Where the undergrowth was less dense, we could hear gruntings and more than once we saw passing herds of the boars which live in these marshes, much as in some promised land. Eagles and sea hawks flew through the clearings, chasing the

ringdoves and the ducks which flew in droves among the reeds."
Circe's island, in fact, had everything that lost and tired sailors
could want—a beach and a secure place for their boat, fresh water,
wood for fuel and for shipwright's work, and plenty of wild
boar and other game. With summer and the sailing season drawing to an end, this would have been as good a place as any in
which to winter.

The rocky height which Ulysses climbed to spy out the land
was probably Lookout Peak, 1,775 feet high which is now scattered with the ruins of an old watch tower. On his way down,
and just as he was nearing a stream, he came across a great
antlered stag and managed to kill it with his spear. A small
stream still flows across the neck of the peninsula, and the Gulf
of Gaeta has more rivers flowing into it than any other part of
this coast. (Among them are the Volturno and the Garigliano,
names famous in the military history of the Second World War.)
The whole area is fertile and luxuriant, and it is Monte Circeo
which dominates the great bay.

One objection which modern commentators have raised against
the identification of Cape Circeo with Circe's Island is that this
is clearly intended by the poet to be an island all alone in the sea.
Against this one may make the charge that a small island, alone
in the Mediterranean, would hardly number stags among its
fauna. To move from classical authorities to the Middle Ages,
Dante had no doubts about this being Circe's island, for in the
famous passage when Dante meets Ulysses in Hell, the latter
describes how he finally left Circe—"She who twelve months
near Gaeta detained me." Standing on the eastern side of the
twin-headed mountain, one sees nothing but the long blue acres
of the Mediterranean all the way south to Sicily. Invisible beyond
the rim of the horizon lie Sardinia, Corsica, and the ill-omened
Straits of Bonifacio. Only, breaking the mist-haze on a warm
summer day, I could just make out the pale bubbles of the Ponza
islands adrift in the sea some fifteen miles away.

Circe, the *Odyssey* tells us, was an enchantress and a goddess.

In mythology she was supposedly the daughter of the sun God Helios by the nymph Perse, and the granddaughter of Oceanus, god of the Great Ocean which encircled the whole earth. The ancestry seems suitable enough for a goddess who inhabited a high mountain on the edge of the sea, and who was destined to tell Ulysses how to reach the Pillars of Hercules and pass into the Ocean. Was there any other reason why this corner of Italy should have been connected with a mysterious goddess, who could change men into beasts? The answer is that only ten miles away down the coast at Terracina there was one of the oldest shrines in Italy, the temple of Feronia, Goddess of the Wild and of the Forest. Her name, Feronia, derives from the Latin *feri*, 'wild animals', but her worship was long pre-Roman. "Feronia had her sanctuary at the opening to this *Valle*, at the foot of Punta di Leano. There stood her sacred grove, her fountain and her temple, the heavy stone foundations of which have survived to this day. It was one of the oldest rural cults in Italy. Primitive worship was practised here among woods held in awe. She presided over the ceremony of freeing slaves: the slave was made to sit down on a stone in the temple: on his head a bonnet was set and then these words were pronounced: 'Be seated, ye slaves that have deserved well! Arise, free men!' "

There is clearly a close connection between Feronia, goddess of the beasts and the forest, and Circe, an enchantress who turns men into beasts and who lives in a glade in the forest. The story, with its poetic elaboration and embroidery, is almost exactly what one would expect to arise out of some sailor's tale about a Goddess of the Beasts whose worship dominated this corner of Italy. There is also, perhaps, a symbolic connection between men who have been enslaved, or turned into beasts, and men to whom the goddess has given back their true shape, turned into free men again.

In the Homeric account, Ulysses after slaying the stag takes it back to his companions, and, as happened before on the island of Favignana, their spirits are immediately raised by fresh meat.

94

They must still have had some Ismarian wine left, for they "washed down the rich meat with mellow wine."

Nowhere in the Odyssey, incidentally, is there any exact figure given for the number of men in Ulysses' ship. We know that six had been lost in the raid on Ismarus, and a further six had perished at the hands of the Cyclops near Trapani. (On that occasion Ulysses had taken a picked group of twelve men ashore with him.) We now learn that, on the morning after their feast of venison, Ulysses divided the ship's company into two bands. He took charge of one party himself and put Eurylochus, "an officer of noble birth" in command of the other which is described as consisting of twenty-two men. Assuming that Ulysses' party was about the same in number, it seems reasonable to conclude that his ship originally had been manned by some fifty to sixty men. This sounds about the right number for a boat with a maximum of ten oars a side. Divided into two watches of twenty each, the remainder would have consisted of nobles and officers (like Ulysses and Eurylochus) who did not take a place at the oars. The Homeric ship was quite small and in no way to be compared with the fifty-oared galleys of classical antiquity. The ease with which the ship of Ulysses is described as being manhandled up the beaches, and his difficulties in anything approaching rough weather, lead me to the conclusion that much of the *Odyssey* is explicable as soon as one realizes how small the ships were.

The sea, from the deck of a small boat, is quite unlike the sea that the modern merchant seaman knows, or that the cruise-line passenger admires. Sailing the Mediterranean with one or two companions in a small yacht, I have noticed how every fluke of wind and weather takes on a real character. High peaks which hurl down squalls become positively evil, one talks to the porpoises as they leap alongside, one associates capes and islands with human characteristics which depend on the kind of weather one has experienced near them, and all the time one listens to the myriad voices of the sea—the wind in the rigging, the quickening pulse of the wake, or the sad slop and sigh when a calm descends.

In Sicily once I heard an old sailor say: "Look! There is the Madonna walking on the water!" He was pointing to those crinkled marks drawn over the surface which indicate the passage of a light air. English sailors call them 'cats'-paws'. The ancient Greeks called them 'The footsteps of Thetis'. There is a great continuity in a sailor's life, and more so in parts of the Mediterranean than anywhere else I know. A great many things which have baffled eminent scholars might have seemed more comprehensible if they had spent a year or two as sailors on this sea.

The *Odyssey* continues with Eurylochus and his men making their way inland towards the smoke which Ulysses has seen rising from Circe's glade. Perhaps because it was early autumn when I saw the smoke standing up from the chimneys of San Felice, I feel sure it was at this season that Ulysses landed there. There is a curiously heavy and fruitful feeling about the whole of this miraculous and evocative passage of the *Odyssey*. It is the still, warm fall of the year when Ulysses strikes down the antlered stag, and there is a hint of approaching winter in that blue smoke rising from the heart of the wood. The landscape has the quality of a Breughel, clear and defined. I seem to hear the apples falling with soft ripe thuds on to grass that is misted with spiders' webs. So Eurylochus and his men came through the forest and "In the clearing of a dell they came upon the house of Circe ... all round it wild animals were roaming—mountain wolves and lions whom the goddess had bewitched with her magic drugs."

The story of Circe was a favourite of classical artists and vase painters, and numerous paintings have survived which show the goddess in the act of transforming Ulysses' men into beasts. One of the finest of these shows the goddess seated calmly on a stool. She is handsome and dark-haired, her tresses confined in a sphendone, a kind of snood. In her left hand she holds the fatal bowl in which her drugs have been prepared, and in her right hand she holds the magic wand. Before her one of the unfortunate Greeks turns away in agony and protest. He is just beginning to change into a beast. We can see the birth of a tail at the base of his spine, and on top of his head a boar's crest is starting to sprout. The contrast between the calm figure of the goddess and the distorted body of the man is strangely moving.

Only Eurylochus, as we know, escaped the fate of being turned into a beast. For, acting in a way which would certainly not have earned him marks for 'officer-like qualities', he allowed his men to go into Circe's palace without him. Suspecting a trap (not for nothing, perhaps, was he a kinsman of the wily Ulysses) Eurylochus preferred to stay outside. As soon as he saw what had happened to his men, he took to his heels and returning "to the good black ship, he told us the fate that had overtaken his party."

This is a moment when Ulysses' character is shown to its best advantage. Far from agreeing with Eurylochus that the sensible thing to do is to make their escape before all of them are captured and transformed, he slings his bow over his shoulder, takes his sword, and sets out to try to rescue his companions. When Eurylochus refuses to direct him to the sacred glade, Ulysses remarks: "Very well then, you stay here and eat and drink by the dark ship. I shall go alone. Such is clearly my duty."

It is at this point that Ulysses' ancestor Hermes makes his appearance, and gives the hero the sacred plant *moly*, which will preserve him against the goddess's drugged potion. The ancient grammarians and scholars had many a tussle attempting to decide exactly what *moly* was. The plant is described as having a black root and a white flower, so it is just possible to identify it with the wild cyclamen which also has a white flower and a dark root. But the fact that it is "hard for mortals to pull up" suggests that one is not supposed to find it in any botanical dictionary. R. M. Henry concluded that the legend of the sacred plant derived from Phoenician or Egyptian sources. Since classical times the name has been applied to a species of garlic (*Allium Moly*) which has yellow flowers. J. E. Harrison commented in his *Myths of the Odyssey*: "Most nations have their herb of virtue, and, curiously enough, the *Allermannsharnisch* of the Germans is a charm against love as well as magic. Its juice is white, and it has

97

a long black bulbous root." Robert Graves in *The Greek Myths* points out that *Allium Moly* was believed to grow when the moon waned, "rather than when it waxed, and hence to serve as a counter-charm against Hecate's moon magic."

Garlic itself has long been associated with magical properties, particularly by sailors. As late as the 14th century, at a time when the magnetic compass was being introduced into all seagoing ships, we find that garlic was reputed to neutralize the lodestone, thus putting the magnetic compass out of action. It was even suggested that sailors should be forbidden to eat garlic to prevent this disaster happening—something that would certainly have caused a mutiny among Mediterranean seamen.

In the village of San Felice I bought some garlic, along with *pasta* and some of that dark-red *salsa*, the tomato paste which the villagers make and dry on the flat roofs of their houses. My garlic was not moly, however, but the more familiar *Allium sativum*, whose brassy smell one must grow to like if one is to live and voyage in the Mediterranean. The padrone of the village inn offered to show me Circe's cave if I came back in the evening when his siesta was over. Cicadas were shouting in the tangled, scented scrub as I made my way down the road from the village to the eastern beach. Hawks still spiralled over the slopes of Circe's mountain. Nothing else stirred in the drug-laden hours of the afternoon.

14

The Lady of Wild Things

I WENT back to the village in the early evening and, after a few glasses of red wine, we set off for the 'Grotto della Maga', the Witch's Cave. It lies on the north side of the 'island' and is not unlike the Cave of Polyphemus in Sicily. But then, I am no spelaeologist. Most caves look much the same to me, smell the same of damp and old ghosts, and are usually—as was this one—haunted by bats. "This is where the Witch lived!" my guide said proudly. I wondered how long they had been telling that tale?—certainly since the 19th century. It is even possible that Roman travellers were regaled with the same erroneous story, although they are likely to have been too conversant with Homer to accept a cave as the home of the divine Circe.

Circe, of course, did not live in a cave but in a comfortable palace, with polished doors and tables, where there were chairs studded with silver, footstools, gold ewers, and silver basins. Homer describes a world of Mycenaean splendour when he brings Ulysses into the palace of the goddess. It is a far remove from the indolent 'Tahitian' land of the Lotus-Eaters, the cave-dwelling barbarism of the Sicilian Cyclopes, or the megalithic city of the cannibal Laestrygonians. The only cave mentioned in this section of the *Odyssey* is the one into which the Greeks put the gear and tackle from their ship after they had dragged her ashore for the winter. But caves alter considerably over the centuries, and it would be pointless to speculate which of the caves around the foot of Mount Circeo may have served the heroes for their winter boat-house.

Ulysses, having taken the sacred herb *moly* from his ancestor Hermes, now entered Circe's palace and was received by the goddess. To her astonishment he drank her potion without any ill effects, being preserved by Hermes' gift, which was an antidote to the drugs that Circe had mixed in the golden bowl. An engraving on a classical gemstone shows one artist's conception of Ulysses at this moment in his life. The hero is naked except for a pointed sailor's cap—not unlike the woollen stocking-caps worn by fishermen in Brittany and in the west of England to this day. In his right hand he carries his sword, and in his left he holds aloft the sacred *moly*. Ulysses, as we know, followed Hermes' directions punctiliously: "When Circe smites you with her wand, draw your sword from your side and spring at her as if you meant to take her life. Now she will fall before you in terror and invite you to her bed. Do not hesitate to accept the favours of the goddess. . . ."

Allowing for all the mythopoeic function of the poet I wonder if I am entirely wrong in detecting a large element of truth in the story of Circe? Throughout the pre-classical and prehistoric Mediterranean world all the evidence seems to show that it was the female function which was reverenced. From the 'white goddess' painted on the walls of the cave at Levanzo, to the goddess figures found in Malta, to the matrilineal customs of Leros in the eastern Aegean (to mention but three places at random)—one gains the impression that matriarchy was once dominant in this sea. Many of the Greek legends similarly seem to show the overlaying of a matriarchal system and of a female goddess by northern invaders, whose religion centred around a male god. The single Muse, for instance, whom Homer invokes, ultimately gives place to the decorative but relatively unimportant chorus who look to the male Apollo as their leader.

In the story of Circe one sees an early nature goddess of the pre-Roman Volscians in the process of being overthrown. It is not, after all, so unlikely that the first sailors who burst into the lands of the Tyrrhenian Sea, acted in just this way. Taking the story of Ulysses as having a genuine element of truth behind it, I visualize him coming ashore in western Italy, and finding himself near the site of a temple dedicated to an all-powerful nature goddess. Being of a race who believed that the male principle is dominant in the world, Ulysses is no respecter of local customs. He is certainly unwilling to accept a priestess as the fount of wisdom.

The accretions of legend upon the story of Ulysses' men being turned into beasts until he overcomes the goddess, are not difficult to sever from the main fabric of truth. Feronia, or whatever the goddess may have been called in pre-Roman times, is likely to have been served by priestesses. The shrine of this goddess of the woods, and wild creatures, will almost certainly have had something akin to a 'zoo' surrounding it. The ancient Egyptians, for instance, kept the animals appropriate to their animal gods in special preserves near the temples. Feronia, similarly, is likely to have had an enclosure of sacred animals as an appendage to her shrine. Now The Goddess of Wild Things was certainly known to both Homeric and pre-Homeric Greeks. She was worshipped in Minoan Crete among other places. Describing Cretan seals and rings which depict the Goddess, H. J. Rose writes: "Several representations of this goddess, or at least of goddesses in similar attitudes and with like attendant beasts have been found. . . . We may think of her as more or less resembling Rhea-Cybele, with power over the wild and the creatures inhabiting it; hence for want of knowledge of her Minoan name, she is referred to as the Πότνια Θηρῶν, the Lady of Wild things."

Ulysses will have treated the priestess and the sacred grove of the beast goddess with scant respect. His ignorant and superstitious sailors may possibly have been willing to accept the local goddess and her priestesses on the same terms that the natives did—but not Ulysses, that embodiment of the rational man. "She had turned them into beasts"—made them subservient to her—but ithyphallic Ulysses was not prepared to bow his head to any woman. He drew his sword. The priestess begged for mercy and invited him to her bed.

Circe's island, if we exclude Ustica, where the daughters of Aeolus lived incestuously with their brothers, is the first place visited by Ulysses where we find any women mentioned. Circe, we know, had her handmaids. They are described as "the daughters of the springs and the groves and the holy rivers that flow into the sea." The combination of springs, groves, and rivers in this passage confirms me even more strongly in my belief that Mount Circeo and the Gulf of Gaeta with its numerous rivers—unusual in Italy—is the place where Ulysses and his men spent their first winter. After the hazards through which they had passed it is hardly surprising that the surviving Greeks were happy to stay in, or near, Mount Circeo. They had found a good dry cave to house their ship throughout the winter, their leader had mastered the local priestess, there was plenty to eat and drink, and there were women.

" 'I know well,' Circe said, 'all that you have suffered on the fishtailed seas and the disasters you have met on the savage land. But now, enjoy your food and drink your wine. That is what I want to see. For you must become again the men that you were when you first left your home in rocky Ithaca. . . .' Such sentiments went down well with my men. And, in fact, we stayed there for a whole year, getting good meat to eat, and plenty of wine to drink."

For the first time it was Ulysses who needed to be reminded that the months were slipping by, and that Ithaca was as far away as ever.

15

Westward
to the Ocean Stream

In the summer of the following year Ulysses, somewhat reluctantly, came to the conclusion that the time had come to get under way again. It seems to have been largely the complaints of his men that drove him to broach the matter to Circe. "They badger me and wear me down with their grumbling whenever you are not here," he said. "I beg you to keep the promise that you made and send us on our way home."

The point is made throughout the whole Circe episode that the Greeks are now completely lost, and in unknown lands and seas. "East and West mean nothing to us here," Ulysses remarks. Until their return to Aeolus' island after being blown back from Greece, Ulysses has been more or less master of his navigation. He has been in uncharted waters, but he has always used his limited knowledge in a logical way. But once the Greeks have left Ustica for the second time they are really lost, and it is only by an error that they reach the Land of the Laestrygonians. With something like a return of his native common sense, Ulysses, has then steered due east—to find himself in Circe's island, with the whole of unknown Italy barring his way to Greece. If he and his companions are to return home, he must rely on local information to get him away from these uncharted shores. But before he can be put on the right track for Ithaca he has to undertake the most difficult part of all his wanderings—the voyage to the Pillars of Hercules and beyond them to the Stream of Ocean itself.

A number of Homeric scholars have come to the conclusion

that the whole of this episode in the *Odyssey* comes from a different source to the main body of the poem. Their argument has been summarized by D. L. Page in *The Homeric Odyssey*: "We have good reason to believe that there was once an independent poem on Odysseus' Visit to the Underworld, wherein the hero met and conversed with Teiresias, with his mother, and with his former comrades-in-arms. This poem was inserted into the *Odyssey*, and more or lesss adapted to it. . . . " This may well be so, and it would surely be pointless to look for the Entrance to Hell on any chart. As Ulysses himself remarks: "No man has ever sailed a black ship into Hell."

Nevertheless this section of the *Odyssey* is not without a substratum of truth, and it seems to me that at this point Homer is surely incorporating the story of some Phoenician navigation into the poem. Robert Graves, who takes the Butlerian view that the *Odyssey* was written by a woman, has this footnote to the story of Ulysses in his *The Greek Myths*: "However, the authoress of the *Odyssey* had little geographical knowledge, and called upon West, South or North winds at random." Now as I have tried to show, all the winds, distances and geographical features so far encountered by Ulysses and his men have 'made sense'. I find the same true for the wind which now drives Ulysses from Circe's island to the Pillars of Hercules, or the Strait of Gibraltar.

If the poet had picked his winds at random, then Circe might well have presented Ulysses with a south wind. This would, indeed, have been useless for sailing a square-rigged boat from Cape Circeo to the Strait of Gibraltar. The Sirocco, or south wind, would either have embayed Ulysses in the Gulf of Gaeta, or would have blown him from cape to cape northwards up the Italian coast. A westerly would have prevented him leaving Cape Circeo at all. An easterly, or Levanter, would have carried him straight back to Corsica and Sardinia, and the dangers of the Bonifacio Straits. But what do we find? Here is Circe giving the Greeks her sailing orders: "Ulysses," the goddess said, "there is no need to linger on the shore just because you have no pilot. Step your mast, hoist the white sail, and take up your place in the ship. The North Wind will blow her on her way...."

Is it accidental that out of the four cardinal winds the goddess should select the only one which would be of any use to a sailor wanting to reach the Straits of Gibraltar from the north-western coast of Italy? The North Wind or Tramontana, (the wind that comes from 'between the mountains') is a welcome gift in this part of the sea. I have spent nearly a whole summer idling down this pleasant coastline, nearly always with winds from the west. This, as the *Admiralty Pilot* confirms, is something that one must expect: "In the summer the winds along the western coast of Italy are mainly onshore, south-westerly or westerly in the northern part.... Strong winds are few and gales rare."

I think it is reasonable to assume that it was late summer or early autumn when Ulysses and his men left Circe's palace and embarked on their long voyage to the west. We know that it was twelve months after their arrival, and this, as I have suggested, is most likely to have been towards the end of summer. The northerly with which Ulysses set sail occurs less frequently, and is usually associated with a depression moving up the Adriatic. A wind from the north will have been ideal for a sailing boat bound for the southern tip of Sardinia—and this would be one's best route before altering to the south-west for the Strait of Gibraltar.

In the late August of 1953 I went by this same route in my 20-ton cutter, bound for the Balearic Islands. Damage to my mainsail in the strong northerlies that were blowing forced me to put into Cagliari at the south of Sardinia to effect temporary repairs. I left again after twelve hours, to find that the north wind had turned into a light north-easter which continued to blow steadily during the next four days of our passage. It was the type of weather that would have suited Ulysses well—blue days and starlit nights, with always a gentle breath from astern to keep way on the ship. In my heavy deep-draught boat I averaged little more than three knots, for she was built for the winds and weather of England's west coast. A long shallow-draught boat, setting a squaresail, would have done every bit as well.

Did the heroes, as we did, trail lines over the stern for fish? Although a stock epithet for the sea in the *Odyssey* is 'fish-infested', there are no references to the Greeks fishing from their ship. They had plenty of meat with them, of course, for when they ran their vessel down "into the good salt water" they stowed aboard the sheep that Circe had given them as a farewell present. One must assume that in those days—as was customary right into the 19th century in sailing ships—they took as much meat as they could 'on the hoof'. But if the Greeks did not fish, then they missed one of the greatest delights of sailing. They will not, as we did, have had the tingling pleasure of running into a great shoal of mackerel just off Cape Spartivento at the southern tip of Sardinia. We were hardly able to get the fish off the hooks quick enough before throwing the lines out again to catch dozens more.

It seems from the *Odyssey* and *Iliad* that the Homeric heroes were pre-eminently meat-eaters, or that they preferred to eat meat whenever they could. But the fact that there are comparatively few references to fish does not really surprise me. Whenever deer or goats or sheep are available, Homer mentions that the Greeks had a great feast, for the reason I feel sure that these occasions were important enough to describe. The fact that they are not described as eating fish while on any of their voyages is not so difficult to explain. When I lived among fishermen in Devon they would never trouble to say that they had eaten a fine piece of fish the night before. But a good steak, now—that was something worth talking about.

Some writers have objected to the idea of the Greeks having taken live animals on long sea voyages on the grounds of its impossibility. Indeed, it is one of the arguments used by Dörpfeld and his followers that Ithaca could not be the island nowadays known as Ithaca, because it would have been impossible to have transported horses and other animals from there across to the mainland. This is an argument that could only have been

Fishing boats at anchor
"I have sailed in the Aegean, and out of Malta and Sicily, in fishing boats much smaller but similar in their general lines to the Homeric craft."

[*The National Tourist Organization of Greece*

A beach on the island of Samothrace
"They will have found some point, cape, or island that gave them shelter from the wind and weather, and then they will have hauled their boats ashore."

[Foto Ernit-Roma]

The harbour of Trapani. Levanzo in the middle distance and Favignana (Goat Island) just visible on the left
"They are lonely islands still, and in Ulysses' day they were uninhabited"

The island of Ustica

[*Italian State Tourist Offic*

"About sixty miles due north-east from Favignana and the Aegadian group lies Ustica, a solitary and steep-to island."

The castle on Mount Eryx

"The high peak of Mount Eryx dominates all this western coastline of Sicily . . ."

Village on the island of Levanzo

"In Levanzo, smallest of the Aegadian islands, there is a cave much older than the story of Ulysses."

Greek temple in southern Sicily

"Ulysses would have seen the cyclamen if he had been here in the springtime of the year. He was certainly the first Greek to set foot on this strange and beautiful coast."

[*Italian State Tourist Office*

The coastline at Cefalù

"I went to Cefalù in Sicily, which Samuel Butler believed to be the city of the Laestrygonians, but the beetling mountain conceals no harbour."

[Radio, Times Hulton Picture Library

In the Bay of Palermo

"It was not long before we reached the Sun-God's favoured

Tunny fishery in northern Sicily

"It is noticeable that one of the first things the Greeks always do

[*Portuguese Tourist Office*

The Atlantic from the headland of Sagres

"They heard of the unending Stream of Ocean which poured away over the world's end . . ."

Siren Land

[*Radio Times Hulton Picture Library*

"Fishing boats in Capri, which has been claimed by some as the home of the Sirens . . ."

Fishing boats hauled ashore
"We brought the good ship into
a sheltered cove, where there was
fresh water to hand, and there the
men disembarked."

[*The National Tourist Organization of Greece*

advanced by men more familiar with their libraries than with the actuality of seafaring. I have travelled in the Aegean in recent years in caiques no more than 40 feet long, carrying mules, goats, sheep, hens, and every variety of live-stock aboard. There will have been no difficulty in tethering sheep or goats to the thwarts or oar-benches of the Homeric ships. They may even have had a small enclosed space forward for the smaller animals.

If we think of Ulysses' ship as being similar, though probably not so seaworthy as the Viking ships, where is the difficulty? In the saga that tells of the first colonists of Vinland we find the line: "When they heard our bulls bellow the Skraelings ran away." Now the balance of opinion today is that Vinland was a part of America near Passamaquoddy Bay, north of Boston. The Skraelings who 'ran away' were the native Indians. If the Vikings could take cattle across the North Atlantic, what difficulty was there for the Greeks of Ulysses to take animals across the far more tractable Mediterranean? The men who colonized Greenland from Iceland did not find it impossible to take their cattle with them across one of the most hostile seas in the world.

The problem of feeding a crew of forty or fifty men at sea in a Homeric ship would have been insoluble if the Greeks were not in the habit of taking as much fresh meat 'on the hoof' as they could safely get aboard. After a few days at sea the bilges will have been foul with animal droppings and urine, with blood from the killings, and with the garbage that was not thrown over the ship's side. Captain Woodget, the 80-year-old son of the famous Captain Woodget (Master of the clipper *Cutty Sark* during her most famous years) recalled in an interview in 1962: "Most of the meat issued to the sailors in the 1890's was salted pork or beef. But the ship also usually carried a few live pigs as a supply of fresh meat. The animals were kept below, but they were taken on deck every morning and hosed down so that they wouldn't smell too much. A strange custom was sometimes observed when a pig was killed. Before the butcher slaughtered it, he pointed the animal's head in the direction from which we wanted a fair wind.

It was probably coincidence, but sometimes a wind did later spring up from that direction." (This idea of a sacrifice to the God of the Winds must surely have been known to the Homeric Greeks.) It is noticeable that one of the first things the Greeks always do when reaching an anchorage, is to run their boat up the beach. This will have been not only for security, but also to scrub her out with sand and salt water. The open fishing boats of the Mediterranean do the same thing to this day.

There will have been little enough comfort or hygiene in the blue-prowed, black ship of Ulysses. Even so she will probably have been sweeter and cleaner than the galleys which ranged this sea in the Middle Ages. Of them we read that, "Calm itself has its inconveniences, for the evil smells which arise from the galley are then so strong that one cannot get away from them in spite of the tobacco with which one is obliged to plug one's nostrils from morning to night." (It is hardly surprising that the Great Plague was brought to Europe in 1347 by Venetian galleys.) Ulysses' ship, manned by free men not slaves, will have been a cleaner and better vessel in which to travel — even if a great deal smaller than the mediaeval galleys, whose oarsmen were compelled to urinate and defecate at the very benches where they toiled in chains.

Before leaving Cape Circeo for the western Mediterranean, Ulysses suffered a further misfortune. The youngest of his crew, Elpenor, was killed by accident. "Not much of a fighting man, and a little weak in the head as well," we are told, so perhaps he was not so much of a loss. Elpenor had retired to bed on the roof of the palace, having got drunk at the farewell party which preceded the Greeks' departure. Waking in the morning and hearing the noise and bustle of departure going on below him, Elpenor, who must have been suffering from an uncommonly bad hangover, forgot to "take the right way down by the long ladder and fell headlong from the roof." The poet clearly had in mind the typical flat-roofed house of the eastern Mediterranean — similar to those one finds all over Greece to this day. The outside ladder is still quite a common feature in country districts, although the more sophisticated outside staircase has mostly taken its place.

How often have I slept out on those flat, white roofs, under a sky dazzling with stars! The brief, sad story of Elpenor has the very ring of truth about it. What more natural place to sleep than on the roof in the summer air, especially if your head is heavy with wine? Fortunately most of us do not make the mistake of forgetting to use the ladder to get down in the mornings. But then, poor Elpenor was not very bright at the best of times.

It was in their usual melancholy mood that Ulysses and his men embarked once more in their ship. "There was not a dry eye amongst us all. . . ." I sometimes wonder how they can ever have stirred themselves sufficiently to leave behind that benevolent corner of Italy, with its good wine, meat, and game, and its obliging young women. Circe, by now, was pregnant by Ulysses, and it seems unlikely that she alone among the handmaids of Feronia was destined to bear a half-Greek child. But, unaware that they would ever see Cape Circeo again, Ulysses and his men ran down their ship into the sea. Then, with the good northerly stretching their sail, they drove down to the channel that lies between Sardinia and Tunisia.

16

The Pillars of Hercules

THE Pillars of Hercules represented the end of the known world. Indeed, throughout classical times—even after the Atlantic was being regularly traversed from Spain to Brittany, and even England—the Pillars of Hercules marked the limits of civilization. Beyond them began the great Stream of Ocean and the fierce tidal systems and currents which proved so strange, and even terrifying, to sailors raised in the Mediterranean. Whether the historic Ulysses ever journeyed this far I very much doubt. About this section of the *Odyssey*—and about this section only—the clear light of geography deepens into the haze of myth and mystery. It is true that Ulysses receives a wind from exactly the right direction to drive him from Italy towards Gibraltar, but afterwards all detail disappears until he returns once more to Circe's island. There are no further indications of times, courses, winds or weather: only that the ship drove on with the favourable wind and "thus she (Circe) brought us to the deep River of Ocean and the frontiers of the world."

Now at the time that Homer was writing, all our evidence seems to show that no Greeks had yet penetrated into the western Mediterranean. After the foundation of Carthage in the 9th century B.C., the Phoenicians, who had established trading posts in western Sicily and in Sardinia, were able to close the sea-gates between the eastern and western Mediterranean to all others. Westward of a line running from Carthage in North Africa to Trapani in Sicily and up to Sardinia, the Mediterranean was, as it were, a 'secret sea'. The monopoly of western trade which the Phoenicians enjoyed, and which they were to expand into one of the greatest sea empires of history, was something that they were naturally determined to keep intact. Any Periplous or Pilot for the area, and any information passed by word of mouth from one sea-captain to another was for Phoenicians alone. Certainly none of it would have been revealed to the Greek traders, who were already active in the Levant and eastern Mediterranean.

There is no reason to doubt that the stories which the Phoenicians allowed to leak out to other interested seamen were deliberately designed to scare away potential competitors. The same thing has happened throughout the whole history of maritime discovery. In the 15th century, when the Portuguese were uncovering the hitherto unknown shores of West Africa, they encouraged the belief among other nations that the world came to an end not far south of the Canary Islands. Long after the Portuguese had been active on these shores, trading in gold and slaves, other European seamen heard only of a sun so hot that it boiled the pitch out of your ships so that they sank. They heard of the unending Stream of Ocean which poured away over the world's end, and of the winds that blew your ship steadily to the south until you were sucked away over the edge of the world. When a few other European nations began tentatively to investigate this mysterious coast, the rumour was spread about that only the specially-designed caravels of the Portuguese could sail safely in these waters. Like the Phaeacians of the *Odyssey*, the 15th-century Portuguese were credited with magic ships, and with mysterious navigational abilities known to no others.

The writer of the *Odyssey* had clearly heard of the Strait of Gibraltar and of the vast ocean that lay beyond it. But for him all this was certainly as remote as fairyland. The Pillars of Hercules were described by the dramatist Euripides as the point beyond which "lies the end of voyaging, and the Ruler of Ocean no longer permits mariners to travel on the purple sea." Now Euripides lived in the 5th century B.C., several centuries after Homer, and yet he was still capable of describing Gibraltar and the Atlantic in almost the same legendary terms.

Calpe, the Rock of Gibraltar, and Abyla, Mount Hacko on the North African coast, were known throughout classical history as the Pillars of Hercules, or Heracles. They formed a natural boundary between the Mediterranean and the Atlantic, beyond which the stream of Ocean was believed to encircle the world. Comparatively few rivers of any size flow into the Mediterranean, and it loses by evaporation two-thirds more than it receives from its rivers. This steady loss is made good by an inflow of water from the Atlantic, the cold 'Great Ocean' flowing in between the Pillars of Hercules. The strait, then, marks the confluence of a sea and an ocean. It is also the meeting place of the old Mediterranean world and of all those other countries and cultures which have since been fertilized from it. When Ulysses is sent to sail into the gates of Hell in his black ship, it is to this mysterious border of the world that he must come.

Whatever was known about the far western corner of the Mediterranean by the Greeks of Homer's time must certainly have come from the Phoenicians. Although the Strait of Gibraltar was associated in classical history with the Greek hero Heracles, the fact remains that this strait was first named by the Phoenicians. The two mountains which face each other across the Strait were called 'The Pillars of Melkarth' by the Phoenicians. They took their name from the twin pillars of the great temple of Melkarth in the city of Tyre. Many of the legends attaching to this Phoenician god were later transferred by the Greeks to their own hero Heracles. Now the principal god, or Ba'al of Tyre, was a solar god in origin. "Later, like the other divinities of Phoenician ports, he added to his primitive characteristics those of a marine god. He was known under the title of Melkarth, 'God of the City'. The Greeks identified him with Heracles." But Melkarth was not only a sea god in Phoenician mythology, he was also Lord of the Underworld, and it was between the pillars of the Strait of

Gibraltar that he was believed to dwell. In this place, which nature had fashioned like a giant archetype of the twin pillars of his temple in the Phoenician city of Tyre, dwelt Melkarth, god of the darkness beyond the world's limits.

Once this Phoenician legend is understood it is easy to see why Circe should have sent Ulysses to the Strait of Gibraltar, for it was here that the god of Underworld had his domain. Beyond the Strait lies the realm of Ocean, (Circe's grandfather) the place where the Sun (Circe's father) sinks nightly into the unknown west. Mythology is far from being, as was once supposed, no more than a pleasant way of telling fairytales. It is almost invariably a kind of shorthand designed to record certain truths about nature, and man, and his place in nature. (An extension of the mythological process are the parables which Jesus told his followers, each of them containing an important truth within the framework of a colourful story that was easy to remember.)

Into this section of the *Odyssey*, which may once have constituted a separate story in its own right, the poet has introduced from some Phoenician source the geographical *fact* of the Gibraltar Strait and of the Atlantic beyond it. I would not look for an actual place on the earth's surface where Ulysses dug his trench and poured libations to the dead. But it would not be absurd to see in the fog-bound Cimmerians who dwell in perpetual darkness, the account of some traveller who had visited the far north of Europe. That there were parts of the earth where for months on end the sun never shone, was something that Homer almost certainly could not have known himself. It is equally improbable that he just 'invented' it.

". . . When the bright sun climbs the sky and puts the stars to flight, his rays can never reach them, for dreadful Night has cast her cloak over the heads of these unhappy people." Sometimes on a winter evening in London, when the street lamps are yielding to the fog, I have thought that Homer had a prevision of our condition—"The fog-bound Cimmerians who live in the City of Eternal Mist." The information, that far to the north people lived in darkness, most probably reached the author of the *Odyssey* from the tale of some amber merchant who traded with the Baltic. Baltic amber was being imported overland into prehistoric Greece centuries before the Homeric period.

Not all Homeric commentators have been content to dismiss Ulysses' visit to Hades without attempting to place it geographically. Victor Bérard would have sited the entrance to Hades near the Gulf of Naples, and it is certainly true that there were several places in the ancient world which were believed to lead down to the grey kingdom of the dead. The most celebrated entrance to Hades was a cave on Cape Taenarus, the southernmost point of Greece. Patrick Leigh Fermor has described visiting it by boat (Taenarus like the Blue Grotto of Capri is a marine cave), and of swimming inside: "I tried all the way round and swam under water to see if there was a submerged entrance to another sea cave beyond. But there was nothing. The ceiling had closed in to about a foot and a half overhead, as I could touch it now with my hand. The air was dark but under the surface the water gleamed a magical luminous blue and it was possible to stir up shining beacons of phosphorescent bubbles with a single stroke or a kick. Strangely, it was not at all sinister, but, apart from the coldness of the water which the sun never reaches, silent and calm and beautiful." Near Enna in Sicily I have been shown the cave down which Persephone reputedly disappeared. The Acheron and the Cocytus, the River of Woe and the River of Wailing, still flow into the Ionian Sea near Phanari on the west coast of Greece. I have swam in the Cocytus—it was muddy and cold, and the mosquitoes were dense as steam over the water. The one good thing that the 'River of Wailing' did for me was to rid my boat of a three month accumulation of underwater weed. I had anchored in the mouth of the stream overnight, and within twelve hours the freshwater killed off all the salt marine growth.

One curiosity about the Homeric account of Ulysses' encounter with the dead is that he is the only hero who did not have to go underground to do so. Having reached the place designated by Circe on the banks of the River of Ocean, Ulysses digs a trench, and pours in his libations of honey, milk, wine, and water. He then sacrifices the finest all-black sheep from the animals that he has on board. Soon the shades of the mighty dead are all about him. Unlike Aeneas, Heracles or Dante—all of whom were compelled to *descend* into Hell—Ulysses remains, throughout his encounter with the dead, firmly on the surface of the earth. An Etruscan mirror shows the meeting of Ulysses with Teiresias, the blind seer from whom he learns his destiny. Teiresias has an epicene, indeed a distinctly androgynous appearance—an allusion perhaps to the story that to Teiresias alone was it given to live both as a man and a woman, and thus to know the secrets of both sexes. (If such are the qualifications for being a seer, there should be plenty available today, when sex-changes are so common as hardly to merit reporting.)

In the twilight world beyond the Pillars of Melkarth, Ulysses now learned his future fate and fortune. He was destined to return to Circe's island. After leaving there, he might yet reach Ithaca with all his companions, provided only that they did not kill any of the Sun-God's cattle. But, if any of these sacred animals were harmed, Ulysses' ship and all his men would be lost. He alone would return to Ithaca, in evil plight, and in a foreign ship. But, in the words of J. E. Harrison, "It is rash to tarry so long in Hades, lest the dim uncertain twilight baffle and daze us, and we behold no longer clearly the light of the upper world."

Leaving the shades of the dead lapping at the dark blood in the trench, Ulysses hastened back to his ship. 'I told my men to get aboard and to cast off the hawsers. Embarking at once they took their places at the oars, and the current carried her down the River of Ocean. . . .'

In the Strait of Gibraltar the greater part of the surface current flows steadily eastwards into the Mediterranean to replenish the salty waters of the sea. I once spent three days trying to beat up to

Gibraltar under sail from Almeria Bay. But Ulysses was bound east, so the current was behind him. "Helped at first by oars, but after that by a friendly breeze," he sailed back into his native sea. The grimmest of his adventures was over. He emerged into the bright Mediterranean sunlight, where we can once more trace his voyage upon a chart.

17

Siren Land

THE return of Ulysses to the island of Circe brings us back into the main story of the *Odyssey*. Even about the visit to Hades, however, two facts emerge which suggest that a grain of truth lies at the bottom of the story. First there is the gift of a northerly wind, the only wind which would serve to drive a square-rigged Homeric boat from Cape Circeo in the right direction for the Strait of Gibraltar. Then there is the statement that the Current of Ocean carried Ulysses' ship safely back into the Mediterranean—which is just what it would do to this day.

"Odysseus' wanderings, however factual their ultimate source, however firmly stated the exact number of days' sail between the ports of call, show how insubstantial was Homer's knowledge of the lands beyond the western horizon. . . ." I would not disagree that the poet himself did not know, and had not visited, the places described. It is the accuracy of the framework upon which the voyage of Ulysses is based that concerns me. From the moment that Ulysses returns to Circe's island, the details of his navigation become explicit. The sailing instructions which he now receives from Circe can be compared side by side with the information in the modern *Admiralty Pilot*.

Upon reaching the island, Ulysses' first duty was to see that the body of Elpenor was suitably buried. Elpenor's spirit had been the first to greet Ulysses across the dark trench beside the waters of Ocean. The Greeks had left Circe's island in such haste that they had omitted to give their dead comrade a proper funeral, and

Elpenor's ghost had implored Ulysses to see that his body was formally buried. He also asked Ulysses to raise a mound to him on the shore of the grey sea, and to set above it the oar he had pulled on the bench alongside his comrades. Ulysses did more than that for the dead sailor, he buried his ashes "on top of the boldest headland of the coast." It is on Monte Circeo itself, then, that Elpenor lies, his ashes long since scattered by the wind. His broad-bladed oar would have been destroyed by sun, rain and insects, within the lifetime of Ulysses.

A bolder monument now marks Elpenor's resting place. A little east of the summit, the lighthouse of Cervia stands up white against the land. All night I lay at anchor under its shuttling fan of light, feeling an obscure companionship with the Italian family who lived in the square house at the base of the tower, and who grew fine cucumbers and tomatoes in their small garden. It was pleasant to come on deck in the dark hours of the graveyard watch, and to know from the blink of the lighthouse that I was not alone in the world. Eastward the light of Gaeta, at the other end of Circe's bay, repeated the warning and, away to the south, the lights of Zannone and Ponza signalled the dangers of their volcanic islets to the mariner. It is easier to sail this sea than it was three thousand years ago when Ulysses and his men buried their comrade.

Circe, goddess or priestess though she was, was not all-knowing. Her first words of greeting to Ulysses were: "What hardihood to have *descended* alive into the House of Hades!" A sensible and practical woman, she did not waste time complaining because Ulysses must now leave her. Circe had always accepted the fact that he was destined one day to return to Ithaca. She did not forget her pride, as Calypso did later, and try to restrain the hero in her island. First of all she ordered her maidservants to bring the Greeks a good meal of fresh bread, meat, and sparkling red wine, the very things they will have longed for after their voyage. Nor did she immediately burden Ulysses with instructions, but begged him and his men to eat, drink, and enjoy themselves. Later, as she explained, she would give Ulysses his 'route', and explain every landmark so that he might avoid the dangers which he would otherwise incur.

In the evening, while the rest of his men lay down to sleep by the dark ship, Ulysses went to the palace with Circe. While she lay beside him, he told her all that had happened since he left for the Pillars of Hercules. Circe in return gave him his sailing instructions for the voyage home. "First of all," she said, "You will come to the Sirens, they who bewitch all men. Whoever sails near them unaware shall never again see his wife and children once he has heard the Siren voices. They enchant him with their clear song, as they sit in a meadow that is heaped with the bones of dead men, bones on which still hangs their shrivelled skin. Drive your ship past the place, and so that your men do not hear their song, soften some beeswax and with it seal their ears. But if you yourself should wish to listen to the Sirens, get your men to bind you hand and foot with ropes against the mast-step. In this way you may listen in rapture to the voices of the two Sirens. But should you begin to beg your comrades to unloose you, you must make sure that they bind you even more tightly."

She then went on to describe the other dangers and perils through which the ship must pass. These do not concern us as yet, for the first thing is to establish the abode of the Sirens. Now Circe was clearly confident that she knew exactly where the Sirens were to be found, for she went on to say, that, once Ulysses had passed this danger, he would "have reached a point beyond which I cannot give you clear directions." She could only indicate the two routes which then lay open to him, between which he must make his choice.

Strabo, the Latin poets, and many classical writers place the Sirens unhesitatingly somewhere in the region of the Gulf of Naples. This makes good sense geographically, for Ulysses will have followed the coast of Italy southward as far as possible, whichever route he intended to take home. Any sailing instructions will have enumerated the islands which the mariner must pass before making the alteration of course that would take him on to the next 'leg' of his journey. The channel between Ischia and Procida, and between Capri and Cape Campanella on the mainland of Italy are certain to have featured in any sailor's description of this coast. Capri has been claimed by some as the home of the Sirens, but the general opinion of classical writers was that the Siren islands should be identified with the Galli islets, which lie at the entrance to the Gulf of Salerno.

The Galli are the last group of islands on the west coast of Italy, and they lie almost due north of the Lipari islands. For my part, if I were instructing a sailor with neither chart nor compass how to get down to Sicily from Cape Circeo, I would be inclined to say: "Keep coasting past the islands," (and I would mention those to be passed—Ischia, Procida, and Capri) "until you come to a small group of islands at the head of a Gulf. There are three of them close together. At this point, take your departure from the coast, and sail south. Keep going south until you sight the volcano Stromboli and the next group of islands—it may take you several days. When you see them, you have two alternatives: either follow the islands westwards until you sight Ustica, and then go round the coast by Trapani; or take the shorter route and carry on southward. This will take you through the Messina Strait."

The Galli at the mouth of the bright bay of Salerno are ideally placed to act as a kind of 'signpost'. It would of course be possible to coast right down the shores of Italy to the Messina Strait. I have done it myself, but it is a long and time-wasting route, for the shoreline trends steadily to the east. Quite apart from that, the coast of Italy from the Galli southward is a dangerous one, offering practically no anchorages. Cape Palinuro and the fishing hamlet of Santa Nicola are about the only two places on this austere coast where even a small sailing boat can find shelter—and that only if the weather is reasonably clement. I lost my dinghy and very nearly lost my boat off this coast in the autumn of 1951. I would have done better if I had followed the sailing directions which

Ulysses received from Circe, and headed due south after leaving the Galli.

"Three stony and desert little rocks" is how Strabo describes the Siren islands. There are, in fact, five of them, but only three lie close together in a group, so the mistake is natural enough. Norman Douglas, lover of Capri though he was, had no doubt that the ancient identification was the right one. "Treeless they are, the Siren rocks; but not flowerless. . . . In the winter months the narcissus dominates; its scent is heavy upon the air and the glossy brown bulbs thrust each other out of the earth; in May the ground is hidden under a radiant tangle of many-hued blossoms that must be seen to be believed. Every flower of Campania seems to have taken refuge on this lonely rock. [The largest of the Galli.] The rapid evaporation of sea-air no doubt contributes to this luxuriance, and also the rich soil of the outer slope. I once attempted to draw up a list of the Galli flowers, but abandoned the idea; they shift with every month."

Unfortunately I have never seen the flowers of the Siren islands. The first time I came here was at night. The second time, it was high midsummer and everything was burned brown. Only the cicadas sang that day, and the scented scrub was almost incandescent, crackling as if it might burst into flame.

It is about seventy-five miles from Cape Circeo to the Galli if one sails direct through the Procida and Capri channels; a little more if, as Ulysses probably did, one follows the coast along the Bay of Gaeta and round the Bay of Naples. Whether under oar or sail it would not have taken him long to sail down this tranquil and golden shore. Even as it is today, studded with the buildings and relics of many civilizations, and varnished everywhere with the deep green of vines, the land still has the air of something slumbering and withdrawn. Wave upon wave of men and cultures have burst over this shore, over these coves and sleeping islands, and yet despite the tide-wrack left behind them, it retains its character. There is an atmosphere here which drowns everything far deeper than 'full fathom five'. I am used to the lethargy and the *taedium vitae* of the Mediterranean—safeguarded I like to think by a devotion to the Samothracian Gods—yet I have come nearer shipwreck here than anywhere else. I am not thinking of the simple shipwreck that I narrowly avoided off Tropea by the Messina Strait, but the shipwreck of energy, of ambition, and indeed, of all desire to struggle for survival.

I sailed down here in a small Dutch-built yacht shortly after the last war. I and my wife were bound for Sicily, Malta, and then on in the following year, to Greece. It was September when we anchored in the small harbour of Capri, and made fast to the quay next to a boat piled high with melons. During the day the owner and his son would spread their ragged mainsail over a pole on the jetty to make an awning, and then sell their fruit to the passers-by. Going on deck at night, in the still damp hours when everything I touched was beaded with the sirocco-dew, I would smell the ripe fruit. Even after I had lit a cigarette, the moist melon-scent—not without a hint of corruption about it—stayed on my palate. Above me in the town the little piazza was spangled with stars and rockets, and the astringent tinkle of the mandolin came out to me across the water. The island was almost deserted in those days, for the post-war tourist boom had not yet started, and there was little enough to eat ashore, nor money to go round. We found a cottage, high up in Anacapri, with its own small garden, a well, and an old vine which shadowed a wooden bench against the south wall of the house. We planned to stay, meditated selling the boat, conjectured how much money we could raise, and ignored the possibility that we would never be able to earn any. A pity, perhaps—Letters arrived, we were due south in Malta for the winter, our seagoing insurance would expire in October, bank managers were cool, lacking any sense of romance, and soon the weather would worsen. So we left. I have been back since, but have never quite recaptured the glamour of those early autumn days. What I heard then was no more than what men usually designate as the 'siren song'; the urge to relinquish ambition, and to withdraw from the arena where life is fought out. Like most of us I had to come back to the big cities and build my sandcastles against the devouring tide. I might have done better to stay. Something fades as we grow older, and the ear does not catch the siren music quite so clearly.

It was, I imagine, a still day with a hint of mist in the air when Ulysses sailed past the steep limestone sides of Capri and headed towards the Galli. In his ears was the pluck of the oars, and the cool chuckle past the steering paddle. But soon he would hear the Sirens calling across the water:

"O stay, oh pride of Greece! Ulysses stay!
O cease thy course, and listen to our lay!
Blest is the man our song ordain'd to hear,
The song instructs the soul, and charms the ear.
Approach! Thy soul shall into rapture rise!
Approach! And learn new wisdom from the wise!
We know whate'er the kings of mighty name
Achieved at Ilium in the field of fame;
Whate'er beneath the sun's bright journey lies.
O stay and learn new wisdom from the wise. . . ."

The Sirens did not hold out any offer of those things for which men customarily fight, toil, and degrade themselves. Neither wealth, women, power, nor even immortal fame. Wisdom was the gift that they promised the hero, that and the "foreknowledge of all that will ever happen upon this fruitful earth." It is the most dangerous of gifts.

"And whoso hears these voices, says Homer, nevermore returns to his home and family, which may be taken to mean that certain persons have rated wisdom higher than domestic bliss; doubtless a poetic exaggeration." But the man who wrote that was never able to escape the Siren islands. The only time I ever saw Norman Douglas out of them—in London, during the last war—he seemed so deep in the dream of his true home that he could not accept his place of exile as having any reality. Fortunately for him he lived long enough to return and die in Capri.

I sometimes wonder whether it was Capri, Procida, Ischia, or perhaps the Siren isles that Petronius Arbiter had in mind when he wrote: "O shore dearer to me than life! Oh sea! How happy am I with leave to come into these lands of mine. How beautiful the day! Here once upon a time I used to swim, disturbing Naiads with my every stroke! And here's the fountain's heart, and there the seaweed waves. This is the haven of my quiet desire. Yes, I have lived! Nor can an unkind fate take from me ever the gifts of that former hour." Certainly the author of the *Satyricon* had the Bay of Naples in his mind when he wrote his great novel, and if he knew the Bay he most probably knew its off-lying islands. Centuries after Ulysses, the 'Arbiter of Elegance' may well have had himself rowed to the Galli, the *Sirenusae* as they were then called. On the largest of them, Gallo Grande, there is the site of a 1st-century villa. A hedonist of refinement, like Petronius, may well have found in this solitary spot a healthful antidote to the debauchery of Nero's Rome.

One argument that has been used against the identification of the Galli with the Siren islands is that Homer only mentions two Sirens, and there are certainly three islands. "*I Galli*," the *Admiralty Pilot* confirms, "are three rocky islets of which Gallo Grande, the easternmost and largest, lies about 1½ miles southward of Punta Sant' Elia and is covered with shrubs. . . ." The other two near by are known today as Castellucio and La Rotonda. The remaining islands in the group, Isca and Vivara, both lie well over a mile away, and in opposite directions.

Did Homer nod, or were there more than two Sirens? It seems as if originally there were many more. Plutarch, and Hyginus, as well as other scholars and poets, have given us the names of ten or eleven. There may well have been two trinities of Sirens: Thelxinoë, the Enchantress; Aglaope, She of the Beautiful Face; and Peisinoë, the Seductress. The other three, and these seem to be our Sirens of the Galli Islands, were Parthenope, the Virgin Face; Ligeia, the Bright Voice; and Leucosia, the White One. In Roman times there were shrines to these three Sirens on this coastline, Parthenope at Naples, Leucosia and Ligeia on the Gulf of Salerno. Virgin Face, White One, and Bright Voice,—these are, I think, the inhabitants of our Galli. Homer mentions no names. He says only that, as their lovely voices sounded across the water, the heart of Ulysses "was filled with such a desire that I nodded and beckoned to my men to set me free."

Apollonius Rhodius, describing many centuries after Homer the Voyage of the Argonauts, tells us that the Sirens all killed themselves when Orpheus sang to them from the deck of the *Argo*. Overcome with hurt pride at being surpassed in their art, they hurled themselves into the sea from the rocks. Apollonius Rhodius was certainly wrong, for the Argonauts preceded Ulysses. (His father, Laertes, was one of the *Argo*'s crew.) Writing so long afterwards, Apollonius either got his facts wrong, or else —which I strongly suspect—the Sirens who attempted to beguile the Argonauts were another set of relations. They lived in a group of islands far from here, most probably in the Echinades, near the mouth of the Achelous in western Greece.

I would hate to destroy any illusions, but the Sirens, however beautiful their voices, were not very attractive physically. Any images one may have of nude and nubile young women swarming over the sides of Ulysses' boat to tempt the sailors as much with their bodies as with their voices, must yield before the truth. Homer does not describe them at all, but the earliest representations show them as birds with the heads of women. In later classical art they were depicted as women with the legs of birds, sometimes with, and sometimes without, wings.

There are many stories as to their parentage, but the oldest suggests that they were the daughters of Chthon, the 'depths of the earth'. They were the companions of Persephone, Queen of Hades, and it was she who despatched them into the realms of men. Like the Harpies, they lived upon human souls. Unlike the Harpies, but rather like the female spider, they needed physical love before they carried the male off to his death. ". . . They served not only death, but also love. A carving in relief shows a

Siren, only the lower parts of whose legs are those of a bird, amorously approaching a sleeping man who resembles a Satyr. The scene is reminiscent of Selene's approach to Endymion. There was something amorous also about the egg-like shape of the Sirens as shown in early pictures of them: the more so as they often clasped small human figures to their bodies. They served not only the goddess of death, but also served human mortals in that they carried men—or, at any rate, men's desires—on golden wings to Heaven." I wonder whether Andrew Marvell had some vision of them in his mind, when he wrote *To His Coy Mistress*:

> "Now let us sport us while we may,
> And now, like amorous birds of prey,
> Rather at once our time devour
> Than languish in his slow-chapt power. . . ."

It was a windless calm, Homer tells us, when Ulysses drew near to these islets. The sail hung down in empty folds, so the Greeks lowered it and stowed it below. They set to work at the oars, while Ulysses kneaded the beeswax and plugged their ears. Then they bound him hand and foot to the mast.

Stillness and calm were always a sign that the Sirens were about, for they loved the hot siesta hours and the breathless nights of late mid-summer. The Sirens were no Valkyries to ride upon the winds of the storm. Indeed, it is not quite certain that they could even fly. Late classical paintings usually show them as wingless. How they ever became bird-like at all is something of a mystery, although one story has it that Aphrodite turned them into birds because—out of a stubbornness fortunately rare in women—they refused to resign their virginity either to gods or to men. They remained proud of their voices, however, and according to one story were once rash enough to challenge the Muses to a contest. When they lost it, the Muses plucked out their feathers so that they could no longer fly.

I think they still had their wing feathers when Ulysses passed this way, for one of the earliest representations of them, on an amphora now in the British Museum, shows Ulysses bound naked to the mast, and lifting his bearded head to hear the Sirens' song. Despite Homer, with whom the painter will surely have been familiar, there are three Sirens depicted—not two. All of them are feathered and winged but, while two of them sing from the rocks, one of them appears to be stooping over the boat like a hawk. On closer investigation, however, it can be seen that her one visible eye is closed. Her bird feet almost touch the rock on which she has been sitting with one of her sisters, and there is something limp and bedraggled about her whole attitude—more like a bird in the larder than on the wing.

"It has not escaped former commentators," wrote J. E. Harrison, "that the whole gesture of the third Siren was rather of despair than attack; but the additional and, I think, conclusive evidence of the closed eye has never, I believe, been pointed out." This Siren, in fact, having failed in her song, is falling dead from the sky—something which might account for Homer only mentioning two of them. Of course, if legend is correct, both her sisters should have died shortly afterwards, for the Sirens were reputedly doomed to die if ever a man passed by them without being lured to death by their song. I do not believe this legend was correct.

In classical art the Sirens were constantly depicted on funeral vases, sarcophagi, and monuments. In this connection they are fulfilling their role as goddesses of death. Often they play instruments—the double flute, the lyre, and cymbals amongst others. Almost as often, they appear as companions of Dionysus and assist in his orgiastic revels, for they are the handmaidens of desire as well as death. On an Apulian vase in the British Museum two Sirens are playing the double flutes while Dionysus holds aloft a vine branch and a wine-horn. On either side of him two satyrs are prancing. On the reverse of this same vase, two Sirens are happily playing the flutes and watching dispassionately while a satyr attempts to rape a reluctant maenad.

It is not until the Middle Ages that we find a blend of Nordic with classical myth has given the Sirens fish-tails and turned them into something like mermaids. The Siren described by Dante, however, was no Matthew Arnold Mermaid, but austere and frightening. She, like the Sirens of Ulysses, was also encountered in the hot, still hours of mid-day.

Their name may well come from the same root as *Sirius*, the Dog-Star, 'the scorching' or 'the glittering one.' Sirius, the brightest star in the heavens, rises as the sun enters Leo, the hottest part of the year. Homer calls it the star of late summer, and also 'the evil star', for its heliacal rising indicated not only the hottest season but presaged the thunderstorms and broken weather that follow in the Mediterranean autumn. The Romans who called the star *Canis*, the Dog, also associated it with this season of the year—a fact which is still remembered in our own expression, the 'Dog-days'.

It was, I believe, in those hot, sultry hours when summer burns into autumn, that Ulysses came into the Gulf of Salerno and heard them singing from the Galli rocks. Across the still sea that carries a bloom on its surface like a grape, the Sirens sang to him. The deaf sailors ignored his struggles to free himself, while Perimedes and Eurylochus obeyed their orders and bound him more tightly to the mast. The oarsmen smote the water and they turned south, setting their course for the Lipari islands. It was not until they were well clear of the enchanted islands that the men removed the beeswax from their ears and set Ulysses free. He had heard the Sirens and he had survived. I think that he never forgot them.

18
What Songs the Sirens Sang . . .

I DO not believe that all the Sirens died after Ulysses had escaped them. Centuries later Parthenope, she of the Maiden Face, was still reverenced in Naples and a torch-race was held there in her honour. Near the Messina Strait, and in other parts of the coastline of Magna Graecia, the Siren cult long survived. It is true, though, that they seem to have lost their former malevolence, becoming gentler and less voracious in their old age. Virgil writing of the Sirens in the *Aeneid* describes them as: "They who were cruel in former days." So one may assume that by the 1st century B.C. they were no longer in the habit of luring sailors to their doom. Virgil, who loved Naples and its bay above all else, and whose body was interred near Pozzuoli, must surely have known the Sirens. Often in his *Eclogues* one seems to catch their voice: "What gifts can I bring in return for a song such as yours? —dearer to me even than the sigh of the South Wind coming, or the shores beaten by the surf, or the sound of the streams as they run through the rocky valleys. . . ."

I do not think that they are entirely dead, but only that their song has been drowned by the roar of the world. Like an old picture they have been obscured by centuries of varnish, smoke, and over-painting. But the X-ray can still discover them, and a careful restorer can bring them swimming back into the light. "What song the Sirens sang, or what name Achilles assumed when he hid himself among women, though puzzling questions, are not beyond all conjecture." Indeed they are not, for we know the burden of the Siren song. They offered to all who heard them the forbidden fruit of the Tree of Knowledge and, as in Hebrew mythology, whoever tastes this fruit shall surely perish. Their victims do not die like other men, but by a slow decline; they waste away until, as Homer tells us, their "withered skin hangs upon their bones." They have learned that life is a tragedy which can have but one ending. Only the gods can endure the burden of this knowledge because, being immortal, they are indifferent.

> "Their words are no more known aright,
> Through lapse of many ages, and no man
> Can any more across the waters wan
> Behold these singing women of the sea."

Certainly I never saw them, but I think I heard them. It all happened a long time ago now. It was the autumn of 1943. Sicily had fallen to the Allies, Italy had surrendered, and the next phase in the Second World War was to be the first major Allied landing on the mainland of Europe. Known by the code name of operation 'Avalanche', this was a seaborne invasion designed to capture the port of Salerno, and Montecorvino airfield at the head of Salerno Bay. It took place on the 9th of September, 1943.

One of the ships detailed to patrol the entrance to the Gulf of Salerno was the escort destroyer H.M.S. *Exmoor*, in which I was then serving. I cannot give an exact date to the following story, but it was certainly within two or three days of the initial landings at Salerno. Unfortunately we were not allowed to keep a diary in those days—to judge from the innumerable 'War Memoirs', of admirals, generals, and air-marshals, this rule cannot have been observed in the upper echelons of the Allied Services.

I had the middle watch (from midnight to four in the morning). It was so calm a night that I could hear the hushing rustle of the bow wave as it broke back, and away over the still sea. There had been some action down by Salerno earlier, but everything seemed to be peaceful at that moment. We were nearly twenty miles from the beach-head, on the northern section of the anti-submarine and radar patrol covering the entrance to the Gulf.

We ran in radar-ranging on a small group of islands; then we turned and ran out again for a few miles. We had to go very close to the islands, for it was just the kind of place that a submarine would try to close, hoping to be protected from our underwater 'ears' by the echoes off the islands and surrounding rocks. It was also the kind of cover that E-boats would fancy for a rendezvous, before making a sudden dart towards the shipping at anchor down the Gulf. The islands were called the Galli.

It was a pleasant watch, with all the south in the idle air. There was dew on the bridge fittings, and the small wooden control deck around the gyro compass was dark with moisture. I do not remember on which leg of our zigzag it was that I first heard the sound. I know well enough, though, that it was when we were at the end of our course towards the Galli, for the islets were close, and clearly visible under the moon. I think it was about two o'clock in the morning when we had just reached the far end of our patrol. The procedure was to lie there stopped for a brief period, while the radar and asdic sets combed the area off the islands.

One's ears, like one's eyes, were sharply in tune in those days. The intervening years have not only blurred my memory but have given me perhaps a greater artifice with words—something always suspect if one is looking for the truth. I fall back then on an account of the incident which I wrote in 1948, only five years afterwards.

"This music crept by me upon the waters. . . . I heard then what sounded like singing. I cannot describe it accurately, but it was low and somehow distant—a 'natural' kind of singing one might call it, reminiscent of the waves and wind. Yet it was certainly neither of these, for there was about it a human quality, disturbing and evocative.

"How could I hear a low singing aboard a ship? The answer

is that most of the time we were patrolling very slowly, and then stopping altogether for quite long periods. It was during one of these periods when we were stopped that I heard the singing. I was just about to call my watchmate's attention to it, when the time came for us to get under way again. On the next leg of our patrol when we were close by the rocks and stopped again, I listened carefully. I heard it again, but much nearer, so it seemed —and now for some unaccountable reason I felt afraid. Who would be singing on a night like this, when the sea was full of warships and down the bay men were doing their best to kill one another?

"I nudged Nobby, and asked him if he could hear anything. 'No,' he said. 'Nothing at all.' Even as he spoke I could hear the singing—it wasn't one voice but several. I could not make out any words, nor any particular tune. Thinking about it later on, I found a word which seemed to me to describe it exactly—'mindless'. There was a kind of 'abstract' quality about it. Just then the Captain came up on the bridge. He, too, could hear nothing. But, as I insisted that I had definitely heard *something*, he agreed to go in close to the rocks and see if we could make out anybody. The idea had flashed through my head that there might be survivors from some sunken craft who had crawled on to the rocks, and were either trying to attract our attention, or were keeping up their spirits with a song.

"We went in as near as we dared to the first of the rocks [probably Gallo Grande, but I cannot remember] and then stopped our engines. Nothing at first—then suddenly it began again. It seemed to have moved, for the sound which I could have sworn originated near this particular rock was now masked by it and seemed to come from one of the others. At first, as I have said, it was 'mindless', a natural song such as the wind might make running through a cave. Then gradually, as I listened it became more personal. Somehow or other I knew that it was feminine, for no man's throat could have made that low, sweet noise.

"So we stopped there—and none of the others could hear it. Neither the Captain, nor Nobby Clarke, my watchmate, nor any of the bridge lookouts. 'You're going round the bend,' Nobby murmured. The Captain said, 'Well we'll take a look all round these damned islands, just in case there is anybody sitting up on them and taking notice.' I told him that it sounded like singing. He made no comment. 'The Angels of Mons all over again!' said Nobby. 'Only this time I suppose they've brought their harps.'

"We circled round every one of those islets and rocks and never saw a thing. Of course, I got my leg pulled, and had to say that I couldn't hear it any more. But this is true—every time we stopped I could hear it. It never came from the rock nearest us, but always seemed to shift away so that there was a distance between us and it.

"Eventually we had to turn back on our 'leg' out into the bay. I'll admit I was glad when we did for I had now reached a point when the singing somehow began to make sense. First of all, it was very old. Don't ask me how I knew that, but I did. And secondly, it had a direct bearing on *me*—of that I felt quite sure. It began to draw me so that I wanted to join it—and this 'joining it', I knew in some obscure way, meant going back into the past. When we stopped by the last of the rocks, just before turning round, I was gripping a stanchion and the sweat was on my forehead. It meant, I knew, going back in time, retreating in some way or another into a different world. I kept getting a picture, as it were, of temples by the shore: white shores under the sun and, where the waves ran up to the land, there was a small temple.

"We never came back that way again. Soon after we had moved off, we got a call to head up towards Salerno and do some inshore work. . . ."

There are plenty of rocky caverns and fissures just above sea-level in the Galli islands, and such places are great originators of moaning sounds, whispers, and far-off wailing voices. But there was no wind on that night, and the sea unruffled.

A logical answer is that at sometime or other, possibly before the war at school, I had read a note or footnote to the *Odyssey* that the Galli Islands were reputed to have been the Siren Rocks. That is quite possible, and I can neither prove nor disprove it. But to my certain knowledge I did not discover this attribution of the Galli until 1949 when I first read Douglas's *Siren Land*.

There is only one sad epilogue to my story. When I came back to the Gulf of Salerno after the war, knowing full well by then what had been written about the Galli and the Sirens, I heard nothing. I was making for Salerno, and I would have explored the islands thoroughly but for the fact that it was windless weather yet again, and the fuel-pump of my small auxiliary engine was giving me trouble. I wanted to get to Salerno while the engine— my substitute for the strong arms and shoulders of Ulysses' oarsmen—still asthmatically coughed away. It was seven years since I had passed the Galli, and perhaps I had changed too greatly for my ears to catch their voices. Certainly it was more than one voice which I heard that night from the bridge of H.M.S. *Exmoor*. We never discovered any reason for what was politely referred to as my 'hallucination'. There were no survivors, no ships sunk that night, nothing that could have accounted for the sounds I seemed to hear. We checked next day—just in case we had left some shipwrecked sailors sitting mournfully on those sea-wet rocks.

Perhaps the reason why I never heard them on my second visit was that I had my wife with me. There is no record of the Sirens ever having sung to a ship that had a woman on board. However old the Sirens may be, and however deep their knowledge of all that passes on this earth and of all that shall ever be, they are still women. They do not want anything from their own sex.

The Wandering Rocks

CIRCE had told Ulysses that, once he had passed the Sirens, two courses lay open to him. One of them would take him between the Wandering Rocks, and the other past Scylla and Charybdis. He elected, as we know, to take the shorter way home, through the dangers of the Messina Strait, rather than go back west-about round Sicily.

We know that he sighted the Wandering Rocks even if he did not go between them. They were, in point of fact, his next 'signpost' in the sea once he had put the Galli Islands behind him. Here is Circe's description of these rocks and their hazards: "When your crew have carried you past this danger [The Sirens], you will have reached a point beyond which I cannot fully guide you. Two ways will lie before you, and you must choose between them as you see fit, though I will tell you both. One leads to those sheer cliffs which the Blessed gods know as the Wandering Rocks. Here blue-eyed Amphitrite sends her great breakers thundering in, and the very birds cannot fly by in safety. Even from the shy doves that bring ambrosia to Father Zeus the beetling rock takes toll each time they pass, and the Father has to send one more to make their number up; while for such sailors as bring their ship to the spot, there is no escape whatever. They end as flotsam on the sea, timbers and corpses tossed in confusion by the waves or licked up by tempestuous and destroying flames. . . ."

Is there anywhere in the Mediterranean which accords with

this description? And if there is, would such a place have come into Circe's sailing directions? The answer to both these questions is—Yes. There is one place and one place alone which accords with her description, and it is exactly at the geographical point where a vessel bound south from the Galli rocks would need to alter course—either to pass through the Messina Strait to the south-east, or to turn west for the other route round Sicily.

One hundred and twelve sea miles from the Galli lies the volcanic island of Stromboli with its attendant islet, Strombolicchio, just under a mile away. This is one of the most important 'sea gates' in the Mediterranean, and Stromboli is still an invaluable landmark for navigators in this stretch of the Tyrrhenian Sea. Here is the *Admiralty Pilot* on the subject: "[Stromboli] is 3,136 feet high, and is wholly formed of a conical volcano. The volcano is in almost continuous activity and the stream of lava, stones, and cinders, which descends steeply to the sea on its north-western side, is in marked contrast to the verdant slopes on the north-eastern side of the island . . . Strombolicchio, about nine cables north-north-eastward is a steep-to, steep-sided rock about 164 feet high, on the summit of which are some rocky protuberances." Circe's description of a place where "the very birds cannot fly in safety" makes perfect sense when one realizes she is referring to an active volcano. So, too, is her description of the "tempestuous and destroying flames". Even the note about the "great breakers thundering in" is relevant, for Stromboli and Strombolicchio stand alone in the sea, well north of the other Lipari Islands. They are exposed to every wind that blows, and to every swell that surges up or down the Tyrrhenian Sea.

Sailing south from the Galli, the first thing that one sights is the awe-inspiring cone of Stromboli, by night alive with fire and by day encircled by a wreathing smoke-cloud. In the days before there were lighthouses built on every promontory, cape and point, Stromboli would have held an even greater importance for the navigator. At night he could have got his bearings from its high and fiery head—a natural Pharos, and in action many centuries before that first great lighthouse was erected off Alexandria.

Sailing south, and one may assume following the general line of the coast, Ulysses would first sight Stromboli on his starboard bow. If he kept on his course and left the volcano to starboard, he would sooner or later find himself at the entrance to the Messina Strait, where Scylla and Charybdis lurked. If, on the other hand, he wanted to go west-about round Sicily, Stromboli and Strombolicchio acted as the 'signpost' that told him it was now time to alter course. Since Strombolicchio lies north-north-east, nine cables or a little under a mile from Stromboli, the passage between the two is approximately on an east-west axis. That is to say, if Ulysses altered course when he saw the volcano on his starboard hand, and went through the passage between it and Strombolicchio, he would automatically be set on a westerly course. Sailing due west from Stromboli for a further 100 miles, he would then sight Ustica, 'floating' all alone in the sea. This would be his next important landmark. He would know that from here a south-westerly course would bring him down to the passage between Favignana (The Isle of Goats), and the westernmost point of Sicily where the town of Marsala now stands.

The importance of these natural 'sea gates' to mariners, in the days before accurate charts, compasses and distance-measuring instruments, cannot be over-emphasized. Like the Bonifacio Strait (the east-west passage between Corsica and Sardinia), like the Messina Strait (the north-south passage between Italy and Sicily), so the Stromboli-Strombolicchio channel was one of vital concern to early navigators. Circe's statement that at this point Ulysses had a choice of 'two ways' makes perfect sense. If he left Stromboli to starboard, he would reach the Messina Strait. If, on the other hand, he went through the passage between the Stromboli and Strombolicchio, he would find himself on the correct westerly course which would bring him back to Ustica.

"Viewed at night-time," wrote the volcanologist Edward

Hull, "Stromboli presents a far more striking and singular spectacle [than during the day]. When watched from the deck of a vessel, a glow of red light is seen to make its appearance from time to time above the summit of the mountain; it may be observed to increase gradually in intensity, and then as gradually to die away. After a short interval the same appearances are repeated, and this goes on till the increasing light of dawn causes the phenomenon to be no longer visible. The resemblance presented by Stromboli to a 'flashing-light' on a most gigantic scale is very striking, and the mountain has long been known as 'the lighthouse of the Mediterranean'."

The island has been in active eruption "from the commencement of history" and is mentioned by Strabo in his *Geography*. I have been past it myself at night and noticed its resemblance to a lighthouse: "As we neared the straits between Vulcano and Lipari the wind began to pipe around us. They were typical island squalls like those we had met in Greece, and they whipped over the dark sea with sudden anger. Squalls at night were frightening. You could not see them coming and only the sudden rise in the wind's note gave you any warning of their approach. Reluctantly we had to lower sails and motor into a rising sea.

" 'Look!' said Janet.

"There was a glow on the horizon, like the light of a distant city—but this was pulsating.

" 'Stromboli.'

"The volcano was always active, but recently it had been erupting violently and we had been warned in Messina not to sail too close to it at any time, for rocks, pumice, and ash were being hurled into the sea around. A thin ribbon of fire fluttered and glowed down one side. . . ."

It was not at night, however, that Ulysses passed this way.

". . . I saw ahead a cloud of smoke and a roaring surf, the noise of which I could already hear. So frightened were my men that they dropped their oars." He was now forced to go round the ship and put fresh spirit into the sailors. At the same time he gave the helmsman his instructions. They are of extraordinary interest, for they give us the exact geographical position of the hero's vessel on that day, some three thousand years ago, when Ulysses sailed past Stromboli. "Helmsman," he said, "these are my orders, and you must understand them clearly, for you have the good ship's steering oar under your control. Give a wide berth to that smoke and surf which you see, and keep close to these cliffs. . . ."

Now the cliffs to which he refers must surely have been the steep sides of Strombolicchio, lying north-north-east of Stromboli, and therefore the first of the two islands to be encountered by any ship sailing southward through this area. The cloud of smoke is understandable enough, but even the reference to the roaring surf is not without its accuracy. Edward Hull, quoting from the great volcanologist Professor Judd, has the following comment: "The explosions of steam, accompanied by the *roaring as of a smelting furnace,* or of a railway engine when blowing off its steam, are said by Judd to take place at very irregular intervals of time varying from less than one minute to twenty minutes, or even more."

Judd visited the volcano in 1874 and described in his work *Volcanoes* not only this roaring sound, but also how a "great volume of watery vapour was at the same time thrown violently into the atmosphere, and with it there were hurled upwards a number of dark fragments which rose to a height of four or five hundred feet." This then was surely the place where the birds could not fly in safety, where flames destroyed ships, and where Ulysses' men were terrified by the noise.

One thing that has puzzled commentators on the *Odyssey,* and led them to infer that the 'Wandering Rocks' existed only in fairyland, is the fact that, if Stromboli is to be identified with these rocks and if a volcano in a state of eruption is so accurately described, why has there been no mention of Vesuvius? Ulysses has sailed down from Circe's island and has passed the Siren rocks. He has come, therefore, right through the Bay of Naples, and yet there has been no mention of Vesuvius.

139

There is no mystery here. At the time when Homer was writing, Vesuvius was not an active volcano. It was not even suspected that the mountain had a volcanic origin until Diodorus Siculus and Strabo, many centuries later, inferred from the appearance of parts of the mountain—"cindery and as if eaten by fire"—that Vesuvius had once been active. The first indications that the mountain was awakening from the sleep of centuries did not come until A.D. 63 when earthquakes occurred in the Naples region. On the night of August 24th A.D. 79 there was a particularly violent earthquake, and the next day a cloud of smoke and steam rose out of the mountain. Shortly afterwards Pompeii was overwhelmed.

But in Homeric times Vesuvius was dormant. In an inverse way I find in this omission of Vesuvius even further proof of the accuracy of the *Odyssey*. As for the description given by Circe of the Stromboli-Strombolicchio channel, and the description of Ulysses' passage past the two islands, it could not be bettered for clarity and definition.

HAVING passed the fire and roaring surf of Stromboli, Ulysses sailed on south towards the Messina Strait. Whatever contrary conclusions may have been drawn over the centuries about other places mentioned in the *Odyssey*, there has never been any suggestion that Scylla and Charybdis dwelt anywhere but in the Messina Strait. The whole of the ancient world agrees unanimously that this was the home of the two monsters whom Ulysses had to pass, before he reached a safe haven on the eastern shores of Sicily.

Since leaving Circe's island, Ulysses and his men had been continuously at sea for over 230 miles. A direct course between Monte Circeo and the Galli rocks is 80 sea miles; from the Galli to Stromboli 112; and from Stromboli to the Messina Strait, 40. The Homeric account makes no mention of the time taken during this part of the voyage, but it is reasonable to assume that Ulysses did not make direct courses—especially between Monte Circeo and the Galli—so it is more than likely that the distance he will have travelled will have been nearer 300 miles. After leaving Circe he had "a favourable wind from astern which filled the sail of the ship," so he sailed the first 'leg' of his voyage. The wind dropped, while he was approaching the Siren islands, for the men had to take to the oars. For the first eighty miles or more he was probably making about three knots, and after that one may assume one and a half to two knots as the speed of his boat under oars. On a rough estimate, Ulysses will have been nearly eight days at sea before he saw the mountains of Sicily, dim-blue in the distance, lifting themselves behind the stretch of coastline that lies between modern Milazzo and Messina. The terror of the Strait now lay ahead.

Too many scholastic iconoclasts have disparaged the dangers of this stretch of sea. It it really so harmless and so safe as has been only too readily supposed? I first came this way in 1943, on our way north for the Allied landings at Salerno. Neither then, nor on many other later occasions passing through the Strait, did I notice anything remotely disquieting. True, I sometimes remarked strange lines of ripples spreading out across the channel at its narrowest point, and the surface of the water nearly always seemed to have a broken 'tidal' look about it, something which one does not see elsewhere in the Mediterranean. But when you are sliding through the sea at twenty knots or more, with vast reserves of power in the turbines beneath your feet, you do not trouble about minor things like eddies and currents. I knew from the *Pilot* that "The currents and whirlpools, famous from antiquity, are such as to necessitate some caution in the navigation of the strait; moreover, in the vicinity of the high land, on either side, vessels are exposed to violent squalls which descend through the valleys with such strength as, at times, to inconvenience even steamers. . . . " But I think that the only navigational hazard to which I ever paid much attention was the bank which lies off Cape Peloro on the Sicilian side. I had no wish to emulate an acquaintance of mine who had managed to ground his vessel at that point.

I liked going through the Strait, seeing Sicily tawny on the one hand, and ruined Reggio on the other, with the mountains of Calabria jagged and grey in the distance. The air off that corner of Sicily seemed always a little fresher than elsewhere in the central Mediterranean, and in winter when the mountains were capped with snow there was that astringent, crystalline taste on the wind, which rinses clean both the head and the heart. When I left the Mediterranean in 1944 the Strait of Messina meant no more to me than those few impressions.

It was not until I came back here seven years later at the helm of my own small sailing boat that I really learned anything about this fabled stretch of sea. In the 20th century, most travellers' impressions are superficial, for the power and speed of the turbines or jet engines which drive them about the world remove them from any real contact with the lands and the seas that they

traverse. Just as the millionaire is insulated by his money from the ordinary texture of life, so the modern traveller is insulated from reality by the immenseness of the power that transports him. To give but one example: I flew recently from London to Malta, the journey accomplished in a few hours. Sitting in a pressurized cabin I ate lunch somewhere over the Alps, and drank a Martini as we passed over Sicily, looking with something like indifference at the long, sunburnt flanks of Etna away on my left hand. It all meant nothing. And yet, I reflected, the same voyage—from England to Malta—had once taken me four months in a 10-ton boat. That, indeed, had meant something, and when I had sailed into Grand Harbour, Malta, on the tail-end of a gale I had felt that I had earned my arrival. Places are little in themselves, you must earn them by your voyage. As Cavafy, the old Alexandrian poet, wrote: "Be sure you are quite old when you drop anchor in Ithaca. Rich with the experience you have gained upon your voyage, do not expect the island to give you riches. Ithaca has given you your wonderful voyage. Without Ithaca you would never have started. . . ." The same applies to all travel—which brings me back to the Strait of Messina, and Scylla and Charybdis.

"The Strait in question," wrote Thucydides, "is the sea that lies between Rhegium (Reggio) and Messana (Messina), the place where Sicily is the least distance from the Continent, and this is the so-called Charybdis through which Odysseus is said to have sailed. It has naturally become accounted dangerous because of the narrowness and of the currents caused by the inrush of the Tyrrhenian sea." Thucydides is quite right when he refers to the inrush of the Tyrrhenian Sea, for it is the difference in temperature and density of the Tyrrhenian and Ionian seas which to some extent accounts for the current in the Messina Strait. Since the Ionian is noticeably colder and more saline than the Tyrrhenian, a current is set up which flows southward through the strait on the surface, and northward below the surface. It is, of course, only the surface current that concerns navigators, and this, especially if the wind is from the north, may attain a speed of as much as one knot. Now in small ships, making anything between one and a half knots and four knots, a current running at one knot is quite considerable. But the principal hazard of the strait is caused by the tides, for this is one of the very few places in the Mediterranean where a marked tidal action is experienced. To early Mediterranean navigators, quite unfamiliar with tides such as those which circulate around the British Isles, the tidal phenomena experienced in the Messina strait must have been awe-inspiring, and even terrifying.

". . . Twice each lunar day," says the *Admiralty Pilot*, "the water level has a maximum slope northward through the strait, and twice each lunar day a slope southward. Though the difference of level is small, amounting to less than a foot at springs, it is concentrated into such a short distance that streams with a rate of 4 knots at springs are generated by it. These streams run with their greatest force where the strait is narrowest and shallowest, viz. between Punta Pezzo and Ganzirri." Now Punta Pezzo is on the Italian side of the strait hard by the village which to this day bears the name of Scilla, and the Sicilian village of Ganzirri lies a little north of Messina, just inshore from the whirlpool of Charybdis. Between Scilla and Ganzirri, then, is the point where the tidal current is experienced at its strongest. A current of four knots would have been something that no Homeric boat could have stemmed, even if the area had held no other dangers for the unwary mariner.

Scylla, 'the Render', and Charybdis, 'the Sucker-down', were the two dangers against which Ulysses was explicitly warned by Circe: "In the other direction [i.e. if Ulysses did not sail westward between Stromboli and Strombolicchio] lie two rocks, the sharp peak of one reaches up to the sky and a dark cloud hangs about it, a cloud that never streams away, not even in summer or at harvest-time. No mortal man could climb it not even if he had twenty hands and feet, for the rock is sheer and smooth as if it had been polished. And in the middle of this cliff is a dim cave which faces toward the West and which runs down to Erebus, the place of darkness. Past this, noble Odysseus, you must steer your ship. Not even the strongest man armed with a bow could reach the cave's mouth with an arrow shot. And it is there that Scylla dwells, she of the terrible bark. Her yelp, it is true, is no louder than that of a new-born whelp, but she is a terrible monster just the same—something that no one could face gladly, not even a god if he were to pass her way. For she has twelve feet which dangle down, and six very long necks, and on each of them a horrible head with three rows of close-set teeth that are full of dark death. She is sunk up to her middle in the depths of the cave, but her heads protrude from the dreadful hollow, and there she fishes, searching about the rock for any dolphin or swordfish she can find, or any of the larger fish which find their living by the thousand in the deep-voiced seas. No sailors can boast that they ever passed Scylla without losing some of their number, for from every passing ship she snatches off a man with each one of her heads. . . ."

Before continuing with Circe's description of the other monster, Charybdis, and before considering any of the mythology which surrounds the figure of Scylla, there are one or two points which this description immediately raises. Now the height and appearance of the rock seem a straightforward case of poetic exaggeration, or rather perhaps of the old sailor's yarn. The rock, today, is only about 200 feet high, although it may once have been higher. Considerable changes have taken place in the land and sea bed in this area even in quite recent centuries. (The whole of the Messina Strait lies on that major fault in the earth's crust which runs through the Ponza Islands to the north, includes Vesuvius, and then divides just south of Stromboli to run westerly through the Lipari group, and southerly to Sicily and Etna.) But what particularly interests me about Circe's description of Scylla is the reference to her fishing activities. Dolphin, the *Delphinus delphis*, is to be found all over the Mediterranean so the reference to dolphin excites no comment. But, if no other authority existed for identifying the haunt of Scylla with the Messina Strait, the mention of swordfish would be a startling clue. For this north-eastern corner of Sicily by the Messina Strait is one of the few areas in the Mediterranean where swordfish are regularly caught. The swordfish-catching industry plays, in fact, an important part in the economy of the families who dwell along the coast between Messina and Milazzo. It is a traditional 'industry' in this part of the world, and the families who live along the coast have the areas of sea opposite their land assigned to them by almost immemorial rights.

When the beautiful great fish close the coast to spawn, they are hunted by the local swordfish-catchers in their special boats. These have a small crow's nest from which the master can con the ship, and give his orders to the hand-harpoonist standing in the bows. I have been out with them north of Messina and have experienced that moment of fabulous excitement when their harpoon bites home, and the great back and the sword-like snout rise shining from the sea as the fish jumps. The harpoonist turns up the line round the wooden bitts in the boat's bows, the rope stands taut out of the sea with the water-drops falling down from it, and then the small open boat takes the strain as the great fish sounds.

It was for swordfish like these that Scylla was accustomed to fish—and where better than here, one of the few places in the Mediterranean where they are to be found?

This area is also remarkable for its variety of unusual marine creatures, dogfish, octopus, and squid among others. Not for nothing was the sea-goddess Scylla reputed to dwell at the narrow neck of this strait. The American biologist Dr. Paul A. Zahn has described the amazing number of rare deep-sea fish which abound in this area. Due to the topography of the sea bed, "waters farther down also feel the solar-lunar tug, and they too begin to move. When these deep-water currents strike the barrier shallows at Messina, they are violently deflected upward, forcibly dragging with them a host of organisms from below. Hence, for these few hours twice a month [during spring tides] the surface waters in the Strait of Messina abound with living or half-living creatures whose habitat is normally down where all is black and still. . . . After a strong onshore wind I have seen beaches along the Strait of Messina littered with thousands of dead or dying creatures whose strange appearance would make even the artist Dali wince."

Now most of these deep-sea fish and organisms are such as would be encountered nowhere else in the Mediterranean, or indeed anywhere in the world without using a deep-sea trawl. For this reason I do not think it too far-fetched to see that there lurked in the horrific Scylla some reference to the extraordinary 'sea-monsters' to be found in this area—the deep-sea squid, for instance, the hatchet fish, and the sabre-toothed viperfish. Octopus, squid, and the jellyfish, *Medusa*, all abound in these waters. It is not stretching a point too far to see some reference to the octopus and the squid in Scylla's twelve feet and six necks. Robert Graves in *The Greek Myths* has the following note: "Since the Cretan Sea-Goddess was also represented as an octopus, and Scylla dragged the sailors from Odysseus' ship, it may be that Cretans who traded with India knew of large tropical varieties, unknown in the Mediterranean, which are credited with this dangerous habit." But even the smallest squid have an alarming appearance, and their habit of flying or leaping across the surface of the sea can be disconcerting. I have often had them leap aboard my boat at night, attracted possibly by the lights. There is something almost diabolic about their sudden arrival, and their appearance is so inhuman as to be a little frightening, even to a rationalist.

Scylla's 'yelp' is something else which must not escape notice. She was portrayed in classical art and mythology with the head of a dog, or dogs, issuing from her belly. But the 'yelp' of Scylla may well have originated in the high piping sounds of the wind in the caves that honeycomb the rock. The noise of the Messina Strait when the wind is in the north and the tide is on the turn—to run northward against the wind—is something that can only be appreciated from a small boat. (I never heard it, for instance, when I went through the strait in a destroyer, nor later in 1953 when I made the passage in a high-powered diesel launch.) Here is an 18th-century Dutch geographer describing a painting which he made of the rock of Scylla: "Scylla is a rock on the Calabrian side which projects into the sea opposite Cape Faro in Sicily: today called Capo. This rock has the figure of a woman, there are big fissures in it as well as deep caverns, in which the wind and the waves make a horrible moaning. . . ."

Combine this noise with the image of squid, octopus, and other deep-sea marine life, add the very real dangers of the tidal currents, the menace of Scylla itself with its off-lying rocks, and you come close to a portrait of the goddess. So much for her possible origins in fact, and now to look at Charybdis, something which is a great deal easier for Charybdis is very much in existence to this day.

Here first of all is Circe's description: "The other cliff, Odysseus as you will see, lies lower than the first and you could send an arrow-shot across between the two. On it grows a great fig tree in full leaf, and beneath it great Charybdis sucks down the dark waters. Three times a day she spouts out the water, and three times a day she sucks it down in a terrifying way. I pray that you are never there when she sucks down the water, for if you were, not even the Earthshaker could save you. So you must take care, and hug the rock of Scylla, and drive your ship through with all speed. For it is better to mourn six of your company than the whole of your crew. . . ."

The most interesting point about this is that, although the poet paints the goddess Scylla as the more dreadful of the two, it is against Charybdis that Ulysses is so specifically warned. Scylla, with the accretions of legend, has assumed divine and awe-inspiring proportions. But if he passes close to her he will only lose six men, whereas Charybdis (who is dismissed in a few lines) is the one who will sink his whole ship if he is rash enough to go near when she is in the process of "sucking down the waters". This is still true, for the dangers of the Scylla rock and of the Italian side of the strait are considerably less than the Sicilian side where Charybdis still spins and whirls. Again, as in every other instance, Circe's directions are completely accurate. To this day a small boat coming down the strait from the north would hug the rock of Scylla in order to avoid the whirlpool of Charybdis and the shoals of the Sicilian cape. I have done it myself on several occasions.

Here is what the *Pilot* has to say on the subject: "Small whirlpools . . . are seen in most parts of the strait especially soon after one or other of the 'Tagli' [tidal bores] has passed. They mark areas where the denser water is sinking. They are commonly accompanied by smooth oily patches . . . where water is welling up from below. The only whirlpools which present any danger even to small craft are those which form always near the same place owing to peculiarities of the bottom. These are:

(a) Off the beach southward of Punta San Raineri.
(b) From 200 to 300 yards offshore abreast Torre Faro.
(c) A few hundred yards westward of Punta Pezzo.

They are stronger and larger at springs; any one of them does not exist continuously but lasts up to about half an hour when it dies away and a new one starts up nearby: (b) is the Charybdis of the ancients; its opposite number Scylla is now very feeble due to changes in the local topography caused by an earthquake in February 1783. There is, however, every reason to suppose that a whirlpool did exist off the town of Scilla and that both it and Charybdis were rather more impressive then than the latter is today."

The Homeric Charybdis no longer swirls a 'bowshot' from the rock of Scylla, but close inshore near the Sicilian coast, and due east of the village Ganzirri. On the same side as Scylla a whirlpool develops, as the *Pilot* informs us, off Punta Pezzo some four miles down the coast. Another minor whirlpool through which I have sailed myself lies just north of the village of Canitello, about three miles from Scylla on the Italian side.

Is there any likelihood that this area was once a great deal more dangerous to shipping than it is today? It is more than likely, it is a fact. As late as 1824, i.e. long after the changes in the sea bed caused by the earthquake of 1783, Admiral Smyth could write: "To the undecked boats of the Rhegians, Locrians, Zancleans, and Greeks, it [Charybdis] must have been formidable; for even in the present day small craft are sometimes endangered by it, and I have seen several men-of-war, and even a seventy-four gun ship, whirled round on its surface. . . ."

Now a seventy-four gun ship would have seemed an unbelievable Leviathan to Ulysses, and if a vessel of this size could be turned around in the whirlpool of Charybdis, what would have happened to a Homeric craft? Ulysses sailed in what we would nowadays call 'a small boat', and Homer wrote for an audience to whom a vessel as large as a 19th-century warship would have been a marvel.

There are still whirlpools in the world violent enough to endanger quite large modern vessels, notably in the Naruto Strait at the entrance to the Inland Sea of Japan, and off the Western Islands of Scotland. It is known that Charybdis was a definite menace to shipping up to the late 18th century, and there is no reason to suppose that it was any less formidable 2000 years B.C. When one remembers the size of the Homeric ships, and the fact that these superstitious early mariners were sailing an unknown and uncharted sea, there is every reason to suppose that the terrors of the Messina Strait were very real to them.

21

Ulysses passes the Strait

ON a sunlit day, well over a week after he had parted from Circe, Ulysses approached the terrors of this unknown strait. Donning his armour, he caught up two long lances, for he hoped to be able to defend himself and his men against the sea-goddess. Circe, in fact, had advised him not to attempt any violence against Scylla. But if he disobeyed her on this point, he followed Circe's instructions to the letter in all other respects. He now shaped his course so as to hug the Italian shore by Scylla's rock, just as she had told him to do.

"So, lamenting, we began to sail up the narrow strait. For on the one hand lay Scylla, and on the other mighty Charybdis in a terrifying manner sucked down the salt sea. When she spewed it forth, she would seethe like a cauldron on a great fire, and the flung spray fell like rain on the tops of either cliff. But when she swallowed down the salt sea-water, one could see right down into the troubled depths. The rocks echoed with the terrifying roar, and the dark sand of the sea-bed was exposed to view. My men turned pale with fear. . . ."

Embroidered in the retelling and then enlivened by the poet's imagination, this is none the less a clear description of a violent whirlpool. But what of Scylla, who, while Ulysses and his men were gazing terror-struck at Charybdis, stretched down from her rock and seized "six of my company out of the hollow ship"? I have suggested that there may well have been some connection between the conception of this frightening twelve-footed, six-necked sea-monster, and the squids and octopus which abound in this region. But it would be wrong to press the analogy too far, for Scylla is clearly far more than a simple representation of some creature or phenomenon of the natural world. It is worth bearing in mind, all the same, that giant squids do exist and that they can be dangerous to man. G. E. and N. MacGinitie of the Kerckhoff Marine Laboratory, California, have recorded some interesting facts about the squid in their *Natural History of Marine Animals*. Of the giant squid, for instance, they write: ". . . one must be particularly careful when handling the large squid, *Dosidicus gigas*, [which] appeared abundantly off the coast of California during the summer of 1934. Net, troll, and set line fishermen from Monteroy to San Diego considered this squid a pest, for the animals stole bait and fouled lines. Those that were captured showered the fishermen with ink, and occasionally one would bite a fisherman severely." Now all squids, like octopods, are predatory and carnivorous. They do, indeed, 'fish' for their food and the largest squids of all are not above doing battle with the whale. Although most Mediterranean squid are quite small, specimens have been found in other seas which are veritable giants. The squid *Architeuthis* is the largest of all invertebrate animals, and one example caught off the Grand Banks of Newfoundland had an overall length of 55 feet. Including its tentacles, it would have weighed some 30 tons. Two arms of another *Architeuthis* were found which were 42 feet long, giving a reconstructed overall measurement of 66 feet, or a sea-giant that would have weighed about $42\frac{1}{2}$ tons. The Kraken of Nordic folk-lore, a monster which was believed to haunt the Norwegian coastline, was almost certainly a huge squid. Whether squids of this size ever existed in the Mediterranean is doubtful, but they did and do exist in eastern waters, as well as in the Atlantic. It seems highly probable that in the legendary aspect of Scylla we have some sailor's account of the giant squid, *Architeuthis*—from a Phoenician who had been trading down the Red Sea and eastwards into the Indian Ocean.

The other curious factor about this passage of the *Odyssey* is Circe's reference to the "great fig-tree with luxuriant foliage" which grows upon the rock below which Charybdis sucks down the sea. This fig-tree is not described when Ulysses and his men sail through the strait, but the fact that it is specifically mentioned by Circe seems to suggest that it had some important connection with the whirlpool. It can hardly be coincidence that there is an identical correspondence in Indian legend. The hero Saktideva, on his journey in search of the Golden City, reaches the island of the fisher-king, Satyavrata, who gives him a ship and agrees to act as his guide. As they sail onwards they see something ahead that looks like a dark mountain rising and falling above the waves of the sea. When Saktideva asks what it is, the fisher-king replies: "It is a fig-tree beneath which there is a whirlpool that drags men down to their death." In this tale, the fisher-king sacrifices himself so that Saktideva can be saved by grasping the boughs of the fig-tree before his boat is sucked down into the whirlpool. J. E. Harrison commented: "What the significance of this recurring fig-tree may be is hard to tell. Possibly its Greek name ἐρινεός may have some connection with Ἐρινύς, the might and destruction of the lower world." It certainly looks as if Charybdis, like Scylla, has received additional embroidery from some eastern folk-lore.

In Greek legend, Scylla was the daughter of a marine god Phorcys by the goddess Hecate. Hecate was a mysterious being who had power over earth, heaven, and hell, and was one of the only Titans to retain her sovereignty after Zeus had over-thrown her fellows. In view of the fact that her daughter Scylla dwelt at the entrance to the Messina Strait with its tidal (lunar) currents, it is not surprising to find that Hecate was a lunar goddess. She taught sorcery and witchcraft, dwelt at the places where roads crossed, and—and in view of her dominion over the lunar cycle—was a goddess much respected by women. Her daughter Scylla is generally represented in classical art as a beautiful woman down to the waist, but with dogs' heads in place of genitals, and with her body terminating in a fish-tail. She was closely related to Lamia, 'The Devourer', a bogy-woman with whom the Greeks used to frighten their children into obedience. Scylla also seems to have been held in great awe by the Etruscans. Like her mother Hecate, she was a triple-goddess—holding dominion over sky, earth, and the region under the earth. This, no doubt, is why her physical attributes are all in multiples of three—twelve feet, six heads, and even the teeth in the heads being set in triple rows.

It is sometimes difficult when trying to equate geographical fact with poetic fiction to realize how, 3,000 years and more ago, men had no conception of those limits which we accept as dividing the world of actuality from the world of imagination. "The limits of human and superhuman, material and immaterial were but dimly realized. There was something in common between gods and men and the beasts of the field and all growing things, and a pathway between the living and the dead. . . . Every stream and oak and mountain was the habitation of a spiritual being whose nature was on the borderland between the human and the divine and partook of both. And so weak was the sense of identity, that with a touch of magic it was felt the barrier might be passed, and a man might become a wolf or a serpent or a hoopoe or a purple lily. He might renew his youth; he might be raised from the dead. With the waving of a branch and sprinkled waterdrops the wizard might bring a rain-shower down the sides of Lykaios. Like Melampous he might understand the language of all living creatures, even the woodworms in the decaying rafters, and say with Alkman 'I know the songs of all the birds'."

In childhood we all know these feelings, but in the childhood of mankind it is possible that men still felt them even when they were adult. It is a faculty which some poets, artists, and men of genius have managed to preserve throughout the ages. William Blake, the "most practically sane, steady, frugal and industrious man" as Samuel Palmer described him, was quite capable of seeing angels singing in trees—and that was in the 'rational' 18th century. A pantheist like Van Gogh could find God as easily in a cane chair or a pair of old shoes as in the clouds and sky over Arles. It may be that artists are those who have retained into maturity the innocent eye of childhood. Scylla may be a cave in a limestone rock to a geologist, and Charybdis a whirlpool of moderate dimensions to a hydrographer, but these definitions do not necessarily disqualify the poet's view. Stromboli has been described by one volcanologist as "an interesting example of a volcano in almost continuous activity," but the child or the poet is equally entitled to see it as the home of a god. There is no proof that the scientific approach to the world is any more 'true' than the poetic. Over the doorway to every library, university, and other place of study or research, I would like to see these words of William James inscribed: "We may be in the Universe as dogs and cats are in our libraries, seeing the books and hearing the conversation, but having no inkling of the meaning of it all."

So while Charybdis is the whirlpool which could well have wrecked Ulysses' fragile boat, Scylla is definitely something more than that. She is above all the sinister aspect of the sea. She is storm, rock, whirlpool, quick-sand, waterspout and sea-monster, all combined. From the Sirens Ulysses had heard the enchanting song which united love and death in a promise of all knowledge. Theirs was the composed wisdom of this sea; that all things have happened before, that all will occur again, and that the course of true wisdom is to accept; to take our ease in the shade, and to cultivate our garden. From Scylla, on the other hand, he heard the dark yelp of the elemental forces that crush a man with the same indifference as they hurl the deep-sea creatures up from the depths, to gasp out their lives on the beaches of the Messina Strait.

It was now that Ulysses learned pity. As the six men were snatched by Scylla from his boat, "they cried my name aloud in their agony." It is in appropriate sea-images that he bitterly recalls their fate: "For just as a fisherman on a headland casts the ox-horn lure into the sea with his long rod—to act as a bait for the little fishes below — and then whips his struggling catch ashore, so she drew them struggling to the cliff. They stretched out their hands, and screamed to me in their death-throes as she devoured them at her cave mouth. And this was by far the most pitiful thing that I have seen, in all my travail over the paths of the sea."

22

Sun-God's Island

So it was that with the loss of six men Ulysses and his crew escaped from the dangers of the Messina Strait. Had it not been for the goddess Circe's instructions he would certainly have lost his whole ship. For the natural thing to do, when approaching a narrow channel like this, is to steer so as to pass through the centre of it—giving the off-lying rocks and shoals on both sides as wide a berth as possible. But if Ulysses had pursued the seaman's normal course, he would have run straight into Charybdis.

Coming through this same strait in the late autumn of 1952 I did exactly as Ulysses had done 3,000 years before—kept close to the Italian coast where the village of Scilla now stands, so as to avoid the broken water and overfalls on the Sicilian side of the strait. I did this because, from Homer up to the latest 20th-century edition of the *Admiralty Pilot*, such has always been the advised course for small vessels under sail. Fortunately for me, no evil goddess with long tentacles or triple teeth lurked on the rock, but there was indeed a hollow booming sound to be heard in the strait. In a small boat under sail, with one's ears attuned to the silence of the sea, one is sensitive to every change in the noise of the waves, of the wind in the rigging, or the sound that the wake makes past the rudder.

"Over on the Italian side, where Scylla had once laid another trap for the unwary, there was nothing stirring. A few broken eddies near the rock, that was all, and the old town looked peaceful under the sun. We came in close by the beach where the

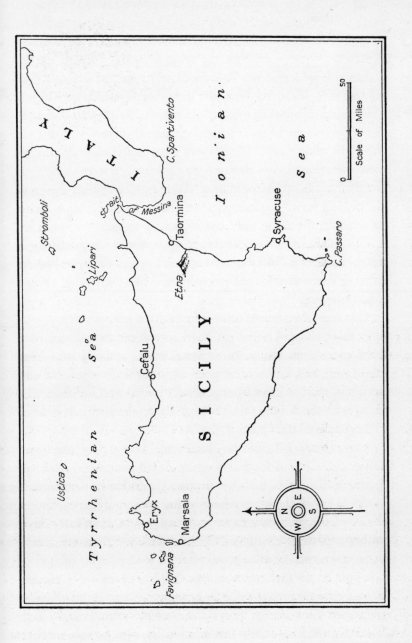

water swirled the waves up the pale sand and the fishing boats were drawn back out of harm's way. There were nets spread to dry along the shore and the smoke from the chimneys was sliding fast to the south." But, on the same occasion, I found on the Italian side of the strait: "a curious swirl on the surface a few cables away. It did not look like the overfalls which we had just left behind. There was a smooth glassy quality about it—and yet the water was moving . . . I could see now that there was a distinct dip in the middle of it, and the small white waves were all moving round and round. We altered course away. We were about four hundred yards off the lighthouse [Faro, on the Sicilian side] and the circling water was moving quite slowly like a gyro-top losing its impetus. Or was it only just beginning to spin?

"The heart of it was just abeam of us, about a hundred yards away. There was froth on the surface all round the boat, but the moving centre had a treacly consistency, like boiled sugar when it is cooling off."

That was Charybdis as I saw it from my small boat, many years after those changes in the sea bed had reduced its violence. But even as it stands today, I can imagine that it could have been frightening to a sailor 3,000 years ago. Yet still the scholars can say: ". . . the Cyclopes belong wholly to the world of fairy tale, along with the Aeolian Isle, Calypso, Circe, the Sirens, Scylla and Charybdis, and the Oxen of the Sun."

After escaping from the 'imaginary' dangers of the strait Ulysses now found himself coasting down the eastern flanks of Sicily, an island which not so surprisingly neither he nor the poet connected with the place where he had previously fallen foul of the Cyclopes. It is easy to see how seamen in those early days, without charts or instruments, were unable to relate one section of an unknown coastline to another. It is facile with the aid of hindsight to say that any man who had landed on the west coast of Sicily would surely realize he was on the same island when he reached its eastern coast. This is just not true. Several times I have found myself temporarily lost when sailing this sea in a modern

160

sailing boat, and in the last war—having made a gross miscalculation in my star sights that morning—I identified completely the wrong section of the Tunisian coastline as being the area off which we were, in fact, steaming. There is no suggestion in the *Odyssey* that Ulysses ever connected the Land of the Cyclopes, which he had visited over a year before, with the island which lay on his right past the Messina Strait.

"It was not long before we reached the Sun-God's favoured island, where Hyperion keeps his fine, broad-browed cattle, as well as his flocks of healthy sheep. . . ." It was natural enough that, having just escaped with their lives, the crew should clamour to go ashore and rest. Ulysses remembered, however, that he had been more expressly cautioned against the Sun-God's island than against any of the other dangers of this sea. Both Teiresias and Circe had warned him that, if any of the sacred animals were harmed, ruin would befall him. His ship would be lost, all his companions would be drowned, and if he survived, it would only be to return home many years later 'in evil plight', alone.

Ulysses repeated this gloomy prophecy to his crew, adding: "So let's drive on in the ship and put the island astern of us." It is not surprising that he was at once faced with something like mutiny, Eurylochus his fellow-nobleman being the ring-leader. "You indeed may be made of iron," Eurylochus protested, "but we are not. It is already getting on for evening. Let us find a place to anchor, and go ashore and cook our supper. Then, in the morning, we can get under way again."

Very reluctantly Ulysses agreed, but not before he had impressed upon them all that they must give him their word not to touch any of the cattle on the island. "You must promise," he said, "to sit in peace and eat only the food that Circe gave us."

By my calculations they must by now have been some nine days at sea, and, although there is no reason why they should not still have had plenty of food, water would probably have been getting low. Their first concern would be to find a secure place to anchor the ship, and then go ashore and find fresh water. This is exactly what we find—"We brought the good ship into a sheltered cove, where there was fresh water to hand, and there the men disembarked."

Before speculating as to where this sheltered cove may have been it is important to consider the objections which have been raised to the identification of the Sun-God's island with Sicily. These arguments mostly stem from the fact that when Teiresias and Circe are warning Ulysses about the dangers of landing there they both refer to the island as *Thrinakia*. Now, *Thrinakia* means the 'Island of the Trident' and it is a term which was never applied to Sicily in classical times. *Trinakria*, however, was the name by which Sicily was commonly known—meaning the 'Three-Angled Island'—this for the very obvious reason that Sicily is an almost equilateral triangle. (To this day, Sicily's crest is the same three-legged symbol as that used by the Isle of Man off Britain.) Now it is quite true that The Island of the Trident and the Three-Angled Island are very different things, but when one considers that it is the change of one letter, the Greek theta instead of the Greek tau and the addition of the second 'r', then I tend to feel that scholars have made something of a mountain out of a molehill. This is particularly the case when it is quite clear in what part of the world Ulysses is now navigating. Of course if we have dismissed Scylla and Charybdis, the Wandering Rocks, the Sirens, and Circe's island, as all being in fairyland then one must look for Thrinakia in fairyland too.

Victor Bérard has the following to say on the subject: "This name [The Island of the Trident] could hardly be given to Sicily by anyone with first-hand knowledge. It implies a mental picture very different from the real one, the picture conveyed by those island-like peninsulae—the Peloponnese and Chalkidike, which from their jagged coasts thrust three sharp rocky arms out sea-wards, spreading in the mariner's path a three-pronged fork in three parallel lines, ending in three promontories lying no great distance apart. From this we must conclude that in Homeric times, neither the rhapsodists nor their listeners had seen the

Sicilian coastline. The Poet or his forerunners did not invent this name, any more than any other linked up with the adventures of Odysseus. Doubtless they had read, in a foreign hand, a name which corresponded to Trinakria and between the facts implied in the name and their mental picture of it, there intervened, either from what they themselves had remembered, or had learned from their race, one familiar stretch on the Achaean coasts. Thus in place of the Sicilian Triangle, they put the Trident of Chalkidike or the Peloponnese."

This seems a reasonable enough supposition, but the whole question is only of concern to those who once argued that Homer must himself have been a sailor in order to write the *Odyssey*. Now this is something that I have never believed. What I do believe—that he based the wanderings of Ulysses on the factual record of a real voyage—is not disturbed by the slip of writing *Thr*inakia when one should have written *Trinakria*. Bigger errors are made by 20th-century writers and publishers every day of the week.

Just as we have found that all Circe's sailing directions lead Ulysses to Sicily—whence he is in a good position to set sail across the Ionian for Ithaca—so we shall find that everything which befalls him from now on fits straightforwardly within this geographical framework. Where, then, was the 'sheltered cove' into which the exhausted and frightened sailors rowed, bemoaning the loss of six of their friends? Some would have it that this was the modern Roads of Messina, the great sheltering arm which spreads out some four miles south of Charybdis. It is not impossible, but I find it unlikely. For one thing, the currents and minor whirlpools are almost as fearsome at this point as they are in the narrows between Scylla and Charybdis. For another thing, it would have meant crossing the strait from the comparatively safe Italian side, only a few minutes after being swept southward by the current past Charybdis. Nowadays one would quite happily cross the strait, knowing that good shelter was to be found in the modern artificial harbour. But not thus I think did sailors act who had just had an appalling fright and who had lost some of their friends at sea. It is far more likely that they would have put that terrifying strait as far behind them as possible before looking for somewhere to anchor for the night. Again, we know that Ulysses told the crew of the prophecies which Teiresias and Circe had made to him, and that near mutiny broke out, in the course of which Eurylochus made a long speech. All this can hardly have taken place in the short length of time which would have elapsed between passing Scylla's rock and crossing the strait to the Roads of Messina. From the description of Scylla and Charybdis, furthermore, it was certainly broad daylight when they passed through the strait. Yet when Eurylochus is speaking, he refers to "the night that is already overtaking us." Several hours have clearly elapsed since their passage between Scylla and Charybdis and the time when they are beginning to look for an anchorage on the Sicilian coast. One can be sure that the current was behind them when they came through the strait, or they would never have been able to make it. So, with this current in their favour and the rowers pulling like demons to get clear of danger, the boat will have been making her maximum speed—four knots, at least.

Southward from the harbour of Messina the coast of Sicily is barren and austere. For some twenty-five miles, there are no real anchorages, and we are looking not for an offshore anchorage, but for a sheltered cove. I have been up and down this stretch of coast at least half a dozen times and there is only one 'sheltered cove' in the whole area. I have been into it on several occasions, and used it once as my point of departure for the Ionian Islands. This anchorage is the Rada di Taormina, the only small indentation on this somewhat featureless coast where small boats can safely shelter from the weather, and with sandy beaches where fishing boats can be drawn up out of harm's way. The cove lies twenty-six miles from Scylla, a little over six hours distant at four knots, and only a little over eight hours at three knots. Whether Ulysses came through the strait at noon or somewhat earlier, Taormina is just about where one would expect to find him towards dusk on an autumn day.

From Messina southward there is nothing else on this coastline that is the remotest bit like a sheltered cove, until one gets down to L'Ognina creek hard by the city of Catania. But L'Ognina is fifty miles from Scylla and Charybdis, and must be disqualified on this score alone. It is a creek, in any case, not a cove. Here is a description of the Rada di Taormina in the impersonal language of the *Admiralty Pilot*: "The small bay, which is entered between Capo San Andrea and Capo Taormina, is divided into two parts by Isola Bella, which is connected with the shore by a shoal flat . . . sand and good holding ground . . . and shingle beach backed by woods. . . ." It is, in fact, an ideal place for yachts, fishing boats, or small coasters to lie at anchor. Furthermore, in an island where water is as precious as gold in summer, two small rivers, the Alcantara and the Minissale, come out into the sea close by. There are springs in Taormina itself, but one can estimate no historical age for springs in an area that is so subject to volcanic disturbance. "A sheltered cove, with fresh water to hand"—such conditions would not be difficult to find on some coastlines, but in this part of Sicily only Rada di Taormina meets the case.

The Greeks anchored their vessel, and then disembarked and made ready their evening meal. It is sad to think they did not know that this small rock-fringed cove holds some of the sweetest lobsters in Sicily. The last time that I was here, on my way south to Syracuse, I bought five of these sea-green beauties for approximately one English pound. Up in the big hotels of the modern resort they will have cost a pound apiece, but there is a brotherhood between those who go down to the sea in ships. And all Sicilians were so amazed to find that my wife and myself sailed our boat alone that their hearts were touched for her plight—"A woman living and working like a sailor!" Our lobsters were the *Palinurus vulgaris*, the Mediterranean lobster, or large crayfish, which lacks the two big pincer claws of the American and north European *Homarus gammarus*. But who cares about that, when they are still damp from the sea, trailing a little weed between their spiny legs and blowing sad bubbles out of their whiskered mouths? At sea that night, a few miles south of Ulysses' sheltered cove, we put them all into a bucket of salt water on the roaring galley stove. One needs little more in this world than a fair wind, the sun going down behind Etna, the sound of the sea, hot lobster, good rough bread, and a little red wine from Taormina. Which brings me back to Ulysses. . . .

After the Greeks had eaten their evening meal and gone to sleep a gale sprang up. They could do nothing in the dark hours, but at the first light of dawn they dragged the ship up the beach and hauled her into the shelter of a cave. There are still caves in plenty in this cove, as well as two or three small beaches. Sudden and alarming gales are common in autumn, for this is the time when the Mediterranean becomes most treacherous. One autumn in Riposto a few miles south from here (it is a man-made modern harbour) I nearly lost my boat when a waterspout came hurling across the sea and burst in a toppling cloud of spray as it hit the land. Thunderstorms tend to build up over the inland mountains, and the sea around the Sicilian coastline is treacherous and dangerous for small vessels. By all my calculations it was just at this time of the year that Ulysses beached his boat at Taormina.

The most outstanding feature of this coastline is undoubtedly the high peak of Etna, soaring up 10,000 feet and more to the south of Taormina. Capped by snows in winter, or wreathed in summer cloud, lazily smoking its pipe of peace, or hurling rocks into the sky while the lava rolls down the plains towards the sea— Etna is the king of this coastline. Returning to Sicily from Ithaca and the Ionian Islands I have seen it from the deck of my small boat while still far out at sea. It meant that my voyage was over, and that within a few hours I would be securely moored alongside the quay in Syracuse, a hundred yards or so from Arethusa's fountain, and with every prospect of a good hot meal ashore. It is strange then, as G. F. Rodwell commented in his history of the mountain, "that Homer, who has so minutely described certain portions of the contiguous Sicilian coast, does not allude to Etna. This has been thought by some to be a proof that the mountain was in a quiescent state during the period which preceded and coincided with the time of Homer. . . ."

Now we know for certain that Vesuvius was quiescent and therefore attracted no attention until many centuries after the Homeric period. It is quite possible that Etna was in a similar state, for the first eruption of which we have record occurred in the 6th century B.C., in the time of Pythagoras, 200 years and more after the poet lived. Pindar (522-442 B.C.) is the first poet to mention "Etna, nursing throughout the year her dazzling snow," and Aeschylus also describes the mountain "on whose highest peak Hephaestos sits." Thucydides reported that there had been three eruptions since the Greeks had inhabited Sicily. Throughout later classical history almost every historian or poet contributed his share towards immortalizing the highest mountain in southern Italy. Our earliest record, however, of any volcanic activity still dates from the 6th century B.C.

This is one good reason why it may have been ignored in the tale of Ulysses' wanderings. But when the hazards of Stromboli and Scylla and Charybdis are so accurately described, does it not still seem curious that Etna—even if quiescent—was ignored altogether? When a small anchorage like that of Taormina is particularized, with its fresh water and its beach where a boat can be slipped, why should something so important geographically as Etna have been overlooked? The answer is simple—the source of Homer's material is a seaman's voyage, and sailors record only those things which intimately concern the safety of their vessel and their crew. Stromboli and the Messina Strait are hazards to navigation, Etna, some ten miles inshore from the coast, is not. In its grandeur and beauty it is a feature which no poet, if he saw it, could ever forget. But Homer never saw Sicily, and the raw material on which he based his account of Ulysses' voyage was not compiled by a poet.

An interesting modern corroboration of this is furnished by the

Admiralty Pilot for Sicily. A small anchorage like that of Taormina (even though it can be of no conceivable interest to modern vessels) occupies over a page of the Pilot—65 lines to be precise. Mighty Etna, the highest volcano in Europe and one of the natural wonders of the world, is dismissed in a bare 19 lines. It is of little or no interest to seamen.

Looking at my own sailing log-books for this stretch of coast I find no references to Etna, except on the one occasion when I used it rather like a leading mark when coming *back* to Sicily from western Greece. I have sailed past here at night even when the mountain was erupting, and when lava streams were like bright ribands down its sides. I have watched the awe-inspiring electric storms playing in the ash-cloud over the peak. Yet I had no worry about the safety of my boat, for the mountain lay too far inland to be a source of danger. Had it been Stromboli in eruption—that would have been quite another matter. The omissions in the *Odyssey* are quite as significant as the things which are recorded with accurate fidelity.

The Cattle of the Sun

ON the first morning in their safe Sicilian anchorage the Greeks secured their boat in the shelter of a cave. It was clear that the weather had broken and that they might be held up for several days. Ulysses called them all together and repeated his warning that, whatever they did, they must not harm a single one of the cattle and sheep which were pasturing near by. Having learned by now that their leader's knowledge of the dangers that were likely to befall them were invariably accurate, his men accepted his order without a murmur.

With the sacred cattle of the Sun-God Helios, or Hyperion as Homer calls him, we are back in the world of myth. "Helios," as Carl Kerényi writes, "was above all a father, and as a father was interwoven with our whole existence: as all-seeing and all-hearing witness of our doings—a sort of higher conscience that hovered over us and could be called upon to testify to the truth—and as a begetting father, from whom continually originate all the days of our lives. Every morning he bestows upon us a day of life, unless he chooses to withhold one or all of these. For example, he withheld for a long time from Odysseus, and for ever from Odysseus' companions, the day of their return home."

This episode in the *Odyssey* is closely paralleled by the Tenth Labour of Heracles, where the hero was required to steal the sacred cattle of the Sun. Homer in the *Odyssey* specifically gives the numbers of these animals, 350 cattle and 350 sheep, and it has not escaped the notice of later commentators that "the number is

that of the days of the year, in which twelve lunar months together constitute an incomplete year of the sun."

These sacred beasts were looked after by two of the Sun-God's
daughters, Phaethousa, 'The Shining One' and Lampetia 'The
Illuminating'. The connection between the all-begetting Sun-
God and cattle, particularly the bull, occurs in many mythologies.
In early Greek legend Helios was described as drawn in his
chariot by bulls—not by horses as he was later depicted. In classical art he was shown as a beautiful, golden-haired youth, not a
rude primeval giant. Thus, in all their mythology, the Greeks
assimilated gods from other sources, hellenized them, and turned
them into gracious anthropomorphic figures. The crude Phoenician giant, Melkarth, becomes Heracles, the recognizable figure
of a noble 'strong man'. Some of Heracles' story is then transferred to Ulysses, who becomes over the centuries not merely a
rough sailor-hero, but an embodiment of applied intelligence.
From the historic Ulysses with his guile, and treachery even, we
finally reach the dedicated intellectual wanderer of Dante—who is
transmuted yet again by Tennyson into a romantic Victorian
explorer.

If mythology ascribed the pasturage grounds of the Sun-God's
cattle to this region of Sicily it is hardly surprising if we find that
even the name of the town upon this site has links with the story
of Ulysses. Taormina, which was a Greek city from the 4th
century B.C., was called by its Greek colonists 'Tauromenion',
later to be changed by the Romans to 'Tauromenium' from which
the modern name derives. Is it only coincidence then that the root
of this name is the Greek word 'Tauros', a Bull. Even if one
entirely disregards the story of the Sun-God who kept his sacred
cattle in this part of Sicily, there is good reason why this area is
always likely to have been a pasturage ground. At this point
between the coast and Mount Etna lies one of the most fertile
areas of Sicily, a plain now cultivated, but which once no doubt
was all grassland. Ten miles away, on the slopes of Etna itself, it is
curious to find that the largest valley on the flanks of the mountain

is called the Val del Bove, the Valley of the Ox. I have been unable to discover at what date this name was applied to this barren and lunar-landscape valley, but there is no doubt that Taormina has been associated with bulls and the Bull-God since the 4th century B.C. This in itself would be striking enough, even if the natural anchorage did not fit in exactly with the Homeric description of the place into which Ulysses brought his ship before the final disaster.

For there was, of course, a disaster. Throughout the *Odyssey* one finds that the crew of Ulysses always act in what one can only call 'a typically human manner'. Some wish to desert in the easy Lotus-Land, others are reluctant to leave Goat Island, while all are eager to go ashore as soon as possible once some danger has been passed. They are 'human, all too human', and one can be sure that, if food begins to run short, no warnings about the sacred cattle grazing on the Sicilian pastures are going to deter them.

Unfortunately, they do begin to run short of food, for no sooner has the offshore gale blown out, than "now for a whole month the South Wind blew steadily." They had a month, then, of what we would nowadays call 'Sirocco weather', and after that "Nothing but southerly and easterly winds." What Ulysses and his men needed to send them back to Greece was a good westerly. Is it only coincidence again that makes the winds equate with geographical facts? A north wind would have blown the vessel down the coast of Sicily towards Malta. An east wind would have embayed them in Taormina, and a south wind would have blown them back to Scylla and Charybdis. They needed a west wind to get to Greece, but all they got was a south wind, and then easterly and southerlies combined. So they were forced to stay in Taormina.

This south wind which "blows for a whole month" is the one most likely to occur in this part of the world in autumn. The Sirocco is always the prevailing wind in this part of the Mediterranean, but it is at its worst during September and October. It is at this period of the year that the North African wind, the

Khamsin, hurls itself over the warm Mediterranean to cause the terrible dust-storms which still devastate parts of Sicily. This wind, which is like the hot blast out of an oven in North Africa, is usually swollen with humidity by the time that it reaches these shores. Those who have never experienced it can have no idea of the effect that it has upon the body, nerves, and temper. I have heard it said that at one time in Sicily, if the Sirocco blew for over ten days, all crimes of passion and violence were ascribed to the weather—and their perpetrators dismissed, as it were, 'with a caution'.

August, September, and October have the highest frequency of Sirocco winds for any months in this part of the world. "On leaving the coast [of North Africa] the hot air soon gains moisture from the sea, and is cooled by contact with the relatively cool sea surface. As a result, the relative humidity becomes very high. The associated weather is warm, hazy, and very enervating; a continuous layer of low stratus cloud is common, while on land the dew is sometimes so heavy at night that the gutters run with water. The 'Sirocco' may occur in any season, but it is most disagreeable in autumn." It was from Taormina in the November of 1921 that D. H. Lawrence wrote: "Here it [the weather] has had a sharp cold touch. But now Sirocco in hot billows of wet and clinging mist. Damn Sirocco." It is not only that the wind is unpleasant on account of its heat and humidity, from a sailor's point of view it is dangerous because the seas in this area have had time to build up all the way from North Africa some 400 miles away. A long and steady Sirocco, such as I have known in both Sicily and Malta, produces conditions at this time of year which are hazardous for even quite large vessels.

So Ulysses endured a whole month of Sirocco. We learn that: "While the bread and wine lasted the men never touched the cattle...." But the provisions which they had brought with them from Monte Circeo, nearly six weeks before, were now almost exhausted. It is hardly surprising to find that, once this happened, the crew began to cast their eyes on the fat flocks in the plain. At first, obeying Ulysses' orders, they contented themselves with trying to catch fish, birds, or any wild game that they could find. But there were about forty men still left in the crew, and forty men take more than a little feeding. Ulysses, we are told, went away by himself to pray to the gods for some relief from the weather. He knew well that disaster must soon overtake him unless he could get his ship away, or his men adequately fed. Unfortunately a natural Mediterranean habit overcame him, and one that is very understandable at this season when the Sirocco has reduced a man to a limp bundle of exacerbated nerves—he fell asleep.

When he woke up he found that the worst had happened. Eurylochus had again been exercising his rebellious authority over the men. "We shall die here anyway from starvation," he had said. "It is better surely to have something to eat first, even if it means that later on we shall all be drowned!" Ulysses heard none of this, but he knew the worst when, on his way back to the vessel, he smelled "the sweet scent of roasting meat on the wind." The sailors, acting under the persuasive tongue of Eurylochus, had gone out into the plain and killed the sacred cattle.

It was too late for Ulysses to do anything about it, and useless to upbraid them. The damage was done. Eurylochus, who had behaved ignobly on Circe's Island, who had been a good friend to Ulysses when they had passed the Sirens, but who had become increasingly mutinous as the voyage went on, had now brought them all to certain disaster. The Greeks had trespassed against life itself. By killing some of the sacred cattle of the year they had cut short their own days, just as surely as if they had committed suicide.

For six days, despite all the warning signs that vengeance was near, the crew continued to feast on the fresh meat. "And on the seventh day the fury of the gale abated. . . ." It was late summer when they had left Circe's Island, and at least nine days had passed before they navigated the Messina Strait to reach the anchorage at Taormina. Since then there had been a month of Sirocco, then more southerly and easterly winds, and now a whole week of gale-force weather. By my calculations we are now in November, and the Mediterranean winter has begun. It is no time to take an open boat to sea for a long voyage.

The Mediterranean, despite its travel-poster advertising (which leads many visitors to believe that it is always like a picture postcard) is an extremely dangerous sea in winter. It is worse for the sailor than many an ocean, for there is always a coastline some-where near by—something that will sink a boat far more swiftly than any Atlantic roller. The American single-handed sailor, Carl Petersen, (who won the Blue Water Medal for a round-the-world voyage in 1953) told me that the worst weather he encountered anywhere in the world was between Crete and Malta in the winter.

The only reason why Ulysses and his men can possibly have decided to put to sea again at this season of the year was that they were convinced they had broken some *tabu*. It is true that they seem to have found in Taormina none of the human comforts which Circe and her handmaidens had provided during their previous winter ashore. (After leaving Circe it is noticeable that the Greeks meet no other human beings at all.) At the same time they had found a safe anchorage, and there was water to hand, as well as fish and game. Superficially, then, there was every reason why with winter coming on they should have stayed ashore. But to confuse fact with fiction in the *Odyssey* is to make a grave mistake, for a true voyage has been 'over-painted' with myth and legend. At any rate, for some reason or other, most probably that they were convinced they had offended the gods, the Greeks elected to set sail for home in the most hazardous season of the year.

As soon as the gale had abated, ". . . We embarked swiftly, stepped the mast, and hoisted the white sail. Then we put out into the open sea."

24

Shipwreck

ULYSSES knew in which direction he had to steer. From Taormina a course of due east would have taken the Greeks back home, bringing them out on the far side of the Ionian Sea, somewhere near the channel between Zante and Cephallonia. However inaccurate their navigation, any course in an easterly direction would have brought them to the shores of Greece.

There is no doubt that they did steer east, for we read that "as soon as we had put the island astern and no other land, only sky and water was to be seen, Zeus drove up a dark cloud which rested over the ship so that its shadow darkened the sea." What is important here is the fact that, after leaving their anchorage, they "put the island astern." Now if they had continued coasting down the shores of Sicily it would have taken them some time to leave the island behind them, for it is all of seventy miles from Taormina to Cape Passero, the southernmost point of Sicily. Clearly they did not sail back again toward the treacherous Messina Strait. They acted logically and correctly, and sailed due east into the open sea where "only sky and water was to be seen."

The slaughter of the sacred cattle had already been reported to Zeus by the Sun-God's daughter Lampetia. Retribution was now at hand. A gale-force wind sprang up from astern, and a sudden squall "snapped both the forestays." The mast collapsed and, as it fell aft, smashed in the helmsman's skull. Homer does not tell us any more than this, nor does he mention whether they were under sail or not, when the gale unexpectedly hit them. It is not difficult, however, to reconstruct exactly what happened since we know how such a type of ship was rigged.

The fir mast was supported by forestays and backstays leading down to the gunwales of the boat at an angle of about forty-five degrees. It was quite a short mast and required no elaborate rigging, having most probably no more than two fore-stays, two backstays, and one main backstay which led right aft in the boat. The object of this main backstay was to give the mast support where it was most needed, when the boat was under sail with a stern wind. This backstay, as we learn from the poem, was made of leather, that being the strongest type of rigging available at the time. Ropes of less importance, possibly the other mast-stays, were probably made of papyrus. Now with a mast set in a three-sided tabernacle and stayed in this manner it will have been inevitable that, if the forestays parted, the backstays—and especially the main leather backstay—will have immediately exerted their leverage, dragging the mast aft and collapsing it into the boat.

The storm that hit the black ship of Ulysses occurred quite soon after they had put the land behind them. They were, I imagine, not far out from Taormina, and therefore just about due south of the entrance to the Messina Strait. It is not a good place at the best of times. But when the wind comes from the west, hurling itself down off the mountains of Sicily, its strength is fearsome. It drops suddenly off the land and on to the sea with all the acceleration lent it by the sudden contrast in temperatures. "With westerly and south-westerly winds," warns the *Pilot*, "especially strong squalls are experienced [in this area]."

It was close on two years since Ulysses and his crew had left Troy, and the real tragedy of the shipwreck is that nothing now lay between them and their home but the comparatively short expanse of the Ionian. It is only about 250 miles from Taormina to Cephallonia and Ithaca. But with the collapse of the mast and the death of the helmsman, the ship must have immediately turned broadside to the waves. Within seconds she began to break up, and the "men were flung overboard and tossed around the black hull like sea-gulls on the waves." What more vivid image could there be of the white faces of the struggling sailors than 'sea-gulls on the waves'?

Some scholars have maintained that the whole shipwreck scene is badly described, unnatural, and in a word that it proves Homer had no knowledge of what he was talking about. Even the speed with which the vessel is overwhelmed has been considered fanciful. But here is Petronius, writing in the 1st century A.D., and describing the loss of a large passenger ship in this very same part of the Mediterranean—south of the Messina Strait somewhere between Sicily and Crotone: ". . . the sea roughened, clouds hurried up from every quarter of the sky, and the day was obscured. The sailors scattered to their posts in a panic and shortened sail before the gale. But the wind veered and drove the waves this way and that, and the helmsman was quite astray about his course. One moment we went skidding fast towards Sicily, but generally the wind came from the north off the shores of Italy, took possession of the abject ship and twirled her in all directions. Also, what brought us worse dangers even than the storm, such pitch darkness gathered and obliterated the day that the helmsman couldn't see the length of the bows . . . the storm was roaring to its height. It shattered and stripped the ship. No mast, no rudder, no rope or oar remained. The hulk tossed and tumbled at the will of the waves like a piece of rough untrimmed timber." The ship whose wreck is described by Petronius may well have been at least 250 tons, a giant compared to the open 'long-boat' of Ulysses.

Dismasted, and at the mercy of the sea, Ulysses' ship disintegrated. A great roller opened the planks, and the ribs started to go. The mast was snapped off 'close to the keel', a little above the mast-step. Ulysses at once seized the leather backstay and used it to lash the mast and keel together. There is nothing 'un-nautical' in any of this, and Ulysses' action is sensible and seamanlike. (With the strongest rope in the ship he lashes together the two strongest and most buoyant pieces of wood to make a raft for himself.) And now "the storm which had come up from the west quickly subsided"—a typical thunderstorm, in fact—"and it was followed by more wind from the south."

Once the temporary interruption caused by the storm was past, the weather reverted to the November conditions which had previously detained Ulysses and his men in their anchorage. But now he was alone, and the prophecies of Teiresias and Circe had been fulfilled. The offence of killing the sacred cattle had been expiated by the loss of the ship and the death of all his crew. Even the headstrong Eurylochus had gone, and only Ulysses was left on his improvised life-raft, drifting at the mercy of the wind and waves.

The wind had gone back into the south. What would one expect to happen to a man adrift on a raft just south of the Messina Strait, with a south wind blowing? That he would be carried by it right back into the mouth of the strait. And what one would expect to happen, given such a situation, is exactly what does happen. "Throughout the night I was carried along, and at daybreak I found myself back again by the rock of Scylla and that terrifying whirlpool. . . ."

At this point there occurs the intrusion of that mysterious fig-tree, that tree of life which overhangs the whirlpool of death. Just like Saktideva in the Indian legend, Ulysses stretches up and grasps the tree. He clings to its trunk like a bat and is saved from the dark maw of Charybdis, just as she is beginning to suck down the water of the strait.

Saktideva was saved to continue his journey to the Golden City by the self-sacrifice of the Fisher-King. Ulysses, on the other hand, has been saved by the sacrifice of all his friends and companions. He, too, will live to reach his Golden City—the rocky island of Ithaca—but it will not be for many years yet. As he clings desperately to the fig-tree, the whirlpool opens beneath him. The mast and keel which have been his salvation are sucked down out of sight into the roaring waters.

25

The Navel of the Sea

Wʜᴇɴ the whirlpool had subsided, the mast and keel and other broken timbers came floating placidly back on to the surface. Ulysses regained his raft and paddling with his hands made off down the strait. No amount of paddling would have been any use if the tide had been flowing to the north. Clearly the ease with which he escaped was due to the fact that the tide had turned and was pushing him southward, at the rate of anything up to four knots. There is no mention of any wind, so one may assume that the Sirocco which had blown him back to Charybdis must have dropped.

"Nine days of drifting followed. . . ." And now we come to one of the most mysterious passages in the whole voyage of Ulysses, his detention in the remote island of Ogygia. Ulysses, so the story goes, drifted for nine days and nights, and "on the night of the tenth day, thanks to the gods, I was washed ashore on the island of Ogygia, home of the fair Calypso. . . ."

The records of the last two world wars have shown that ship-wrecked men can indeed survive under the most terrible conditions, and for lengths of time that 19th-century scholars would have thought impossible. It is quite probable, for instance, that one man on a raft could have stayed alive for close on ten days—provided always that he had water to drink. Some form of food would have been necessary, but this would be a secondary consideration. One must assume, then, that Ulysses had had the forethought to lash some waterskins and some food to his improvised life-raft before his ship sank beneath him in the Ionian Sea. It is unthinkable that the 'wily one' will not have had these practical considerations in mind when he was left alone aboard his sinking ship. Water, then as now in many parts of the world, was carried in bladders or in goat-skins—well capable of keeping their contents intact throughout wind and weather and even submersion in the Strait of Messina. Grain and meat was also carried in hide satchels that would have preserved it. (I have eaten *biltong*, the sun-dried meat of South Africa, that had been days in the saddle-bags of our horses. It was unpalatable but life-sustaining.)

Assuming then that Ulysses really managed to keep afloat and alive on an improvised raft for nearly ten days, where was the island on which he was washed ashore? The question was debated by scholars and geographers throughout the classical period. It was, indeed, questions like this that prompted the philosopher Seneca to attack "the minutiae of the literary craft" and to jeer at the "laborious superficiality of the schools (e.g. such themes as how many rowers did Ulysses have?)." Let Seneca and all the scholars since his time have their laugh. Nevertheless let us see at this point in the *Odyssey*—and at this point alone—whether all reason deserts us.

A raft adrift on the eastern shoreline of Sicily will inevitably have had an impulse towards the south. The basic structure of this sea has not changed in many thousands of years, even though minor variations have occurred such as the diminution of the whirlpools in the Messina Strait. Ulysses will have drifted south because there is a distinct south-going current along the whole of the eastern coast of the island. "Along the eastern coast of Sicily, southward of the parallel of Monte Etna, a south-going current flows, in summer and autumn, at a rate of about 0·2 knots; this current, quite noticeable near the coast, extends from one to one and three quarters of a mile offshore; at a short distance beyond it there is usually no definite current. This south-going current seems to be caused by the south-westerly current along the southern coast of Italy impinging on the coast of Sicily in the vicinity of Monte Etna. . . ."

Now Ulysses could only have left the Messina Strait with the tide behind him, and it would not have taken long for him to be within the grip of the general coastal drift in this area. No mention is made in the *Odyssey* of the wind during this part of Ulysses' adventures so—even though it would be a convenience to assume a northerly—it is only right to forget wind directions altogether. It is quite likely that after the Sirocco and the broken weather, there will have followed some of those misty autumn days when nothing stirs but 'cats' paws' sidling back and forth over the water.

There are no islands today off the eastern coast of Sicily. There are rocks, but they are all too small even to be dignified by the name of 'islets'. There was once a small island off this coast, however, and this was Ortygia on which the city of Syracuse was built. It has been claimed, both in antiquity and since, as the Ogygia of Calypso and the scene of Ulysses' detainment for some seven years. Ortygia is a very small island connected with the mainland, at least since classical times, by a mole. Today it is at most about one cable, or 200 yards, from the mainland of Sicily. Even allowing for the fact that, with subsequent building and siltage, the distance has been reduced, Ortygia must always have been only an 'almost-island', like the home of Circe. But an 'almost-island' is just what the home of Calypso was not.

The term which is used to describe Calypso's island is 'the navel of the sea'. Ortygia on which Syracuse stands could never have been described in these words. Another thing which stands out is the fact that Ulysses was unable to escape without the help of Calypso. But if he had been marooned on Ortygia he would have been quite capable of swimming across to the shore of Sicily, for Ulysses as we know was a good swimmer. He had no difficulty in reaching his raft when it was thrown up again by Charybdis in the Messina Strait, and later in his story he was able to swim for a long time before reaching the land of the Phaeacians. Yet we find him in Calypso's island looking out across 'the desolate acres of the sea', and unable to escape until Calypso herself showed him where to find the wood and materials with which to make a raft. This can never have been the island on which Syracuse is built, even if Ortygia had ever been able to support the descriptions — 'lonely', 'in the middle of the sea', and 'well-wooded'.

There are no islands in the Ionian Sea between Sicily and the offshore islands of western Greece, so one must look further south. It is important to remember that the south-going current still flows today just as it did 3,000 years ago. A man on a raft off this shore would drift steadily southward, always provided that it was windless weather or that the Sirocco did not blow against him.

The island of Ortygia is inacceptable for the reasons shown, and there are no other islands off this coast except the minute *Isola Correnti*. This lies just off Cape Passero at the southernmost point of Sicily, and suffers from the same disadvantages as Ortygia. It is too close to the land, and again it could never have been described as 'well-wooded' or 'alone in the midst of the sea'. Beyond Sicily there is nothing else but the Maltese archipelago, and the long blue acres of the Mediterranean until one reaches the North African coast.

Malta, the nearest island to Cape Passero at the southern tip of Sicily, is about 150 miles from the Messina Strait. At a speed of 1 knot, nine days and nights plus one whole day gives a distance of 228 sea miles. At half a knot, nine days and nights plus one whole day gives 114 miles. At nearly any point then between these two possible speeds it would seem that a man, drifting on a raft from the Messina Strait, could have reached the Maltese archipelago.

The main objection which has been raised against the identification of Malta or its sister island, Gozo, with Calypso's home is that the *Odyssey* very clearly says that it was "alone in the sea." How could one call either Malta or Gozo "alone", when they are close together and surrounded by attendant islets like Comino and Filfla? This question puzzled Samuel Butler: "I have now only to find the island of Calypso, which in the *Odyssey* is called the 'navel' of the sea, a metaphor absolutely impossible of application to any but a solitary island, and prohibitive of either Gozo or Malta, or of the other two small islands of the same group. Calypso lives by herself and is cut off from everyone else— Ulysses cannot be supposed to have other islands in sight as he sits on the sea shore weeping and looking out upon the waves. . . ." Butler then goes on, in accordance with his Trapani theory of the origin of the *Odyssey*, to find Calypso's island in Pantelleria. The great objection to this is that Pantelleria lies nearly 300 miles from the Messina Strait. It is more than unlikely that Ulysses could have covered this distance on his mast-and-keel raft and survived, let alone in nine and a half days. A further argument against this identification is that the raft, after drifting south down the Sicilian coast, would then have had to alter course and drift almost due west for 150 miles. This is just possible, but highly unlikely. As we have seen, the south-going current would have carried him down Sicily, but from the southern coast of Sicily "there is usually a slight south-east going current." This current, though it would help Ulysses down to Malta, would be in quite the wrong direction for driving him towards Pantelleria.

On all grounds of meteorology, geography, and oceanography I can find no island or group of islands conceivable as Calypso's home except the Maltese archipelago. What, then, is one to make of the term, "alone in the sea", which Butler found prohibitive of Malta or Gozo? It is prohibitive certainly if the poet had ever travelled the route which he describes and seen the places concerned. But no one supposes that he had. His information came from a sailor's *Pilot*, from some navigator's mnemonics of the Mediterranean, or just conceivably from the original account of Ulysses himself which had been handed down by word of mouth over the generations.

As far as Ulysses was concerned, he might just as well have been on an island alone in the sea. Whether he was ship-wrecked on

Malta or Gozo does not matter for the moment. Whichever island it may have been, he would have been able to swim across the Comino strait to the other island—it is no difficult feat for I have done it myself, and I am a poor swimmer. Once landed on the other island (whether Gozo or Malta), he would still have found 'the barren acres of the sea' confronting him on all sides. He would have been no nearer Ithaca, and in no way better off.

I can find no ancient authority for the belief that either Malta or Gozo were the home of Calypso. "The annalists of the islands," wrote Vittorio Boron, "have also claimed Gozo as the Ogygia of Homer. . . . By this statement, no doubt, they wished to secure, like historians in the Middle Ages everywhere, a good place for their own particular country in the geography—whether real or imaginary—of the classics; and in this way, indeed, the fair Calypso has had quite twenty island homes placed at her disposal. Anyway, we find Gozo called by the Maltese the Island of Calypso, and her Grotto may there be admired today by the uncritical."

I have admired it myself, a pleasant cave in an enchanting place, but I remain as unconvinced by it as by all caves. The most one can say is "Yes, it could have been—but so could a dozen more other caves in either Malta or Gozo." I am not concerned with this piece of typical Mediterranean folk-lore. I am interested in the Maltese archipelago because it seems to me that these are the only islands to which a man on a raft could have drifted from the Messina Strait in ten days. That there is more than one island does not alter the fact that they are indeed 'alone in the sea', far from any mainland, and many miles from Ulysses' longed-for home.

Ogygia, the name given to Circe's island, has been found by some commentators to be derived from the same root as 'Oceanus', the Ocean. The mythical first ruler of the Greek city Thebes was Ogyges, and this introduces two curious facts. Firstly, the Great Flood was said to have occurred during the reign of Ogyges. Secondly, it was in Thebes that the first use of the alphabet was reputed to have been introduced into western

Europe from Phoenicia. Is there any reason to connect Malta or the Maltese archipelago with either the legend of the Flood, or the Phoenicians? There are several. The Maltese archipelago was inhabited many centuries before the basin of the Mediterranean was flooded, as is shown by the remarkable evidences of neolithic civilization on the islands. Malta is the fragment of an old land bridge that once united Italy and Africa. It is a place, therefore, where the legend of the Great Flood might well have been handed down from generation to generation. Secondly, and by far more important, there is every reason to connect Malta and its attendant island with the Phoenicians. It was the Phoenicians who first used Malta's magnificent harbours, and who kept the secret of them hidden from the Greeks for centuries.

"The first arrival of the Phoenicians [in Malta] dates from the beginning of the last millennium B.C.," writes T. D. Kendrick, "but the period of the foundation of the towns is later, that is to say, about the 7th or 8th century B.C. The island was clearly an important colony, and the Phoenician remains are of considerable interest." Malta, that is to say, was becoming very important in the Phoenician world at about the time that Homer was writing—yet it had been known to the Phoenicians for several centuries before this period.

It was the Phoenicians who first gave the island its name, Maleth or Malet—the Shelter, Haven, or Hiding Place. Centuries later, when Phoenician and Carthaginian power declined, the Greek traders who then came to Malta corrupted the Phoenician word into Melita, Honey—a product for which the island was famous. (It was known as Melita until the Arabic occupation when it gained its present name.) Now the word 'Calypso' in Greek means 'hidden' or 'hider', and the Homeric words for Calypso's isle, *Neesos Kalupsous*, can best be translated in English "The Island of the Hiding Place." *Neesos Kalupsous* is, therefore, no more than a Greek translation of 'Maleth'. Homer had heard of the Haven or Hiding Place somewhere remote in the sea, but had no idea where it was, or that it was part of a small group of islands.

Carl Kerényi in *The Gods of the Greeks* describes Calypso as one of the children of Oceanus and says that "Kalypso [stands] for the sheltering cave." She is the Goddess of the Cave, on the island of Maleth, which is the Shelter or Haven, the Hiding Place in the depths of the sea.

The curious but distinctive description of Calypso's island as being the "navel of the sea" can apply to only one place in the Mediterranean. Fifty miles south of Sicily, commanding the main channel through which all shipping between east and west must pass, the Maltese islands are almost equidistant from Gibraltar, on the one hand, and Cyprus on the other. Malta's importance as the finest harbour in the dead centre of the Mediterranean sailing-routes was readily appreciated by the Phoenicians —just as it was by Sultan Suleiman the Magnificent, over 2,000 years later, when he planned that as master of the whole Mediterranean he, or his successor, "may dictate laws, as universal lord, from that not unpleasant rock, and look down upon his shipping at anchor in its excellent harbour."

It is not surprising that the Phoenicians who first used the harbours of Malta were determined to keep the island a 'hidden place' from their rivals. There is nothing comparable to the Grand Harbour of Malta in the whole of this sea, and it is a natural harbour. It has never needed man's artifice to make it a perfect anchorage, something that was of inestimable importance in the days before men learned how to construct efficient artificial harbours. Malta was important to the early Phoenicians for another reason—it was only 200 miles from the North African coast, along which they navigated from their home ports of Tyre and Sidon. It gave them a perfect watering-place and shelter on their way north to Sicily. In later days, after the foundation of Carthage, it was ideally situated in 'the navel of the sea', either for a voyage down to North Africa, or up to their new colonies in Sicily. It is little wonder that 'Maleth' was a name to be recorded in their *Pilots*, or passed on by word of mouth from one sea-captain to another.

If, for all these reasons, Malta fulfils the role of Calypso's island, it would be too much surely to find that it had similar connections with a mother-goddess worship such as existed at Monte Circeo? But all the evidence seems to show that this was exactly what did exist in Malta, both prior to the Phoenicians' arrival in the island, and subsequently. The most striking of all the statuettes and statues which have been found during excavations in Malta are those which show the so-called 'Cabeiri' —"figures fat as Tunisian Jewesses, seated on the ground like Chinese *poussahs*. These," as W. K. R. Bedford wrote, "have assuredly more to do with Ceres than with Vulcan, with abundance and fertility than with subterranean toil. There is also preserved in the [Malta] museum an altar, and the sacred slab is ornamented with an egg-shaped figure between two volutes symbolizing the Universe."

These figures and this altar were excavated at Hagiar Kim, the Stone of Veneration, towards the end of the 19th century. They clearly connect this ancient shrine with a worship of that Mother Goddess whose shadow can be perceived to lie all over the Mediterranean prior to the ascendancy of the Greeks and Romans. "There is another large temple in good preservation scarce a quarter of a mile from Hagiar Kim, a strong evidence to the existence of a large population in the vicinity and the whole of the range of eminences which rise on the southern and western shores . . . are honeycombed by caves, dwellings, and tombs dating from the period of Phoenician occupation." Here, then, if one must look for the cave of Calypso is our place. Is it just another coincidence that one should find the Greek hero detained here by a sacred priestess who lives in a cave?

Something else links Ulysses' visit to the Pillars of Heracles at the Strait of Gibraltar with Calypso's island. This is the cult of Melkarth, or Heracles, which the Phoenicians also established in Malta. It was in Malta that a bilingual inscription was found in the 17th century, which by its Greek translation following upon the Sidonian characters helped to provide some of the first clues for the translation of the Phoenician language. In this inscription "My Lord, Melkarth, Lord of Tyre," is invoked (the Greek translation substituting "Heracles" for Melkarth).

There is a further point which seems to establish the Phoenician connection between Calypso's cave and Malta. A number of authorities have seen in Calypso a Death-Goddess—something she was almost certainly not. But the fact remains that, quite unlike the Greeks who either buried or cremated their dead, the Phoenicians were in the habit of interring them in *caves*, usually horizontally, and with their feet towards the west.

Homer has heard from one source or another of a hidden island, presided over by a goddess-priestess. Unlike Circe's island, however, where the priestess dwelt in a temple or palace, the priestess of this other island dwells in a cave. Now the principal temples of Phoenician, as well as pre-Phoenician, Malta all have a cave-like appearance, even where they are not literally excavated out of the rock. With such an abundance of clues all pointing in the one direction, I cannot doubt that Malta was the island of Calypso. It was here that Ulysses was washed ashore on his improvised raft.

Calypso

FOR seven years Ulysses was detained in the island by the fair Calypso. The number of years in itself means little, although it is just possible that it may bear some relation to the lunar cycle, and would provide a further link with the mother-goddess. The female principle whom Calypso, or the priestess, served in Malta seems to have been a double goddess (like Isis and Nephthys in Egypt), for a number of the Maltese temples are built in pairs. There is a double shrine at Borg en Nadur and another at Tal Bakkari. M. A. Murray in his *Excavations in Malta*, came to the conclusion that: "In Malta the divine pair was probably female," and describing one of the statuettes he goes on to say, "the figure stands with one arm hanging down, the other being laid across the body below the breasts. It is an attitude common to divinities (usually goddesses) in the eastern Mediterranean."

If the 'divine Calypso' who shared her couch with Ulysses for so many years did in fact look like the female statuettes which have been found on the island, one can perhaps understand his eagerness to return to the embraces of Penelope. These figures are uniformly steatopygous, with the immensely fat buttocks and thighs which the pigmies of Africa still consider to be the criterion of female beauty. Curiously enough, despite thousands of years of foreign occupation, this racial type can still be seen in the island. During the year in which I lived in the village of St. Paul on the east coast of Malta I saw 'Calypsos' every day of my life—the lady at the grocery store, the one behind the local bar, and the wife of the baker, who sat knitting all day on her doorstep. Everywhere I looked, in fact, I saw among the fertile and fruitful married women exactly the same short-legged, steato-pygous figures as the 3,000-year-old statuettes now to be seen in the Malta museum. As young girls, however, the Maltese are often slim and enchanting, and it is only after some years of marriage and child-bearing that their figures spread into such ponderous proportions.

It is noticeable that Ulysses, who seems to have been perfectly happy with Circe—indeed he had to be badgered by his companions into leaving her island—does not seem to have felt at all the same way about Calypso. Rather like Edward Lear, another solitary who visited Malta (and portrayed the island in some of his finest water-colours), Ulysses "weeps by the side of the ocean, he weeps on the top of the hill. . . ."

Perhaps it is not too flippant to suggest that the lady had lost her attractions after child-bearing, for some classical commentators maintained that Calypso bore Ulysses twin sons, Nausithous and Nausinous—Impetuous Sailor and Wily Sailor. Others credit her with having also borne him a third son, Latinus, the founder of the Latin race. It is presumably to be taken as a proof of the hero's masculinity that at no time did Ulysses father daughters—Penelope bore him Telemachus; Circe, Telegonus; and now Calypso at least one, possibly three sons.

In Greece to this day, as in other parts of the eastern Mediterranean, it is considered the worst of misfortunes not to have sons. An old fisherman in Levkas once told me that he had no children, only to be slyly reminded by the local harbour-master that he had three daughters. "I don't count females," the old man replied. But whatever misfortunes Ulysses suffered in his life, he was never accused of having fathered girls.

Despite some of the natural discontents of home-life, one feels that after his hard years at sea Ulysses might have been content to stay in the island. The description of Calypso's troglodyte home is one of the most charming passages in the poem: "The cave was sheltered by a verdant copse of alders, aspens, and fragrant cypresses, which was the roosting place of feathered creatures, horned owls and falcons and garrulous choughs, birds of the coast, whose daily business takes them down to the sea. Trailing round the very mouth of the cavern, a garden vine ran riot, with great bunches of ripe grapes: while from four separate but neighbouring springs four crystal rivulets were trained to run this way and that; and in soft meadows on either side the iris and the parsley flourished. . . ." But the water-shift and the sea-surge haunted Ulysses. He remembered the waves like glass on a dazzling morning, the scent of pitch-pine and the tar, laid thick as a sailor's finger along the keel. He could not remain for ever wedded to the earth.

If I were to consider looking for Calypso's home on Malta I would settle for somewhere on the western coast, perhaps in the region of Dingli, or near the present site of Verdala Palace. The rainfall is heavier on this side of the island, and the scenery in places is almost lush—something which comes as a surprise to the visitor who is more familiar with the barren lands around Grand Harbour, and the North African bleakness of so much of the east coast. The cliffs which stoop into the sea on the western side of the island are honeycombed with caves—from those made by neolithic man, to Phoenician burial vaults, and so on through all the centuries, right up to the caves occupied by refugees during the Second World War.

But Homer had never seen the island, and the poet is only indulging in a pleasant flight of fancy, calling up before his listeners' eyes a vision of all that is dearest in the parched eastern Mediterranean —grapes and luxuriant trees, lush pasturage and crystal springs.

With surroundings so pleasant, and after his years on the barren acres of the sea, one might have expected Ulysses to be happy. What with wine and fruit, and the good fish that still haunt these waters—tunny, *lampuki*, and the dappled mullet—a ship-wrecked sailor should have been content. Ulysses, one feels, must at some time or other, perhaps in the first year, have congratulated himself on his good fortune. Looking out from Calypso's cave, he may even have anticipated the *Careless Gallant's Song*:

"Fish dinners will make a man spring like a flea,
Dame Venus, love's Lady, was born of the Sea;
With her and with Bacchus we'll tickle the sense
For we shall be past it a hundred years hence."

But the point about the *Odyssey*, perhaps the basic essence of the poem, is that it is the story of the good 'family-man', and the good family. The poet clearly intends a contrast between the story of Agamemnon, Clytemnestra, and Orestes, (the unhappy family), and Ulysses, Penelope, and Telemachus—father, wife, and son, who each in their respective ways serve as models of domestic virtue. It is only with Circe that Ulysses for a few brief months seems to forget his duty to his family, and his kingdom. But as Sacred King to the Priestess-Goddess Calypso, he is never made to seem either happy or content.

He was wise not to believe her offers of immortality, for no doubt he knew the fate of Tithonus. Even without the gift of immortality, Ulysses will have known something of the tedium that afflicts the gods. Gazing over the hot island in summer and across the endless blue of the sea, he may have sighed with Tennyson's 'Tithonus':

"I wither slowly in thine arms
Here at the quiet limit of the world. . . ."

After seven years of exile he was saved by his ancestor Hermes, who had been despatched by Zeus to order Calypso to let Ulysses return home. Calypso's meeting with the Messenger of the Gods gives us some indication of Homer's real feelings about the immoral immortals. "When Hermes had spoken, Calypso answered with feeling: 'How cruel you are, you gods, and how unparalleled for jealousy! You cannot bear to see a goddess sleeping with a man, even if she does it without any concealment and after having made him her legitimate husband'!"

Calypso is nevertheless constrained to obey the dictates of

almighty Zeus. Although she protests that she has no ship in which to send Ulysses on his way, she is forced to promise that she will give him the means to sail home, and "such directions as will carry him safe and sound to Ithaca." After Hermes has gone, she makes her way to the seashore where she knows that she will find Ulysses. He has long given up any pretence of being happy in her island. One might describe his behaviour as ungallant in the extreme: "His eyes, as always, were wet with weeping. All the sweetness of life was flowing away in the tears he shed for his lost home. It was a long time since the Nymph had brought him any pleasure. True, at night he had to sleep with her under the roof of her cavern, but he was no more than a cold lover with a passionate woman. Always the daytime found him sitting on the rocky strand, gazing with tearful eyes across the wastes of water, tormenting himself with sighs and groans of anguish. . . ." It is not difficult to feel some sympathy with Calypso, and under the circumstances she behaves extremely well.

Without reproaching Ulysses for his ingratitude, she at once gives him the necessary directions to make his escape. Suspicious to the last, Ulysses does not hesitate to say that in suggesting he makes a raft and embarks on the high seas, the goddess may have something other than his survival in mind. His suspicion of her motives only confirms him in her affections. Anyone who has ever lived in the Levant will recognize the respect that is everywhere accorded to guile and craftiness. The qualities which are supposedly embodied in King Arthur, Charlemagne, or Abe Lincoln, are not those which are held in the greatest reverence in the eastern Mediterranean. Some of Ulysses' actions which may seem to us despicable rather than admirable, would have been viewed quite differently by Homer's audience—or, indeed, by a group of Aegean islanders to this day.

Calypso now proceeds to show Ulysses to a corner of the island where trees are growing which are suitable for shipbuilding. There are alders, poplars, and firs and—although the poet does not tell us so—I am fairly sure that it was the firs which Ulysses felled first with the 'double-bladed bronze axe' that Calypso so thoughtfully provided. He cut down twenty trees and then, with the adze and augers which Calypso had also given him. proceeded to build himself a raft. The Homeric account of the raft-building is as factual and accurate as an extract from a manual on the subject. "Twenty trees in all he felled, and lopped their branches with his axe; then trimmed them in a workmanlike manner and trued them to the line. Presently Calypso brought him augers. With these he drilled through all his planks, cut them to fit across each other, and fixed this flooring together by means of dowels driven through the interlocking joints, giving the same width to his boat as a skilled shipwright would choose in designing the hull for a broad-bottomed trading vessel. He next put up the decking, which he fitted to ribs at short intervals, finishing off with long gunwales down the sides. He made a mast to go in the boat, with a yard-arm fitted to it; and a steering oar too, to keep her on her course. And from stem to stern he fenced her sides with plaited osier twigs and a plentiful backing of brush-wood, as some protection against the heavy sea." With cloth which Calypso provided he then made a sail. After which he stepped and rigged the mast, and arranged the sheet-leads.

The whole question of Ulysses' methods and techniques was thoroughly investigated by E. H. Warre, who also produced quite a convincing drawing of the completed raft. The voyage of the famous Kon-Tiki raft has made millions of modern readers familiar with the elements of raft construction, as well as with the strength and endurance of this type of craft if it is well constructed. It remains only to say that there seems to me nothing unconvincing about the Homeric description. It is a clear and succinct account of exactly the methods which one would use to build something similar to this day.

The raft described by Homer is very akin in construction, although on a miniature scale, to the barges still used on the Nile. It is perfectly possible that the poet may have heard of such vessels from Greek sea-raiders who had been down to Egypt. Rafts of a somewhat similar type have also been used on the Euphrates since time immemorial, and the Phoenicians will certainly have been acquainted with such sailing-rafts long before the Greeks.

"Calypso does not produce a magical ship," writes H. L. Lorimer in *Homer and the Monuments,* "and Odysseus could not build an ordinary one single-handed; a raft he might in favourable circumstances achieve, and does so, apparently following the Egyptian Nile-Boat as a model. His adventures on the raft are well within what we have lately learned to be the range of human endurance; even his ordeal on the spar [from Messina to Malta] does not greatly surpass even in duration things which we know men to have undergone and lived to recount."

Many of the 19th- and early 20th-century objections to the plausibility of the voyage of Ulysses were based on ignorance. Scholars of those days had little idea what the human being can endure and survive. Just as there is nothing unseamanlike about the raft of Ulysses, so there is nothing in all his adventures on the sea which seems incredible to the survivors of our own century.

It is noticeable that the author of the *Odyssey* does not ignore those important details so often forgotten in poetry—food and drink. No sooner had Ulysses got his raft ready and dragged it down on rollers to the sea, than Calypso was at hand with his victuals. She put into his boat two leather skins, one full of wine the other of water. Here again one notices the practical touch— "It was the larger one that was full of water." Exactly! For stimulating and pleasant though wine is, it is no thirst-quencher, and a man embarking on a long raft-voyage would rather have plenty of water than plenty of wine. Calypso also gave him a leather sack full of corn, and plenty of "appetizing meats'. Sensible, like all the women in the *Odyssey*, she had also given him a good bath beforehand and a new set of robes.

Clean, and in fresh clothes, with plenty of provisions, water, and some wine—Ulysses was ready to leave. He had everything that a man could want who was setting out on a long, single-handed voyage.

27

Across the Ionian

IT was most probably summer when Ulysses left Calypso's island. It would not be too hazardous an undertaking to attempt to cross the Mediterranean on a well-built pine-log raft at that time of the year. I have sailed round Malta in an open dinghy in July, and have known of a crossing from Sicily made by two young men in a folding canvas canoe.

Calypso, true to her promise, not only enabled him to make his craft but also gave him his sailing directions. After the long and complicated instructions given him by Circe, these were simplicity itself. There was no reason why they should not have been, for all that the sailor has to do to reach Greece from Malta is to sail east. Any course between east and north-east will bring him out somewhere on the western coast of Greece, and once Ulysses reached the west coast—whether it was off the Peloponnese or further north by the islands—he knew his way home. The west coast of Greece was his native sea, and he had sailed all round the Peloponnese on his way to the Trojan war some nineteen years before. There were no Siren Rocks, no dangerous volcanoes, and no whirlpools to warn him against. Between Malta and Greece the deep Ionian holds no hazards, except the normal ones of wind and weather.

Calypso's instructions to Ulysses were that he should keep the Great Bear, or the Plough, "on his left hand as he made his way across the open sea." So long as he kept this constellation, "the only one that never bathes in Ocean's Stream," to port, or on the left of his line of advance, he would reach his home. This was absolutely true, and if one were to set off from Malta to Greece today in a small boat without any compass this is exactly what one would do. By keeping the constellation of the Plough on one's left hand, one would automatically be sailing east.

Another and not unimportant point arises from these instructions. A sailor, and this I am sure must have held true at any period of the world's history, considers everything with relation to his line of advance. It is this which is important to him, and if you instructed a modern yachtsman, say, "To keep such-and-such a star or light to port," he would not think that you meant *"Anywhere* on the left, from ahead to almost astern." In general practice he would steer so as to hold the object at about forty-five degrees from his line of advance. Now, as we have seen, it was quite enough for Ulysses to get back to Greece if he merely sailed east. But his instructions, were in fact, a little more explicit: He was to keep the Plough "on his left hand," which will almost certainly have meant then, as it would now, somewhere to port of the bow, probably about forty-five degrees. This was an even more useful sailing direction, for it gave him a course of north-east—and the Ionian islands lie north-east from Malta.

So Ulysses left the island. Taking a general direction from the sun by day, and a fairly accurate direction from the Plough at night, he headed out across the Ionian Sea. Calypso, one may presume, having concealed her grief at his departure, returned to her sacred grotto where her handmaids were awaiting her. There, no doubt, two or even three small half-Greek boys were playing about in the sand.

It was with a "warm and gentle breeze," Calypso's final gift, that Ulysses left the island and "with a happy heart he set his sail to catch the wind." The wind is more than likely to have been a westerly, for the highest percentage of winds off Malta blow from this quarter in summer. A westerly will have been ideal for the course he had to sail, giving him either a quartering or a stern wind. The voyage passed uneventfully, and one must assume that for long periods of time, most probably during the day, Ulysses lashed the steering oar while he had a sleep. At night it was essential for him to keep awake in order to steer by the Plough. But so long as the westerly held, he could have hauled down his sail while he took a rest, for there are no real currents in the central Ionian except those set up by wind action. These local currents can be quite strong if the wind has been in one quarter for a number of days, so he could easily have slept while the gentle easterly drift eased him on his way towards Greece. Homer, in fact, says that "he never slept," but kept his eyes on the stars and particularly the Great Bear. But I take this as confirmation that he did his real sailing at night when he could navigate more accurately. No man could keep awake for seventeen days and nights, and that was the length of time which it took Ulysses to reach the western shores of Greece from Malta. ". . . For seventeen days he held his way, and on the eighteenth there came into view the shadowy mountains of the Phaeacians' country."

I am confident that the land of the Phaeacians was Corcyra, or Corfu as it is now better known. Just assuming for the moment this to be so, let us look at the raft voyage in terms of wind, weather, and the distance from Malta to Corfu. Now the direct course for the voyage is north-east from Grand Harbour, Malta, to a point off the north-western coast of Corfu. The distance is 330 sea miles. Clearly one cannot calculate the speed of a raft for which one has no hull—or sail—dimensions, no knowledge of exactly what courses were steered, and no information as to the wind-strength and direction. But, on the limited data available— the length of time taken by Ulysses on the voyage, and the distance between Malta and Corfu—then a seventeen-day voyage for a course of 330 miles gives a distance made good of a little under twenty miles per day. That is to say, Ulysses' raft has an average speed for the whole voyage of about three-quarters of a knot.

This is slow, but perfectly reasonable, for a small raft with one man on board, and one somewhat inefficient sail. Clearly there must have been times when the raft was making two knots or more, while at other times it may well have been almost stopped, or even losing ground. If Calypso had instructed Ulysses to keep the Great Bear on his *right* hand, or to steer straight for it, then one could indeed have said that "all this takes place in fairyland." It would have been absurd if Ulysses had made the voyage in five days. It would have been most improbable that he could have taken as long as fifty—even if a small raft could have accommodated enough water and stores for so long a voyage. But seventeen days is highly likely from every point of view.

"The land looked like a shield laid on the misty sea. . . ."—a miraculous description of Corfu as one approaches it. But no sooner did Ulysses get within sight of the Ionian islands than, as before, the weather broke. It is clear from what follows that when he sighted Corfu, he was somewhere to the north of the island, probably in the Faro-Corfu Channel, which is always a dangerous place when the Bora blows. I have discussed the weather conditions in this area already, so there is no need to say any more than that thunderstorms, squalls, and sudden gales are a feature of this part of the Ionian.

Poseidon, we are told, had been on a visit to the Ethiopians and was returning to Olympus, when he saw Ulysses on his raft drawing near to the land of the Phaeacians. The Sea God knew that this was the place where Ulysses was "destined to bring to an end his long ordeal," so he immediately raised a great storm. "East Wind and South Wind and the violent West all combined together. . . ."—So much, perhaps, for poetic licence. But the line "From the North came a white squall, rolling before it a huge sea" returns us to probability. The most dangerous wind in this part of the Ionian is the Bora, the north wind that blows all the way down the Adriatic from Trieste (where I have known them rig safety-lines in the city streets to prevent people being blown off their feet).

In the confusion, a mountainous wave sweeps down on the raft of Ulysses, the steering-oar is torn from his hands, the mast, yard-arm, and sail go overboard, and he himself is swept into the sea. He swims frantically after his raft and it is fortunate for him that the sail has gone, or he would have known the horror of watching his one chance of salvation disappearing away from him down-wind. But he manages to regain the raft and crouches there, "squatting amidships where he felt safe from immediate death." He is now at the mercy of the wind and the waves, but luckily he is still within sight of the coast.

At this point in the story Ulysses is saved by the intervention of Leucothea, the White Goddess, a marine divinity possibly associated with the flashing 'white' of the wave crests when the sea runs high. "Strip off your clothes," she tells him, "and take this veil and wind it round your waist. Then swim for the shore." The goddess appropriately enough appears in the disguise of a sea-mew. Having given him her veil and her advice, she dives back again into the sea—just as a gull seems to do when the lift of a wave carries it out of one's sight. Although the magic veil is no more than a poetic touch, the White Goddess's advice is sound enough by any standards. The shore is in sight, his raft will soon break up, and the best thing for Ulysses to do is to take off his heavy robes. They have already been described as "weighing him down" when he was washed off the raft. Ulysses, it seems quite clear, has decided that he had better get out of his waterlogged clothes and swim for the shore.

He is just on the point of doing this when he has second thoughts and, considering how far away the land looks, decides to remain on his raft as long as possible. He will stay with it until it begins to break up, naturally hoping that before this happens he will have been carried a little closer to the coast. But only a few minutes later a huge wave rears itself over his raft and bursts aboard. Under the impact of the collapsing water, the dowels and joints which hold the planks together give way. As the raft disintegrates Ulysses throws off his robes, winds the veil around him, and lays fast hold on one of the planks.

The initial violence of the storm is over. The confused seas subside, and the wind comes steady from the north. For two days and nights Ulysses drifts before it on his plank. "But on the morning of the third day there was a beautiful dawn, the wind dropped, and a dead calm fell on the sea." Now he will have known the wonderful sensation of the sun warm upon his back, and of his water-crinkled skin reviving as the salt dried white on his body. Even so his troubles were not at an end, for the land towards which the swell was driving him was steep-to and rocky. There was no beach or cove where he could land.

The heavy swell left over by the gale was thundering against an iron-bound coast. Explosions of spray threw drifting mist veils into the air, and ahead he could see jagged rocks fringing a sheer cliff. He was already getting into the boom-and-sizzle of the surf, feeling the undertow plucking beneath him. A bursting roller lifted him forward and he was carried in towards the rocks. Striking out on his own (presumably having abandoned his plank) he managed to break clear of the wave, and to lay hold of a large rock which jutted out into the sea a little beyond the shoreline. A few seconds later, as the greater roller swept back from the coast, he was torn from the rock and carried seaward by the undertow. "Pieces of skin stripped from his strong hands were left sticking to the rock, like the pebbles that stick to the suckers of an octopus when he is hauled from his hole in the rocks. . . ."

The backwash of the roller carried Ulysses well clear of the breakers. Wisely deciding to avoid this treacherous part of the land he swam down the coast, always keeping to seaward of the heaving surf. Presently he saw a change in the surface of the sea ahead of him—a different feeling, no doubt, in the water on his body. It was the coolness of a stream flowing out into the sea. Now wherever a river runs into the sea there is a clean entrance to the land; and wherever a river enters the sea, its current will flatten the waves round about.

Ulysses swam landwards into the mouth of the sweet, freshwater stream. He was safe at last. After nineteen years he set foot once more on one of the Ionian islands.

28

The Land of the Phaeacians

"THE land looked like a shield laid on the misty sea. . . ." Such is the description of Scheria, home of the Phaeacians, as first seen by Ulysses from his raft. The words could never have been applied to an island as large, say, as Sicily. They suggest that the whole of the island is in sight, and that the sea frames it on either side. Equally, the term could never be applied to Ustica, Stromboli, Monte Circeo, or any of the other islands so far encountered by Ulysses. Ustica suggests, perhaps, a helmet; Stromboli is a cone of fire; and Monte Circeo a breast. 'A shield' suggests a gradual curve, rising to a main central boss, and sloping away all around. This is exactly what Corfu does look like when approached from the west or north-west, with Mount Pandocrator (nearly 3,000 feet high) forming the boss of the shield. Corfu was also known in antiquity as Drepanon, the Sickle, for it lies in a half-moon shape over against the Albanian coast. I have sailed down to Corfu from the heel of Italy and can confirm the Homeric simile. It is as accurate as it is evocative.

Ulysses, as the poem makes abundantly clear, made his landfall after crossing the Ionian Sea somewhere to the north of the island. Now anywhere north of Corfu is a most treacherous place, for it is right in the mouth of the Adriatic, and when the Bora blows, a violent sea and a huge swell roll down to hurl themselves against the island. It was under exactly these circumstances that the raft of Ulysses was wrecked, and he himself swept away to come ashore first of all on one of the many rocks that fringe the north-western coast of the island. I suspect that the sheer cliffs which are described may well have been Akra Angelokastro which, as the *Admiralty Pilot* remarks, "rises from the sea in bold precipitous cliffs." The whole of this part of the coastline is starred with off-lying rocks and dangers, and with minute spray-whited islets.

The decision of Ulysses to keep well outside the line of breaking surf is typical of his common sense. There had been a gale blowing from the north for several days. The surface current will therefore have helped to sweep Ulysses southward down the island coast. Naturally, he swam with the current, and after an unspecified length of time he found himself near the mouth of a small river. The river is one of the easiest things to find in the whole *Odyssey*. It is easy because small rivers or even streams are so rare in this part of the world that any mention of one is a clue that not even Dr. Watson could overlook.

The northern coast of Corfu is distinguished by sheer cliffs which are fringed by many rocks. Homer now describes a stream some way further south from this hostile stretch of coast. The stream has 'never-failing pools', and it enters the sea at a point where there is an attractive beach. Ulysses, as we know, having dragged himself ashore and fallen asleep, is woken next day by laughter and women's voices. Nausicaa and her maidens have come to the stream to wash clothes. Then they spread them on the pebbles to dry and, having finished their work, proceed to play ball on the beach.

Just twelve miles south of Akra Angelokastro, the north-western cape of Corfu, the land swings round into a gentle bay, and at the head of this bay the Ermones flows out into the Ionian Sea. "Ormos Ermones, the entrance to which is about half a mile wide, lies close northward of Akra Ayios Yeoryios; a small stream flows through a fertile valley into the head of this bay. . . ." It is one of the most enchanting and idyllic places in the Mediterranean and it is the only place in Corfu which could correspond with the Homeric description. Furthermore, this is just where a man would be washed ashore with a northerly swell behind him, for the current would sweep him round safely into the bay. No one in their senses would try to land on the north-western part of Corfu under the conditions described, for they would be dashed to pieces. But where could one find a better place to come ashore than in the Bay of Ermones—in the mouth of a stream, and with a safe beach at hand!

With his arrival on the island of Scheria, the long travail of Ulysses is really over. At the same time it is important for all my geographical conclusions that the identification of Scheria with Corfu should be correct. Having sailed here across the Ionian, having approach the island from the north, and having at a later period sailed all down the western coast of Corfu—and indeed right round the island—I have no doubts whatever that this is the land of the Phaeacians. At the same time it is reassuring to find that I have ancient authority on my side. The voice of antiquity is almost as unanimous about Scheria being Corfu as it is about the Messina Strait being the home of Scylla and Charybdis—or about Troy having existed exactly where Schliemann subsequently found it.

Some scholars are as reluctant to accept the simple version of things as are the followers of the rancid Baconian heresy. Thucydides, however, had no doubts about Scheria having been Corfu, nor did Strabo. More recently, Alexander Shewan has written: ". . . there is in the Homeric text no real reason for believing that there is anything supernatural about Scheria or the Phaeacians. Here I shall urge that the picture is not imaginary, that the poet was describing a people who dwelt on earth, and that Bérard is right in locating them, where the ancients put them, on the island of Corcyra." I maintain that if there is anything 'supernatural' about Nausicaa, then we might as well throw all the literature of the world on the fire.

Olive trees abound in Ermones Bay—and it was under the shelter of an olive that Ulysses dragged himself and fell asleep. The basins into which the river Ermones plunges were used in comparatively recent times for watermills, but they must always have been used by women for the family washing. I have clambered down all the way by these basins to reach the beach and the mouth of the river. It is a sand and shingle beach, and this, I feel sure, is where Nausicaa and her maidens laid out their clothes to dry under the hot Ionian sun.

The city of the Phaeacians lies just as it was described by Nausicaa to Ulysses, "with an excellent harbour on each side and approached by a narrow causeway." It is about seven miles away on the eastern coast of Corfu. There one finds the two natural harbours on either side of Garitsa, the modern suburb of Corfu. One of them is suitable for the summer months, and the other sheltered at all seasons of the year. And it was near here, in the long-vanished palace of King Alcinous, that Ulysses told the story of his wanderings.

Aided by Nausicaa—the most enchanting young woman in all history—Ulysses, the Sacker of Cities, the Wanderer, and the archetype of all explorers, is welcomed and entertained in her father's court. From here he is assured of his passage home in one of the Phaeacians' ships. The vessel in which he is to return to Ithaca is clearly something much larger than the one in which he has wandered the central and western seas of the Mediterranean. She has fifty-two oarsmen (twenty-six a side) but she is similar in being 'black', or tarred, in the leather thongs for the oars, and in her white sail.

Whether the Phaeacians were an early Phoenician colony, as some have maintained, does not affect my belief that in Corfu we have the Homeric Scheria. It is certain that Corfu, at the meeting-point of the Adriatic and the Ionian, commanding the strait between the island and Albania, and with access to the route to southern Italy, will always have been—as it was in classical times—the most important island in this part of the world. For what other reason, indeed, did the British make it the capital of their Ionian confederation in the 19th century? Corfu is fertile and fruitful beyond the measure of any of the other Ionian islands, and there is nothing in the Homeric description of Scheria's beauties and natural luxuriance that could not be said about Corfu to this day.

Restored to health, Ulysses boards the ship that King Alcinous has put at his disposal. After all his years of wandering and hardship, having been commander of a squadron of twelve ships, and finally reduced to a shipwrecked sailor alone in the world, he is about to be returned to his beloved Ithaca. "He lay down quietly, while the crew settled to their benches like men born to the work, and they cast off the rope from the pierced stone that secured it." A passenger for the first time in his life, Ulysses relaxed and let others do the sailing and the navigating. A wonderful deep sleep, "the counterfeit of death," sealed his eyes as the oarsmen bent to their task. The great ship, more like the galleys of the Phoenicians than the simple Viking long-boats that Ulysses knew, swept down the channel between Corfu and the mainland.

They passed Paxos and Antipaxos, small grey humps in the dark—islands where the knotted olives clung to the harsh soil like wrestlers. Centuries later, in the reign of Tiberius, the pilot of a ship bound for Italy heard off Paxos the words which proclaimed the death of the pagan world. The pilot's name was Tammuz, and as he coasted past here in the still night a voice called out to him "Tammuz! Tammuz! Great Pan is dead!" From that moment onwards:

"The Oracles are dumb;
  No voice or hideous hum
  Runs through the arched roof in words deceiving. . . "

But when the sleeping Ulysses passed this way, the gods still spoke out of every cave and rock. They revealed themselves in the flight of birds, in the way the mist lifted off a mountain, in the dolphin and the flashing wave, and in every mood and movement of the sea. Ulysses himself was fulfilling an oracle in this return to Ithaca, "alone, aboard a stranger's ship, after twenty years of absence."

They neared the white cliff at the end of the promontory of Levkas, and then there opened up before them the narrow channel between Ithaca and Cephallonia. They altered course to port to reach the harbour on the eastern coast of Ithaca. The night began to yield before the dawn, and off the craggy island there came the scent of pine trees and damp grass. "When the bright star, that heralds the tender dawn, lifted in the sky," the Phaeacians ran their ship ashore in the Bay of Phorkys on Ithaca.

Following the most likely route from the ancient harbour of Corfu, inside Paxos and Antipaxos islands, and through the Levkas-Ithaca channel, the distance is about seventy miles. A large galley would have had no difficulty in making this passage over-night. We do not know exactly when they left Corfu, but it was clearly some time in the evening, for the sun had just set when Ulysses appealed to King Alcinous to send him on his way. Bearing in mind the south-going current which normally flows in this area, and the prevailing north wind, a twelve-hour passage in a fast galley is quite feasible. The Phaeacians not only rowed, but also set their sail. With the northerly wind behind them as well as the current, they could easily have made the necessary six or seven knots.

The Phaeacians laid the sleeping hero on the sand in the Bay of Phorkys. Safe at last, in the twentieth year since he had left Penelope and the infant Telemachus behind him, Ulysses was on Ithaca again.

After the completion of their goodwill mission the Phaeacians manned their ship and set off back to their own island. But just as they were nearing the harbour of Scheria, Poseidon, vindictive to the last, turned their boat into stone for having given assistance to his old enemy Ulysses. You can still see Pondikonisi, Mouse Island, if you have a mind for such stories, for it lies just off the entrance to the ancient Phaeacian harbour. If one looks out towards it in the evening, just as the sun is sliding behind the hills of Corfu, the illusion that it is a ship making for the safety of the bay is very strong. But people have managed to find the petrified boat of the Phaeacians in many other places. Samuel Butler found it off Trapani, and it is only natural that certain small islets should have suggested petrified boats—even to those who were not on the look-out for them.

When Ulysses finally awoke he saw the hill-paths of his home, the indented bays, and the high, wooded peak of Mount Neriton. He had yet to meet Penelope, to stand side by side with Telemachus, and to revenge himself upon the suitors. But his voyage was over. With his scarred hands, his boar-wounded thigh, his jutting beard, and his indomitable heart, he stands there on the scant soil of his native island—Ulysses found.

The Flowers of
the Sea

THE end of the *Odyssey* leaves Ulysses in triumph, with the suitors killed, and the Ithacans accepting his authority. He is reunited with Penelope, and with Telemachus and old Laertes. The hero has mounted his pedestal, and it would seem that no more need be said about him. "He lived happily ever after. . . ." But the story of Ulysses, the idea of the Great Wanderer, so obsessed men's minds that they were unwilling to let him rest. Consequently his old age and death were matters that engaged the attention of innumerable commentators, mythographers, and also great poets.

There is nothing in the Homeric account to suggest that Ulysses had anything other than a happy and peaceful old age. When Teiresias spoke to him across the dark trench at the end of the world he prophesied that "Death will come to you in his gentlest form, out of the sea. When Death comes, you will be tired, after a comfortable old age, and surrounded by a prosperous people. This is the truth that I tell you."

But according to some later story-tellers, Ulysses was killed by Telegonus, Circe's son, who had landed in Ithaca in search of his father but failed to recognize him when he saw him. (Here we have something parallel to the Oedipus legend, since Telegonus was afterwards supposed to have married Penelope.) According to yet another legend, Ulysses in later years was banished from Ithaca to the mainland where he died. None of these additions to the story need concern us, for they have no bearing on the

Ulysses who made the great voyage and who returned to triumph in his island kingdom.

It is only when the later invention springs from a great genius that one need pay any attention to embroideries on the *Odyssey*. Here I would echo the words of Leigh Hunt: "Talking the other day with a friend [Keats] about Dante, he observed, that whenever so great a poet told us anything in addition or continuation of an ancient story, he had a right to be regarded as classical authority. For instance, said he, when he tells us that characteristic death of Ulysses in one of the books of his *Inferno*, we ought to receive the information as authentic, and be glad that we had more news of Ulysses than we looked for. . . ."

Dante, in his descent into the Inferno, found Ulysses among the Counsellors of Fraud. Among the hero's listed sins was the fact that he had carried off the Palladium by trickery out of Troy, that he had invented the stratagem of the Wooden Horse, and that he had lured Achilles away from the island of Skyros. Nevertheless Ulysses was a figure for whom Dante clearly felt the greatest regard, and the passage where Dante meets him in Hell is one of the finest in the whole *Divine Comedy*. It influenced Tasso and Tennyson, and helped to turn Ulysses for all time into the archetype of the Eternal Wanderer, the Questing Spirit of Man.

Dante sees amid the flames two peaks of fire twisting and turning together, one of them is Diomedes who helped Ulysses to carry off the Palladium from Troy, and the other is the hero himself. He is represented as the 'loftier horn' amid the flames.

> "Then of that age-old fire the loftier horn
> Began to mutter and move, as a wavering flame
> Wrestles against the wind and is over-worn;
>
> And, like a speaking tongue vibrant to frame
> Language, the tip of it flickering to and fro
> Threw out a voice and answered. . . ."

The tongue of fire that is Ulysses tells Dante how he was detained twelve months by Circe near Gaeta, and how, after his return home:

> "No tenderness for my son, nor piety
> To my old father, nor the wedded love
> That should have comforted Penelope
>
> Could conquer in me the restless itch to rove
> And rummage through the world exploring it,
> All human worth and wickedness to prove."

He put to sea again and sailed westward. He passed Sardinia, touched the Moroccan coast, and finally reached Spain and the Pillars of Hercules. He sailed out into the Atlantic Ocean and turned southward down the coast of Africa. Dante, writing in the 14th century with all its new geographical knowledge, was able to describe how the Southern Cross lifted at night above the horizon, and how the Pole Star, which had always before been Ulysses' guide, sank out of sight. Ever southward Ulysses sailed, until at last the mountain of the Earthly Paradise hove up on the horizon ahead of his dark boat.

> "Then we rejoiced; but soon we had to weep,
> For out of the unknown land there blew foul weather,
> and a whirlwind struck the forepart of the ship:
>
> And three times round she went in a roaring smother
> With all the waters; at the fourth, the poop
> Rose, and the prow went down, as pleased Another,
>
> And over our heads the hollow seas closed up."

One must agree with Keats, and with Dante, and with Tasso, and with Tennyson that such seems a fitting end for Ulysses. Whatever his faults—and they were many—he was never a man to "rust unburnish'd, not to shine in use!"

From the demi-god, worshipped in classical times on his native

Ithaca, he was to become the symbol of man's aspirations for knowledge. One sees the loom of his gigantic shadow behind innumerable artists. From the Romantic Revolution onwards, Ulysses becomes the figure or the image against which men measure themselves. Poets as remote from one another in time and temperament as Byron and Matthew Arnold, Baudelaire and Rimbaud, catch something of his voice. Byron with melancholy:

"So, we'll go no more a-roving
so late into the night. . . ."

Arnold with envy:

"Yet on he fares, by his own heart inspired."

Baudelaire with admiration:

"Mais les vrais voyageurs sont ceux-là seuls qui partent
pour partir. . . ."

And Rimbaud with the certainty of one who means to emulate him:

"Mais pourquoi regretter un éternel soleil, si nous
sommes engagés à la découverte de la clarté divine—
loin des gens qui meurent sur les saisons."

Ulysses has become a part of all human consciousness, and even those who may never have read the *Odyssey* have felt him lean over their shoulder. "To be sure," wrote Admiral Boscawen during the Seven Years War, "I lose the fruits of the earth, but then I am gathering the flowers of the sea." It is not surprising that sailors throughout all ages, and in every country, have found a model in Ulysses. But he has become the embodiment of far more complex and diverse aspirations than the simple conquest of the sea. In the words of Henri Bergson, "I only know one way of finding out how far one can go, and that is by setting out and getting there."

Even in the field of human emotions—one which Ulysses was

inclined to treat with a blunt sailor-like disrespect—one seems to catch an echo of his spirit. "Circumstances are of little importance," wrote Benjamin Constant, "Character is everything; breaking with objects and other beings is of no avail—you cannot break with yourself. You can change your situation; but into each situation you carry the torment from which you had hoped to rid yourself; and, as you do not mend your ways when changing scenes, you discover that you have merely added remorse to regrets and sins to suffering."

Whatever the mythological aspects of Ulysses and of his voyage, my only purpose has been to try and show that the voyage which is described by Homer had its origins in fact. I have spent most of the best years of my life sailing the Mediterranean and I never intended to make an incursion into the sacred grove of classical studies. It merely happened that during these years I found myself time and again seeing harbours, anchorages, islands, and stretches of coastline, through other eyes than mine. At times the sensation was as uncanny as if I had suddenly found a pair of strange binoculars put before my eyes—to give me a new, un-usual, and detailed view of something that I had previously thought familiar. Imagination! Yes, but then I hold, unfashion-ably perhaps, that "The imagination may be compared to Adam's dream,—he awoke and found it truth."

Ulysses had known the click of light in olive branches far from Ithaca, the black beaks of the dolphins as they rose with rasping sighs alongside his boat, winds of fig and grape, and the stars big as moons on hot, still nights. He had heard the Sirens singing across the cat's fur of an autumn sea. He had known the sand dimpled like hand-beaten copper on lonely islands, and looking down from his boat into the waters of uncharted anchorages had seen among the weed-wigged rocks the movement of strange-coloured fish. He had felt Sicilian amber smooth between his fingers, and had known both as lover and as sacred King the mysteries of the Beast-Goddess and of the great Earth-Mother.

"For every desire has enriched me more than the possession —always false—of the very object of my desire." I do not believe that he was content. One night they slid the black ship down into the water and unloosed the mooring rope from the pierced stone. They turned the eyes of the ship towards the west, and sitting all in order they smote the grey sea-water.

Select Bibliography

Bérard, V., *Did Homer Live?* trans. B. Rhys, 1931.

—— *Introduction à l'Odyssée*, 3 vols., 1924.

—— *Les Navigations d'Ulysse*, 5 vols., 1929.

Browne, H., *Handbook of Homeric Study*, 1905.

Butler, S., *The Authoress of the Odyssey*, 1897.

Dörpfeld, W., *Alt-Ithaka*, 1927.

Farrington, B., *Samuel Butler and the Odyssey*, 1929.

Finley, M. I., *The World of Odysseus*, 1956.

Gell, Sir W., *Topography and Antiquities of Ithaca*, 1807.

Graves, R., *The Greek Myths*, 1955.

Gruppe, P., *Griegische Mythologie*, 1906.

Guerber, H. A., *The Myths of Greece and Rome*, 1929.

Harrison, J. E., *Myths of the Odyssey—Art and Literature*, 1882.

Hole, R., *Essay on the Character of Ulysses*, 1807.

Jebb, Sir R., *Introduction to Homeric Studies*, 1887.

Kerényi, C., *The Gods of the Greeks*, 1951.

Larousse Encyclopaedia of Mythology, 1959.

Leaf, W., *Homer and History*, 1915.

Lorimer, H. L., *Homer and the Monuments*, 1950.

Page, D. L., *The Homeric Odyssey*, 1942.

Rodd, Sir R., *Homer's Ithaca*, 1927.

Schliemann, H., *Ithaque, la Péloponése, Troie*, 1869.

Shewan, A., *Homeric Essays*, 1935.

Taylor, E. G. R., *The Haven-Finding Art*, 1956.

Thomson, J. A. K., *Studies in the Odyssey*, 1914.

Wace, A. J. B. and Stubbings, F. H., Ed. *A Companion to Homer*, 1962.

Webster, T. B. L., *From Mycenae to Homer*, 1958.

Whitman, C. H., *Homer and the Homeric Tradition*, 1958.

Admiralty, Hydrographic Dept. *Mediterranean Pilot*, vols. I-IV, 1951-7.

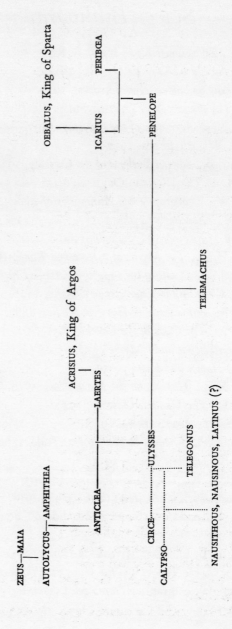

Genealogy of Ulysses

Chronology of Ulysses' Voyage

Fall of Troy circa 1200 B.C.
1st Year of Voyage

Ulysses leaves Troy and raids Ismarus,   Spring?
city of the Cicones, in Thrace.

A gale from the north drives him southward through the Aegean.

He attempts to double Cape Malea and
head north for Ithaca, but is swept "for
nine days" across the Mediterranean.

"On the tenth day" he reaches the Land
of the Lotus-Eaters.

He leaves there almost immediately, and   Summer
sails to the Land of the Cyclopes, making
his landfall on Goat Island.

Encounter with Polyphemus, six of his
crew are killed.

He leaves Goat Island and comes to the
Island of Aeolus where he stays for a
month.

He leaves with a favourable west wind,
and "for nine days" he sails until "on the
tenth" he is in sight of his homeland.

Driven back from Greece by adverse
winds he returns to Island of Aeolus.

"For six days" his squadron rows across
Mediterranean, and "on the seventh"
reaches the Land of the Laestrygonians.

All the ships are destroyed and all the men
killed by the Laestrygonians, with the
exception of Ulysses' ship and crew.

"In due course", he reaches the island   Autumn
home of Circe.

He and his men spend the winter ashore.   End of 1st Year

In Circe's island.	*2nd Year of Voyage* Spring
To the Pillars of Hercules and back to Circe's island.	Summer
He passes the Sirens and the Wandering Rocks.	Autumn (September?)
Scylla and Charybdis.	
He reaches "a sheltered cove" in the Island of the Sun.	
"For a whole month the South Wind blew, and after that nothing but southerly and easterly winds."	
He leaves the Sun-God's island and his ship is sunk in a storm.	Late Autumn/early Winter
"All through the night" he is carried on his improvised life-raft back to Scylla and Charybdis.	
He is swept clear of Scylla and Charybdis, and "nine days of drifting" follow. "On the tenth" day he is washed ashore on Calypso's island.	*End of 2nd Year*
Ulysses is detained in Calypso's island for seven years.	*End of 9th Year*
He leaves Calypso's island on a raft and for "seventeen days" sails on his way. "On the eighteenth day" he sights Scheria, Land of the Phaeacians. His raft is wrecked and "for two days and nights" he is adrift on a log. "On the morning of the third day" he is washed ashore "in the mouth of a fast-running stream."	*10th Year of Voyage* Summer (?)
Ulysses leaves Scheria and after one night's journey is restored to Ithaca.	

218

APPENDIX II

Ithaca and Levkas

PROFESSOR P. GARDINER in an essay "The Troad and Phrygia" wrote of Homeric geography that "the investigator may feel at times as though he were climbing a hill of sand or wading through a deep morass. . . ." Nowhere is this sensation more acute than when one comes to the Ithaca-Levkas problem. The fact remains that no such problem existed for the ancients. They accepted without reserve that the home of Ulysses was the island which they themselves called Ithaca, and which is called Thiaki in modern Greek. Since my book is concerned only with Homeric geography in terms of the hero's voyage, I have omitted any reference to Ithaca and its particular geographical problems. But it is true to say that, until the arrival on the scene of the eminent scholar and archaeologist Dr. W. Dörpfeld early in this century, no one had even suspected that there was any 'Ithaca problem'.

The basis of Dörpfeld's theory (that the Homeric Ithaca was really the island now known as Levkas) rested on certain discrepancies in the *Odyssey*. These led him to conclude that, at some time before the classical era, pressure of invaders from the north had driven the old inhabitants of Levkas (Ithaca) to the south, where they settled in Ithaca (Same). They thereupon gave Same the name of their former home. The greatest weakness of this theory is that it is necessary to presuppose these 'invaders from the north', for whom there is no historical evidence. If this is conceded, it must be admitted that Dörpfeld's theory that Levkas was the Homeric Ithaca, and Ithaca was the Homeric Same, has some attractions to it. It has had sufficient impact on modern scholarship for H. L. Lorimer to write in *Homer and the Monuments*: "When we turn to the *Odyssey* itself we find that the account which Odysseus gives of his home is in every vital respect inapplicable to the island which as far back as we can trace its history has borne the name of Ithaca, or, in modern form, Thiaki. Only the forces of tradition and prejudice could have sustained the orthodox identification wholly unmoved by Dörpfeld's contention that Homer's Ithaca was Leucas. . . ."

The arguments and objections have been summarized by H. Browne in his *Handbook of Homeric Studies*.

" 1. Those who defend the Homeric description of the island point out many congruities while they perhaps slur over difficulties. . . .

" 2. Homer mentions four islands: three (Zacynthus, Same, Ithaca) can be recognized without difficulty—there still remains Dulichium, and various attempts have been made (not perfectly satisfactory) to decide its identity. . . .

"3. Ithaca is said to be the most westerly of the group: this is not absolutely correct, but the error can be fairly accounted for in a case where maps are still unknown.

" 4. It is said to be "low-lying" ($\chi\theta\alpha\mu\acute{\alpha}\lambda\eta$) a more serious error.

" 5. A rocky islet is said to lie between Ithaca and Same; and this cannot be satisfactorily identified."

Among British scholars who were won over by Dörpfeld's theory was Walter Leaf, whose arguments can be followed in his *Homer and History*. Opposing him, among others, was Sir Rennell Rodd, whose book *Homer's Ithaca* I find the most convincing of all the many essays, books, and theses which have been thrown up by Dörpfeld's *Alt-Ithaka*. Like Sir Rennell Rodd, I have spent a number of weeks sailing round and about Ithaca and the near-by islands, and confess myself a complete traditionalist. I cannot agree with H. L. Lorimer that "the account which Odysseus gives of his home is in every vital respect inapplicable to [Ithaca]." On the contrary, in every vital respect Ithaca seems to me to meet the Homeric requirements. (I have described my impressions of the island in my book *The Greek Islands*.)

It is never wise to press local identifications too far, but in my opinion the modern Thiaki meets almost all of the Homeric requirements. Even over the much-vexed question of Asteris Island I find the modern Daskalio, in the channel between Ithaca and Cephallonia, every bit as convincing as Dörpfeld's identification of Arkudi Island with the Homeric Asteris. Levkas was a promontory, as far as we know, until the Corinthians bored a channel through the isthmus in the 7th century B.C. Strabo, Thucydides, Polybius, Livy, and Pliny were of this opinion and, in more recent times, so was Bérard.

The problem raised by the fact that Ithaca is referred to as "low-lying" is far from insoluble. "Low-lying" the island does seem to be, when you sail up from the south and see Ithaca against the high peaks of Cephallonia on the one hand, and the promontory of Levkas beyond. (This has been well illustrated by W. H. D. Rouse in his *Homer*, plate facing page 120.) On the other hand, Levkas could neve conceivably have been described in the words of Telemachus: "There is no room for horses to exercise in Ithaca, nor are there any meadows. It is a pasture land for goats and more pleasant than those lands where horses roam." Levkas has wide flat plains ideal for horses. This description could, in fact, only fit Ithaca-Thiaki out of the main islands in the group. Another reason which Dörpfeld gives for his identification of Levkas with the Homeric Ithaca, is that the recurrent line "In what vessel did you come here, for I cannot suppose that you came here on foot?" could only apply to Levkas. (It is so close to the mainland that a traveller could practically wade across the channel.) I fear that this is an example of the Germanic inability to see a joke. How often during the last war did I hear sailors in harbour say to a visitor from another ship: "How did you get here, mate? Walk?" Such simple jokes are timeless and quite in the epic spirit. Then there is the question that Ithaca is said to lie "highest up in the sea towards the gloom". But so indeed it does, once one accepts the fact that Levkas is not an island but a peninsula. I have shown elsewhere that Homeric terms for east and west refer only to general sectors and not to compass points.

All this is not to deny that there are many (probably insoluble) problems involved in Homeric geography. But when the bulk of the evidence all points in one direction, and when the general consent of antiquity is that Ithaca was indeed Ithaca, then I feel that it is merely wasting one's time to pursue elaborately-contrived theories. The Baconians may rage, but Shakespeare endures—and so, as far as I am concerned, does Ithaca. The fact that Ithaca is small, and comparatively barren, has sometimes been held against its having been the home of the leader of the island confederation. But the size of an island has little to do with its importance, as we know from the case of Delos in the Aegean. Ithaca, commanding the sheltered channel between itself and Cephallonia, and dominating the channel eastwards to the mainland, is most likely to have been the principal of the island confederation.

Notes

Introduction

p. vii. Quotation from John Livingston Lowes, *The Road to Xanadu* (1927).

Chapter 1

p. 3. *Olysseus*. Robert Graves in *The Greek Myths* suggests that his name derives from Oulos, a wound, and Ischea, a thigh, in reference to his having been wounded in the thigh by a boar. I have preferred the derivation given by Professor J. A. K. Thomson in his *Studies in the Odyssey* (1914). The dialect form was "Olixes", first found in the poet Ibycus of Rhegium *c.*530 B.C.

Chapter 2

p. 7. Odysseus. "I am at present angry . . ." I am indebted for this derivation to A. R. Burn, who also pointed out to me similar derivations in Eurymedon, Kerystonikos, and Telemachus.

p. 9. *About 1200 B.C. the City of Troy was sacked and burned....* This seems to be the now generally accepted date (naturally approximate) for the destruction by fire of City VIIa, the Homeric Troy on the mound of Assarlik. Vid. C. H. Whitman, *Homer and the Homeric Tradition.* H. L. Lorimer, *Homer and the Monuments.*

p. 10. *The Madness of Ulysses.* Robert Graves in *The Greek Myths*, vol. II has the following interesting comment: "What he [Ulysses] did was to demonstrate prophetically the uselessness of the war to which he had been summoned. Wearing a conical hat which marked the mystagogue or seer, he ploughed a field up and down. Ox and ass stood for Zeus and Cronus, or summer and winter; and each furrow, sown with salt, for a wasted year. Palamedes, who also had prophetic powers, then seized Telemachus and halted the plough, doubtless at the tenth furrow, by setting him in front of the team: he thereby showed that the *decisive battle*, which is the meaning of Telemachus, would take place then." [Telemachus, however, means 'Fighter Afar'.]

Chapter 3

p. 18. "*The pitch wells of Zante . . .*" Quotation from my *The Greek Islands* (1963).

p. 20. ". . . *ten oars a side.*" Many writers on the subject of ships in the Homeric period, and the navigations of Ulysses, have been confused by the images of classical galleys and triremes. (18th- and 19th-century painters were also particularly prone to this error. But it is noticeable that the few representations of Ulysses' vessel in classical art mostly show small, open boats.) It is unlikely that the Homeric warships were any bigger than the Viking ships. ". . . It is not probable that the largest Viking ships had more than ten oars a side. As these ships must often, against a contrary wind, have had to row both day and night, it seems reasonable to imagine the crew divided into three shifts which would give twice as many men available to fight on any occasion as to row. Thus a 20-oared vessel would carry 60 men. But some 40 men per ship seems, for this period, nearer the average. In 896, it is incidentally mentioned in one place that five vessels carried 200 Vikings, an average of 40 per ship. Elsewhere about the same time we read of 12,000 men carried in 260 ships, an average of 48." ['Vikings'—*Encyclopaedia Britannica*, 14th Ed.] Larger Viking ships than these undoubtedly existed. The sagas mention ships with forty to sixty oars. A. R. Burn has pointed out that geometric vases depict as many as 22 oars on 'long' ships. At the same time, if one bears in mind a typical Viking ship with 10 oars a side, one has a fair picture of the vessels likely to have been used by the Homeric Greeks. It is unlikely, however, that the Homeric ship will have been as well constructed as a Viking longboat.

p. 23. *Construction of Homeric ships.* Phillipe Diolé in his *4,000 Years Under the Sea* has given some interesting data including spectrographic and X-ray analyses, relating to the construction and metal fittings of ancient ships.

p. 24. *Sailing techniques in bad weather.* My friend Arthur Oliver, who sailed an open Sicilian fishing boat from Palermo to England in 1953, told me that he and his crew adopted the Homeric practice. Whenever bad weather threatened, they ran their boat up the nearest suitable beach and waited there until conditions had improved.

Chapter 4

p. 26. *Homer's silence about the Aegean islands.* Samuel Butler in *The Authoress of the Odyssey* made some play with this Homeric omission, and used it as one of the props to his theory of the Sicilian origin of the poem. But, to shift the argument to the 15th century, one does not deduce from the Portuguese chronicler Azurara that he was a native of Africa simply because it was Africa's geography which he described, and not Portugal's . The Portuguese of that century wanted to know about the mysterious and 'new-found' lands, not about those with which they were familiar. The same argument may equally have applied to Homer and his audience.

p. 29. *Ancient wines*. Quot. from Phillipe Diolé's *4000 Years Under the Sea*, trans. G. Hopkins (1957).

p. 29. *That the 'Odyssey' was written by someone without any real knowledge of the sea*. This theory has been most elaborately developed by B. Farrington in his *Samuel Butler and the Odyssey* (1929). I cannot agree with any of it, for the many reasons given in this book.

p. 31. *Course of the Greek Fleet after leaving Troy*. Nestor's Story. *Odyssey*, Book III.

Chapter 5

p. 34. Cythera. An alternative—and better-known tradition—gives Aphrodite's birthplace as Paphos in Cyprus. It would seem that the Phoenicians first imported the worship of Astarte (Aphrodite) into Cythera.

p. 34. *The islet of Marathonisi*. Quot. from P. Leigh Fermor's *Mani. Travels in the Southern Peloponnese* (1958).

p. 36. Mycenaean trade-goods, back to c. 1500 B.C., have been found in Lipara and as far afield as Wessex. But there is no evidence that they reached their 'markets' direct from the eastern Mediterranean. Early Chinese porcelain reached 18th-century England, but no one suggests that Chinese sailors brought it.

p. 36. *Phoenician inscriptions in Sardinia*. Quot. from H. L. Lorimer, *Homer and the Monuments* (1950).

p. 37. *Scylax of Caryanda*. Not to be confused with the Greek historian (521–485 B.C.), but a 4th-century B.C. geographer who compiled a Periplous or Sailors' Pilot of the Mediterranean.

Chapter 6

p. 43. *The North Star*. Quot. from Professor E. G. R. Taylor, *The Haven-Finding Art* (1956).

p. 44. *Coleridge and the 'Ancient Mariner'*. Quot. from John Livingstone Lowes, *The Road to Xanadu* (1927).

Chapter 7

p. 49. *Description of Goat Island.* Quot. from *Odyssey*, Book IX, trans. by E. V. Rieu (1960).

p. 50. *Mirrors of the Sea.* Quot. from V. Bérard, *Did Homer Live?*, trans. Brian Rhys (1931).

Chapter 8

p. 56. *The cave of Levanzo.* Quot. from my *The Journeying Moon* (1958), in which I described my first visit to this cave, shortly after it had been discovered.

p. 58. *The cave of Polyphemus.* The *Grotta del Toro*, which Butler describes lying near the modern Saltpans, would be in the right place for Polyphemus' cave, but I would not press the identification. There are many caves along this, as along nearly all coasts.

p. 61. *Did Polyphemus have two eyes?* Quot. from Samuel Butler's *The Authoress of the Odyssey* (1897).

Chapter 9

p. 65. *Beowolf compared with the 'Odyssey'.* The translation is from Professor R. K. Gordon's *Anglo-Saxon Poetry* (1926).

p. 70. *The magnetic compass.* The first description of the magnetic needle is to be found in the work of an English monk, Alexander of Neckham, in the 12th century.

p. 70. *Definitions of east and West in the ancient world.* Quot. from Professor E. G. R. Taylor's *The Haven-Finding Art* (1956).

Chapter 10

p. 74. *Squalls in the islands.* Quot. from the Admiralty *Mediterranean Pilot*, vol. III (1957).

p. 75. *A thunderstorm off Ithaca.* Quot. from my *The Wind off the Island* (1960).

Chapter 11

p. 69. *The harbour in the land of the Laestrygonians.* Quot. from the *Odyssey*, Book X, trans. E. V. Rieu (1960).

p. 80. *Horace and Cicero believed that Formiae was the city of the Laestrygonians.* "nec Laestrygonia Bacchus in amphora Languescit mihi." Horace, Carm. Lib., iii, 16, 34.

"At hercule in agris non siletur; nec iam ipsi agri regum vestrum ferre possunt. Si vero in hanc τηλέπυλον veneris Λαιστρυγονίην (Formias dico) qui fremitus hominum! quam irati animi!" Cic. ad Att., ii, 13.

p. 82. *Cannibalism for the satisfaction of hunger.* Quot. from 'Cannibalism'—*Encyclopaedia Brittannica*, 14th Ed.

p. 82. *The short nights of mid-summer in northern latitudes.* Samuel Butler, who placed the Land of the Laestrygonians at Cefalù in Sicily has a cleverly contrived explanation of this passage. *The Authoress of the Odyssey*, p.186. Ingenious though Butler's theory is, I find it unsatisfactory for the reason that many other places, apart from Cefalù, in this part of the world are similarly blessed by nature.

Chapter 12

p. 86. *Bonifacio in Corsica and Ciudadella in Minorca.* If, as I suspect, the information about 'the excellent harbour' (of Bonifacio) reached Homer from Phoenician sources, it is interesting to note that Ciudadella—which so much resembles Bonifacio in miniature—was also used by the Phoenicians. The town was a Phoenician settlement.

Chapter 13

p. 89. *Circe's island and Monte Circeo.* Alexander Shewan, among other scholars, has criticized the identification. "No one can approach a peninsula or an island near the coast from the sea without perceiving that it adjoins the land! And be it added that it is far from certain that Circe's island is Mount Circeo. So far as my observation goes, the belief among those competent to judge only becomes more pronounced, that the fairy adventures of Odysseus, as distinguished from the voyagings in Greek seas, will never be identified with known parts of the earth" p. 87, *Homeric Essays* (1935). The first part of this comment is adequately taken care of by my quotation from the Admiralty *Pilot for the Mediterranean*, vol. II, p. 353 (1954). As for 'the fairy voyagings of Odysseus'. the least explicit are those which occur in 'Greek seas'.

p. 92. *Feronia's sanctuary.* Quot. from Moulin de la Blanchère in V. Bérard's *Did Homer Live?*, trans. Brian Rhys (1931).

p. 96. *Circe depicted in classical art.* The vase painting to which I refer is illustrated (plate 18b) in J. E. Harrison's *Myths of the Odyssey* (1882).

p. 97. *The sacred plant moly.* R. M. Henry investigated the origins of the plant in *Class Rev.* (Dec. 1906), p. 434. Like so many other things in the *Odyssey*, it would seem to have stemmed from Phoenician or Eastern legend.

Chapter 14

p. 100. *Ulysses depicted on a classical gemstone*. Illustrated in J. E. Harrison's *Myths of the Odyssey*, plate 20b.

p. 100. *Matriarchy once dominant in the Mediterranean*. The Great Mother has, of course, survived to this day. She has been absorbed into the person of the Virgin Mary. In most areas of the Christianized Mediterranean the other members of the Christian hierarchy are noticeably subordinate to the Mother.

p. 101. *The Goddess of Wild Things*. Quot. from H. J. Rose's 'Religion' in *A Companion to Homer* (1962). Three illustrations of Minoan seals and gems in this volume show the goddess in company with her sacred beasts.

Chapter 15

p. 108. *Conditions in mediaeval galleys*. Quot. from the Memoirs of Barras de la Penne—E. Hamilton Currey's *The Sea Wolves of the Mediterranean* (1910).

p. 109. *Circe's child by Ulysses*. Later commentators on the *Odyssey* ascribed a son to Ulysses' liaison with Circe. He was Telegonus, Last-Born, the reputed founder of Tusculum.

Chapter 16

p. 112. *Melkarth and Heracles*. Quot. from J. Delaporte 'Phoenician Mythology', *Larousse Encyclopaedia of Mythology* (1959).

p. 114. *Contact between Greece and the Baltic in the pre-Homeric period*. Evidence for this is referred to by H. L. Lorimer in *Homer and the Monuments*, p. 16.

p. 114. *Cape Taenarus, the entrance to Hades*. Quot. from P. L. Fermor *Mani* (1958).

Chapter 17

p. 117. *Homer's knowledge of geography*. Quot. from H. Thomas and F. H. Stubbings in *A companion to Homer* (1962).

p. 121. *The Siren Islands*. Quot. from Norman Douglas's *Siren Land*. Douglas illuminates the whole of this corner of Italy in the one true handbook for all Siren-lovers.

p. 125. *The Sirens in ancient art.* Quot. from Carl Kerényi's *The Gods of the Greeks* (1951).

p. 128. *Derivation of the word 'Siren'.* Some scholars derive this from the root *Seirazein*, "to bind with a cord" (R. Graves, *The Greek Myths*, p.249). Others derive it from a Semitic root meaning "to sing" (J. E. Harrison, *Myths of the Odyssey*, p.175).

Chapter 18

p. 129. *Virgil on the Sirens.* "Jamque adeo scopulos Sirenum advecta subibat/Difficiles quondam multorumque ossibus albos", Virgil, *Aeneid*, v. 864.

pp. 131–133. The incident described in these pages is quoted from a 'war book' which I wrote in 1948. I was serving at the time as a sub-lieutenant R.N.V.R. aboard the escort destroyer H.M.S. *Exmoor*. Her captain was Commander J. Jefferis, D.S.C., R.N. The *Exmoor* was senior ship of the 22nd Destroyer Flotilla.

Chapter 19

p. 135. *The Wandering Rocks.* Quot. from the *Odyssey*, trans. E. V. Rieu (1960).

p. 138. *Stromboli.* Quot. from Edward Hull's *Volcanoes: Past and Present* (1892). Strabo's reference to the island is as follows: "Strongyle a rotundate figurae sic dicta, ignita ipsa quoque, violentia flammarum minor, fulgore excellens; ibi habitasse Aecolum adjunct", Strabo, Lib. vi.

p. 138. *Stromboli today.* Quot. from my *The Wind off the Island* (1960).

p. 140. *No mention of Vesuvius in the 'Odyssey'.* Devotees of Sherlock Holmes will need no reminder of the case of 'Silver Blaize', recorded in his memoirs. For those unfamiliar with the great detective, I quote the relevant passage, when Inspector Gregory asks Holmes: " 'Is there any other point to which you would wish to draw my attention?'

" 'To the curious incident of the dog in the night-time.'

" 'The dog did nothing in the night-time.'

" 'That was the curious incident,' remarked Sherlock Holmes."

Chapter 20

p. 145. *Scylla and Charybdis.* Quot. from the *Odyssey*, trans. E. V. Rieu (1960).

p. 147. *Marine 'monsters' in the Messina Strait.* Quot. from Dr. Paul A. Zahn's *'Fishing in the Whirlpool of Charybdis'*, *The National Geographic Magazine*, Nov. 1953.

p. 148. *An 18th-century view of Scylla*. Quot. by J. E. Harrison in *Myths of the Odyssey*, (1882).

p. 150. *Charybdis in the early 19th century*. Quot. from Admiral Smyth's *Sicily and its Islands* (1824).

Chapter 21

p. 155. *The world of actuality and the world of imagination*. Quot. from Professor J. A. K. Thomson's *Studies in the Odyssey* (1914).

Chapter 22

p. 158. *Scylla and Charybdis today*. Quot. from my *The Wind off the Island* (1960).

p. 160. *The world of Fairytale*. Quot. *A Companion to Homer* (1962).

p. 162. *Thrinakia*. Quot. from V. Bérard, *Did Homer Live?'* trans. Brian Rhys (1931).

p. 164. *Anchorages on the Sicilian coast south of Messina*. The *Mediterranean Pilot* mentions only one—'Off the village of San Alessio'— until one reaches Taormina. But the anchorage off San Alessio is only an open roadstead, not a sheltered cove.

p. 165. *L'Ognina Creek*. I have anchored here once, it is a safe place for small boats. It is known locally as Porto Ulisse, Sicilian folk-lorists having claimed it as Ulysses' 'sheltered cove'. It is too far from the Messina Strait, however, for him to have reached it in one day.

p. 167. *No allusion to Etna in the 'Odyssey'*. Quot. from G. F. Rodwell's *'Etna, A History of the Mountain* (1878).

Chapter 23

p. 169. *Helios, the Sun God*. Quot. from Carl Kerényi's *The Gods of the Greeks* (1958).

p. 170. *The number of Helios' cattle*. Quot. from Robert Graves's *The Greek Myths* (1955).

p. 172. *Frequency of the Sirocco in autumn*. Quot. from the *Mediterranean Pilot*, vol. I, p.41.

Chapter 24

p. 177. *A storm off Sicily described by Petronius*. Quot. from Petronius, *The Satyricon*, trans. by Jack Lindsay (1960).

Chapter 25

p. 180. *A south-going current along the eastern coastline of Sicily.* Quot. from the *Mediterranean Pilot* vol. I, p. 9.

p. 184. *Ogygia and Oceanus.* Robert Graves, *The Greek Myths* vol. II, p.368 (1955).

p. 185. *The Phoenicians in Malta.* Quot. from T. D. Kendrick—'Malta' (*The Encyclopaedia Britannica,* 14th Ed.).

p. 187. *Goddess worship in Malta.* Quot. from W. K. R. Bedford's *Malta* (1903).

Chapter 26

p. 189. *Temples of the goddess in Malta.* Quot. from M. A. Murray's *Excavations in Malta,* Part III, p.29 (1929).

pp. 191 and 194. Quot. from the *Odyssey,* Book V, trans. E. V. Rieu (1960).

p. 194. *The raft of Ulysees.* The construction of the raft was most thoroughly investigated by E. H. Warre in *The Journal of Hellenic Studies,* V (1884).

Chapter 27

p. 197. *Winds off Malta in summer.* This information, confirmed by personal experience, is taken from the 'Climatic Tables' in the *Mediterranean Pilot,* vol. I, p. 58.

Chapter 28

p. 202. *Scheria/Corfu.* Several classical scholars have made the same observation as myself, that Corfu does indeed have the appearance of 'a shield laid on the misty sea.' For a full analysis of the Corfu/Scheria question Alexander Shewan's *Homeric Essays* (1935), are of the greatest interest. Shewan considered all the various theories that had been propounded, and came down firmly on the side of the Corfu identification.

p. 203. *The Stream Ermones.* Quot. from the *Mediterranean Pilot,* vol. III, p.148.

p. 204. *Corfu compared with the other Ionian islands.* In my *The Greek Islands* (1963) I have given a more detailed account of Corfu's topography and archaeology.

Chapter 29

p. 210. *Leigh Hunt, Keats, and Dante.* This story was told by Leigh Hunt in *The Indicator,* no. IX, 8th December 1819.

pp. 210–211. The translations from the *Divine Comedy,* Canto XXVI, are from the version by Miss Dorothy L. Sayers (1957).

Index

The page references in italic figures refer to illustrations.

231

237

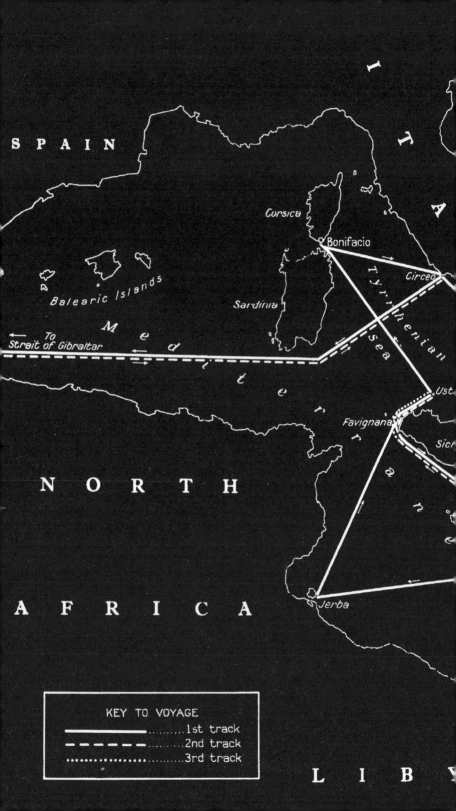

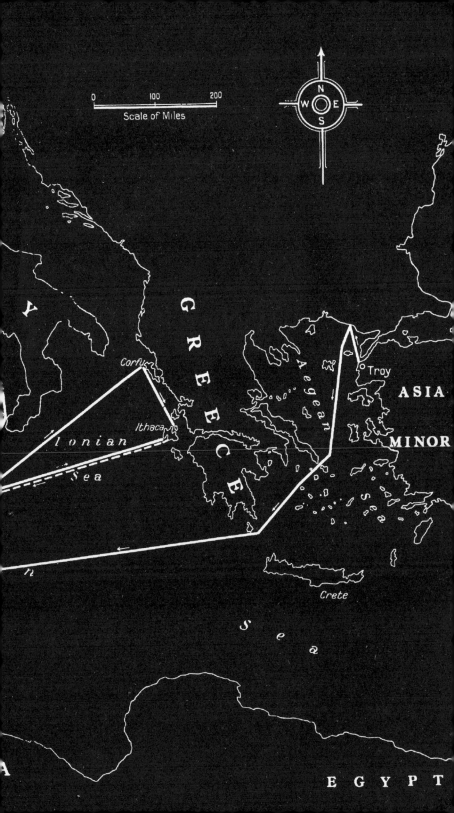